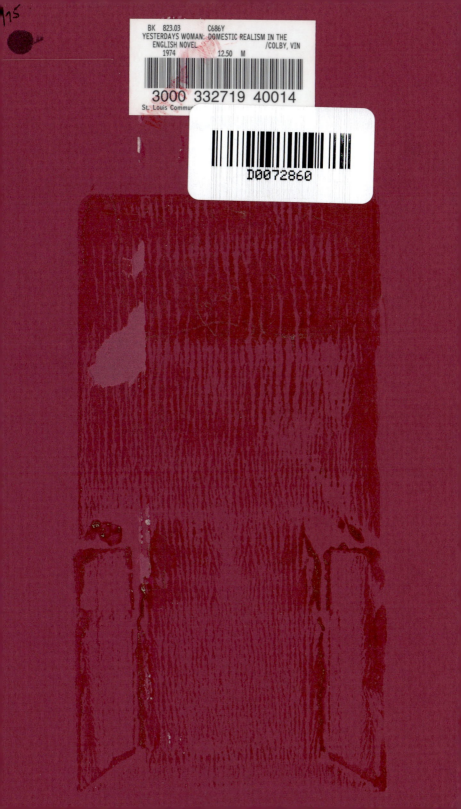

Yesterday's Woman

Domestic Realism in the English Novel

Vineta Colby

Woman

Domestic Realism in the English Novel

Princeton University Press

LIBRARY OF CONGRESS CATALOGING IN PUBLICATION DATA
WILL BE FOUND ON THE LAST PRINTED PAGE OF THIS BOOK

PUBLICATION OF THIS BOOK HAS BEEN AIDED BY A GRANT
FROM THE ANDREW W. MELLON FOUNDATION

THIS BOOK HAS BEEN COMPOSED IN LINOTYPE CALEDONIA

PRINTED IN THE UNITED STATES OF AMERICA BY
PRINCETON UNIVERSITY PRESS,
PRINCETON, NEW JERSEY

Acknowledgments

THANKS to the rich resources of libraries in the New York area—mainly the research divisions of the New York Public Library, the Fales Collection of New York University, and, going a little farther afield, the Beinecke Library at Yale and the Firestone Library at Princeton—I have been able to track down most of the material for this book. I am grateful to Mimi Penchansky of the Queens College Library for inter-library loan service and to Florence Waldhetter and the staff of the Queens College Graduate Division for typing assistance. Lillian Feder, my colleague in the Queens College English Department, and R. Miriam Brokaw and Marjorie C. Sherwood of the Princeton University Press have given me generously of their time, knowledge, and sympathetic interest. My chief indebtedness is to my colleague and sometime collaborator Robert A. Colby, for whom I must borrow some lines from Lady Sarah Pennington's *An Unfortunate Mother's Advice to her Absent Daughter* (1761):

". . . the Weaknesses, the Pains of the Body may be inexpressibly alleviated by the Conversation of a Person, by Affection endeared, by Reason approved; whose tender Sympathy partakes of your Afflictions, and shares your Enjoyments; who is steady in the Correction, but mild in the Reproof of your Faults; like a guardian Angel, ever watchful to warn you of unforseen Danger, and by timely Admonitions prevent the Mistakes incident to human Frailty, and Self-partiality. . . . Happy is her Lot, who in an Husband finds this invaluable Friend!"

Contents

Yesterday's Woman

Domestic Realism in the English Novel

"Oh, Sir Austin," she ejaculated, "it is surely our Education which causes us to shine at such a disadvantage! You make dolls of us! puppets! Are we not something—something more?"

"Aren't we yer mothers?" shouts the M'Murphy.

—George Meredith, *The Ordeal of*
            Richard Feverel (1859)

Introduction

THIS study is an attempt to explore and illuminate that grey area in the history of the English novel, the first half of the nineteenth century. The towering presences of Jane Austen and Sir Walter Scott dominate the era, yet, like giants among pygmies, they are not wholly representative of it. We remember the age far more for poetry than for fiction, for genres than for individual novels; but mainly we mark time between, say, 1818, when the last of Jane Austen's works was published, or perhaps 1824, when with *Redgauntlet* Scott published his last widely read novel, and that flowering decade of the 1840's which saw the emergence of Dickens, Thackeray, the Brontës, and Mrs. Gaskell.

Among the scores of novels that filled the artistic vacuum of this almost half-century were many of considerable interest and a few of real literary merit. Not neglected masterpieces, they nevertheless deserve rereading and close study for their intrinsic qualities and also for what they tell us about that glorious and seemingly miraculous rebirth of the great novel in the mid-nineteenth century. They were the minor novels that both the major novelists and the large novel-reading public read in their childhood and youth. They do not account for the creative genius of the major novelists, but they provided themes and ideas, they shaped styles and formed attitudes toward a still new art form that, in spite of the prestige given it by Scott and Austen, remained morally and aesthetically suspect.

It is the contention of this study that the most important contribution made by these novels was in the emergence of domestic realism, understood here in its narrow sense as simply a literary manner and, in its larger sense, as a whole artistic conception or vision of life. The single most striking feature of the major Victorian novel is its essentially bourgeois orientation. It is anti-romantic, un-aristocratic, home- and family-centered. Its values, its subjects, and its principal characters are drawn from middle-class life. It is domestic by the standard dictionary definition of the word "domestic"—"of or pertaining to a particular country," as this type of novel tends to be local, even provincial; "adapted to living with or near man, tame," as it deals almost exclusively with human relationships within small social communities; "of or pertaining to the home or family," as it draws its subjects mainly from the daily life and work of ordinary people: courtship, marriage, children, earning a living, adjusting to reality, learning to conform to the conventions of established society and to live within it tranquilly, if not always happily.

Not surprisingly, therefore, the emerging novel is female-dominated. The large number of women novelists, the far larger and ever-increasing number of women readers, the tendency even among men novelists to refine their subjects, soften their language, and write about bourgeois family life, all suggest that "female domination," a popular phrase during this period, would be a fitting subtitle to this study. Even the wildest flights of romantic imagination in the Victorian novel were launched from the female-dominated hearthside: *Wuthering Heights* with its housekeeper-narrator relating a chronicle of middle-class (however a-typical) family life; the heroines of *Jane Eyre* and *Villette* realizing their romantic dreams ultimately in domestic reality, Jane as the wife of a chastened, reformed rake, Lucy as a spinster schoolmistress. Dickens' imagination soars above the realities of middle-class family life, but invariably descends to them at the end. His untamed romantics like Steerforth and Carton are doomed, and Pip pays bitterly for his misguided romanticism. In Thackeray's social satire, while smug bourgeois values are constantly challenged, the female imperatives of home and hearth win out. After all

4

his *weltschmerz* has been released, Arthur Pendennis settles down at the family fireside to watch his young friend Clive Newcome follow a similar but more painful course. Even Becky Sharp is at last tamed and domesticated. Indeed, in the last glimpse we have of her, going to church and charity bazaars, is she not perversely but unmistakably the archetype of female domination?

It is tempting to see this tendency as crowned by the dominant female image of Queen Victoria herself, but history does not tolerate such over-simplifications. Numerous studies of this period have demonstrated that change and reform were emerging even in the Regency period, long before a modest and delicate-looking young girl ascended to the throne of England. As over the years the Queen developed into an ample matron, she created many images—all of them reflected in the novels as well as in the life-styles of her subjects—devoted and submissive wife, loving mother, grieving widow, dominant matriarch, ruling empress. But her image was reflecting rather than formative. The novel that developed in her reign owed nothing to her active influence but much to the social and moral developments of the early nineteenth century that influenced and molded her as they did all her subjects.

I have attempted to isolate some of these developments for closer scrutiny and to study their influence upon the fiction of the first half of the century. Specifically, I have examined the changes in manners and mores from the Regency into mid-century as registered in the novel of high society, focussing on Mrs. Gore and her contemporaries; new directions in educational theory, as reflected mainly in novels by Maria Edgeworth and Susan Ferrier about young men and women growing up to the responsibilities of mature life; the profound alterations in religious thinking and practices recorded in evangelical literature from the didactic tales of Hannah More and Charlotte Elizabeth to the novels of religious conscience and self-examination of Elizabeth Missing Sewell and Charlotte Yonge; and, finally,

5

changing attitudes toward reality itself as mirrored in the love story, now domesticated into stories of human relationships in community, home and family life, and illustrated here primarily in Harriet Martineau's *Deerbrook*. Wide and scattered as these areas may be—society, school, church, community, and home—they come together under the rubric of domestic realism. Other developments in the nineteenth-century novel, some equally or perhaps even more significant—such as regionalism, social realism, sensationalism—are beyond the scope of this book. I have, however, been aware at all times of the complex inter-relationship of ideas, issues, and literary influences that produced the domestic novel under study. The beauty of the nineteenth-century English novel is its sensitivity to its total world. That, alas, is also in the long run its chief peril to students, who can never hope to grasp and encompass its dimensions. At best we can only map trails and chart its outlines and tentatively explore its depths.

I

Ut Pictura Poesis: The Novel of Domestic Realism as Genre

Our little habitation was situated at the foot of a sloping hill, sheltered with a beautiful underwood behind and a prattling river before; on one side a meadow, on the other a green. My farm consisted of about twenty acres of excellent land, having given an hundred pound for my predecessor's good-will. Nothing could exceed the neatness of my little enclosures, the elms and hedge rows appearing with inexpressible beauty. My house consisted of but one story and was covered with thatch, which gave it an air of great snugness; the walls on the inside were nicely whitewashed, and my daughters undertook to adorn them with pictures of their own designing. Though the same room served us for parlour and kitchen, that only made it the warmer. Besides, as it was kept with the utmost neatness, the dishes, plates and coppers being well scoured and all disposed in bright rows on the shelves, the eye was agreeably relieved and did not seem to want richer furniture. There were three other apartments, one for my wife and me, another for our two daughters within our own, and the third, with two beds, for the rest of my children.

The little republic to which I gave laws was regulated in the following manner: by sun-rise we all assembled in our common apartment, the fire being previously kindled by the servant. . . .

—Oliver Goldsmith, *The Vicar of Wakefield,* ch. 4

I

ENGLISH domestic realism may have been invented in this passage from *The Vicar of Wakefield* in 1766. Proudly describing his modest home—"the little republic to which I gave laws"—Reverend Primrose epitomizes and apotheosizes the eighteenth-century bourgeois ideal. No classic pastoral landscapes, no romantic vistas, no epic flights of the poetic imagination here. This idyll is home-based and family-centered.

Generations of English novel readers and novel writers grew up on *The Vicar of Wakefield*. It is unlikely that a single major Victorian novelist did not know the book and probably, at least in his youth, love it. If in his sophisticated maturity he laughed at its sentimentality or winked at its cynicism, the Victorian continued to cherish its basic images of home and family life. In this characteristic paragraph Goldsmith captured the spirit of simplicity, intimacy and privacy, immediacy and precision of detail, that informs English domestic realism. Size is modestly scaled down—"little habitation," "little enclosures," "one story," "three other apartments." Spaces are small and enclosed—the house "at the foot of a sloping hill," "sheltered," "covered with thatch," "an air of great snugness." Inside and outside there is "neatness," "nicely white-washed" walls decorated only with home-made pictures, no "richer furniture." Order and symmetry prevail—a meadow on one side, a green on the other, the well-scoured dishes arranged "in bright rows." Dreamy and idyllic as the scene is, it is also filled with specific material detail—size, function, price—"twenty acres," "an hundred-pound for my predecessor's good-will," the sleeping arrangements of the family, the uses to which the rooms are put. As we read on, we get a precise account of the family's living routines from morning prayers to sunset.

Apart from its faithful attention to physical detail, this descriptive passage is interesting for its aesthetic and moral implications. The total picture is both pleasant and good. The Vicar's evident self-satisfaction reflects his judgment that his laws (which are also God's laws) are right. The neatness and order, the comfort and security of the homestead prove him so. Nature and man live in a harmony to which the physical beauty of the landscape and the modest attractiveness of the house testify. Because it is pious and virtuous, the Vicar's simple life is also beautiful, a work of art. For the Victorians it literally became so, inspiring many of the leading painters of the age. Thus domestic realism stretched from the printed page to the painted canvas. Hollins, Maclise, and Frith painted the Primroses in various scenes from the novel. In 1844 Mulready added his painting of the family to an already proliferating number, provoking Thackeray's good-humored outburst in *Fraser's Magazine* that although he had vowed to notice no more pictures from the novel, the work of Mulready "compelled the infraction of the rule, rushing through our resolve by the indomitable force of genius, [and] we must as the line is broken, present other Vicars, Thornhills, and Olivias, to walk in and promenade themselves in our columns, in spite of the vain placards at the entrance, 'VICARS OF WAKEFIELD NOT ADMITTED.'"[1]

The working relationship between the artist and the novelist was never closer than during the period in which the domestic novel flourished. Dickens gave much personal attention to the illustration of his novels. Some novelists, like Thackeray and George Du Maurier, illustrated their own work. Other novelists wrote art criticism professionally—Henry James, Mrs. Oliphant, and Thackeray again. These and still other novelists—Charlotte Brontë, George Eliot—

---

[1] 29 (June, 1844); rptd. in *Works of W. M. Thackeray* (Biographical Centenary ed.), XIII, 419-45. Illustrated editions of *The Vicar of Wakefield* were steady bestsellers; among the more distinguished illustrators were Bewick (1798), Rowlandson (1817), Westall (1819), Cruikshank (1832), Mulready (1843), Hugh Thomson (1890), and Arthur Rackham (1929).

introduced painters as characters and discussed painting in their novels. What caught the artist's imagination and moved his heart was much the same as what inspired the novelist—domestic life, portrayed in the simple reality of its day-to-day course. "The heroic, and peace be with it! has been deposed," Thackeray proclaimed in 1843, "and our artists, in place, cultivate the pathetic and the familiar."[2] In 1855, viewing a Paris exhibition of English painting, Baudelaire was struck by its "intimate glimpses of home," and another visitor to the show, Richard Redgrave, observed that to walk from the salon containing French and other continental paintings into the British gallery "was to pass at once from the midst of warfare and its incidents, from passion, strife and bloodshed, from martyrdoms and suffering, to the peaceful scenes of home."[3]

Bourgeois genre painting, as Mario Praz has written, had "an addiction to narrative." Other styles of painting—religious, allegorical, and symbolical—that draw upon mythology, epic, and history transcend mere circumstantiality. They invite multiple interpretations, but offer no simple explanations. Genre, however, is drawn from the everyday reality that can be described, explained, accounted for. It is therefore anecdotal.[4] This woman is reading a letter, taking a music lesson, nursing a child, preparing a meal, dressing in a cluttered and shabby bedroom. She is an ordinary woman—not the Virgin receiving the Annunciation or holding the Christ child. We are free to speculate: does she have a lover? what was she doing a moment before? what is she thinking about? Victorian novelists were especially attracted to this style of painting because of its air of "truth,"

[2] "Letters on the Fine Arts," *Stray Papers*, ed. Lewis Melville (Philadelphia, n.d.), p. 214.

[3] Graham Reynolds, *Victorian Painting* (London, 1966), p. 94.

[4] *The Hero in Eclipse in Victorian Fiction* (Oxford, 1956); *Mnemosyne: The Parallel Between Literature and the Arts* (Princeton, 1970), Ch. 1; and *Conversation Pieces: A Survey of the Informal Group Portrait in Europe and America* (University Park, Pa., 1971).

its concern with subjects that could be instantly recognized and verified by the experience of the viewer. "Dutch realism" is a recurring phrase in nineteenth-century art and literary criticism. In *Adam Bede* George Eliot cited it as justification for her whole approach to fiction: "It is for this rare, precious quality of truthfulness that I delight in many Dutch paintings, which lofty-minded people despise. I find a source of delicious sympathy in these faithful pictures of a monotonous homely existence, which has been the fate of so many more among my fellow-mortals than a life of pomp or of absolute indigence, of tragic suffering or of world-stirring actions" (Ch. 17).

Among the "lofty-minded" was Henry James, novelist and art critic, deploring, as many others did and still do, the excesses of genre—its sentimentality, triviality, and banality— every bit as much the plague of the novels as of the paintings. It is significant that James's condemnation embraces the novel as well. Reviewing the Royal Academy's exhibition of 1877, he observed: "The pictures, with very few exceptions, are 'subjects'; they belong to what the French call the anecdotical class . . . they are subjects addressed to a taste of a particularly unimaginative and unaesthetic order —to the taste of the British merchant and paterfamilias and his excellently regulated family. What this taste appears to demand of a picture is that it shall have a taking title, like a three-volume novel or an article in a magazine; that it shall embody in its lower flights some comfortable incident of the daily life of our period, suggestive more especially of its gentilities and proprieties and familiar moralities, and in its loftier scope some picturesque episode of history or fiction which may be substantiated by a long explanatory extract in the catalogue."[5]

Whether for aesthetic good or bad, genre, Biedermeier, domestic realism swept over Germany and France in the early nineteenth century as powerfully as the countervail-

[5] "The Picture Season in London," in *The Painter's Eye*, ed. John L. Sweeney (Cambridge, Mass., 1956), p. 148.

11

ing force of romanticism had swept Europe in the last decades of the eighteenth century. In England its effects on
painting were pervasive and long-lasting. Its effects on the
novel were more curiously mixed. A newly emerging art
form, the realistic English novel was in a state of rapid evolution and development throughout the nineteenth century.
It was plastic and flexible. Its history was far shorter than
that of painting and its public vastly larger. To draw close
parallels between the two art forms, however inviting such
efforts may be, is perilous. Far too many histories and critical studies of the nineteenth-century novel make reductive
and simplistic generalizations about its bourgeois-sentimen-
tal character. *The Vicar of Wakefield*, a kind of archetype
of the domestic novel, illustrates the pitfalls of the genre approach. Is it, as it appears to be, a glorification of home,
family, and church? Or is it, as we may also read it, an acid-
etched satire on those same honored institutions? Its implications are less profound than those of the Book of Job,
from which Goldsmith took his theme, but no less ambiguous. Genre painting is a fixed scene on canvas. We may
speculate on the action and circumstances involved, but we
usually know what we see. Fiction, however, involving the
complexities and ambiguities of language and concept, is
open-ended and resists critical generalizations.

A novel of wit written by a notoriously sophisticated man
of letters, *The Vicar of Wakefield's* enduring popularity
cannot be accounted for only by its simple sentimental appeal. Those elements of domestic realism—privacy, enclo-
sure and warmth, precision of detail—that we noted in a
single descriptive passage are more than accidental literary
effects. Goldsmith knew the nature of the public for whom
he wrote and the nature of the society about which he was
writing. *The Vicar* was widely imitated in lower-class fiction up through the mid-nineteenth century. Working-class
readers, crowded into industrial towns, in dreary slums and
dingy factories, devoured pastoral-domestic idylls of rustic
life. Titles like *The Cottage Girl, The Pride of the Village,*

The Maid of the Village, or the *Farmer's Daughter* dot the bestseller lists of the 1840's.[6] Although that same public was reading a variety of fictional genres—latter-day romances and gothic tales—the modest attractions of domestic fiction seem to have had special staying powers. The mass public was at last discovering what realistic novelists from Defoe onwards had known, namely, the pleasure of recognition and identification, the appeal of homely detail, precise and specific and recognizable to the average reader. One of the shrewdest and most perceptive witnesses to nineteenth-century cultural developments was Harriet Martineau, who, writing of her youth, attributed the great success of Miss Mitford's sketches of rural life, *Our Village* (1824-1832), to her exploitation of "that new style of 'graphic description' to which literature owes a great deal":

"In my childhood, there was no such thing known, in the works of the day, as 'graphic description,' and most people delighted as much as I did in Mrs. Ratcliffe's [sic] gorgeous or luscious generalities—just as we admired in picture galleries landscapes all misty and glowing indefinitely with bright colours—yellow sunrises and purple and crimson sunsets,—because we had no conception of detail like Miss Austen's in manners and Miss Mitford's in scenery, or of Millais' and Wilkie's analogous life pictures, or of Rosa Bonheur's adventurous Hayfield at noon-tide. Miss Austen had claims to other and greater honours; but she and Miss Mitford deserve no small gratitude for rescuing us from the folly and bad taste of slovenly indefiniteness in delineation."[7]

Homely descriptive detail became increasingly graphic in the early nineteenth century. In the most popular novelist of the period, Sir Walter Scott, it served the special function of recreating the dead past of history with activities

[6] Louis James, *Fiction for the Working Man* (Oxford, 1963), p. 103.

[7] *Autobiography*, ed. Maria Weston Chapman (Boston, 1878), i, 315-16.

13

and interests recognizable in the living reality of his readers. Scott resolved, he wrote in his introduction to *Waverley*, to throw the force of his narrative on "those passions common to men in all stages of society, and which have alike agitated the human heart, whether it be throbbed under the steel corselet of the fifteenth century, the brocaded coat of the eighteenth, or the blue frock and white dimity waistcoat of the present day." Sharing almost equal time with his battling knights in armor, feuding clansmen in tartan, and dramatic highland scenery, are the "broth, onions, cheese" and the roasted yearling lamb—"It was set upon its legs, with a bunch of parsley in its mouth, and was probably exhibited in that form to gratify the pride of the cook, who piqued himself more on the plenty than on the elegance of his master's table" (*Waverley*, Ch. 20). Jeanie Deans, that noblest and homeliest of Scott's heroines, is as remarkable for her cheese-making and the contents of her pantry ("in which she kept her honey, her sugar, her pots of jelly, her vials of the more ordinary medicines") as for her integrity and courage. The daily living habits of the rugged Highlanders were in fact a subject of endless fascination to Scott and, evidently, to his readers. In *Old Mortality* we get a faithful account of the dinner offered to the Laird of Milnwood's domestics:

". . . old Robin, who was butler, valet-de-chambre, footman, gardener, and what not, in the house of Milnwood, placed on the table an immense charger of broth, thickened with oatmeal and colewort, in which ocean of liquid was indistinctly discovered, by close observers, two or three short ribs of lean mutton sailing to and fro. Two huge baskets, one of bread made of barley and pease, and one of oatcakes, flanked this standing dish. A large boiled salmon would now-a-days have indicated more liberal housekeeping; but at that period salmon was caught in such plenty in the considerable rivers in Scotland, that instead of being accounted a delicacy, it was generally applied to feed the servants. . ." (Ch. 8).

14

Rob Roy, a veritable travelogue of the wild remote regions of the north, balances the flamboyantly romantic adventures of its hero with documentation on the realities of life in a rough highland public house:

"The interior presented a view which seemed singular enough to southern eyes. The fire, fed with blazing turf and branches of dried wood, blazed merrily in the centre; but the smoke, having no means to escape but through a hole in the roof, eddied round the rafters of the cottage, and hung in sable folds at the height of about five feet from the floor. The space beneath was kept pretty clear, by innumerable currents of air which rushed towards the fire from the broken panel of basketwork which served as a door, from two square holes, designed as ostensible windows, through one of which was thrust a plaid, and through the other a tattered great-coat; and moreover, through various less distinguishable apertures, in the walls of the tenement, which, being built of round stones and turf, cemented by mud, let in the atmosphere at innumerable crevices" (Ch. 28).

Jane Austen, on the other hand, seems to revert to the eighteenth century with its fondness for typology and generalization. Much as we *think* we know her world—landscapes, interiors, and the habits and activities of her characters—we discover that she gave scant space to physical description of any kind. Pemberley, Rosings, Mansfield Park are magnificent houses, but we know surprisingly little about their details—their size, furnishings, numbers and arrangements of rooms. Nevertheless, Jane Austen utilized the techniques of domestic realism. Having so thoroughly mastered her art, with a few economical strokes she achieved what lesser novelists needed paragraphs for. "She stimulates us to supply what is not there," Virginia Woolf observed, or, as Margaret Lane points out, ". . . she takes such an immediate grasp of our attention, so firmly trains our imagination on to her characters and the exact social milieu in which they have their being, that our inner eye obediently supplies everything that she has economically left out."[8] The eye for domestic detail, for example, with which she sees the squalor of Fanny Price's home in Portsmouth is cruelly perceptive: "She sat in a blaze of oppressive heat, in a cloud of moving dust; and her eyes could only wander from the walls, marked by her father's head, to the table cut and knotched by her brothers, where stood the tea-board never thoroughly cleaned, the cups and saucers wiped in streaks, the milk a mixture of motes floating in thin blue, and the bread and butter growing every minute more greasy than even Rebecca's hands had first produced it" (*Mansfield Park*, III, ch. 15).

She characterizes with domestic detail: fussy, talkative but loving Miss Bates worries about her niece's failing appetite: ". . . and she really eats nothing—makes such a shocking breakfast, you would be quite frightened if you saw it. I dare not let my mother know how little she eats—so I say one thing and then I say another, and it passes off. But about the middle of the day she gets hungry, and there is nothing she likes so well as these baked apples, and they are extremely wholesome, for I took the opportunity the other day of asking Mr. Perry; I happened to meet him in the street. Not that I had any doubt before—I have so often heard Mr. Woodhouse recommend a baked apple. I believe it is the only way that Mr. Woodhouse thinks the fruit thoroughly wholesome. We have apple-dumplings, however, very often. Patty makes an excellent apple-dumpling" (*Emma*, II, ch. 9).

In her domestic arrangements practical Charlotte Collins reveals her determination to make the best of her marriage

---

[8] "Jane Austen," in *The Common Reader* (London, 1925), p. 174; *Purely for Pleasure* (London, 1966), p. 102. See also Karl Kroeber, *Styles in Fictional Structure* (Princeton, 1971). On the basis of tabulations of word usage, Professor Kroeber confirms that Jane Austen uses little physical description, but he also demonstrates, through a close analysis of her style as it relates to theme and characterization, that her art "consists of subtle complexities . . . presented in a simple, lucid, even conventionalized manner" (p. 19).

16

to an insufferable bore. She chooses a small back room for her private parlor: "Elizabeth at first had rather wondered that Charlotte should not prefer the dining parlour for common use; it was a better sized room, and had a pleasanter aspect; but she soon saw that her friend had an excellent reason for what she did, for Mr. Collins would undoubtedly have been much less in his own apartment, had they sat in one equally lively; and she gave Charlotte credit for the arrangement" (*Pride and Prejudice*, II, ch. 7).

The use of itemized domestic description for social "placing," for satire, for special effects of all kinds, was firmly established by the first quarter of the nineteenth century. Long before Dickens lampooned the bourgeois prosperity of the Podsnaps, Susan Ferrier in *Destiny* (1831) impaled the Ribleys, a London couple "whose household gods were all united in one, and that one—comfort," with an inventory of the furnishings of their drawing-room: ". . . with its little serpentine sofas and formal circle of chairs; its small elaborate mirrors, stuck half-way up the wall; its high mantelpiece, decorated with branching girandoles and Dresden shepherds and shepherdesses; its Brussels carpet, with festoons of roses; its small bare satin-wood tables; its tall twin fire-screens, embroidered forty years ago by Mrs. Ribley's own hands; not a vestige of a book or work, or any such lumber was to be seen in this room, appropriate solely to the purpose of sitting in bolt upright. . ." (Ch. 72).

With catalogues and price lists of fashionable London shops and menus of exclusive clubs and dinner parties, Mrs. Gore set her Regency aristocrats and parvenus firmly in their scene. Maria Edgeworth placed her socially ambitious Irish Lady Clonbrony, trying to make an entree into fashionable London society, with the advice of her interior decorator, Mr. Soho, "the first architectural upholsterer of the age": "You fill up your angles here with *encoinières*—round your walls with the *Turkish tent drapery*—a fancy of my own—in apricot cloth, or crimson velvet, suppose, or *en*

17

flute, in crimson satin draperies, fanned and riched with gold fringes, *en suite*—intermediate spaces, Apollo's heads with gold rays. . ." (*The Absentee,* ch. 2).

Descriptive detail, however, is merely a utility device of the fiction of domestic realism. It serves the needs of the novelist who is seeking to portray a way of life, a milieu in which his characters can move. The impression of family life that stamps itself upon the reader of the pastoral, idyllic opening pages of *The Vicar of Wakefield* is graphic but unreal because the family is not engaged in believable activity. They are described in detail but not in motion. In many late-eighteenth- and early-nineteenth-century family portraits we notice that everyone is either engaged in some appropriate activity or so represented as to suggest his or her identification with specific duties and activities—the mother with a baby in her lap while older children cling to her skirts, the father holding a book or an implement identifying his line of work, the children with balls or toys, sometimes even the family cat ready to pounce on a caged bird or the dog caught silently in the act of yapping.[9] We have a sense of life arrested, caught in a moment of normal activity and about to resume that activity the moment that the sitting ends. These are not Keats's "Cold Pastoral," frozen in sculpture. Goldsmith himself ridiculed the allegorical posturing of the Vicar's family when they sat stiffly for their family portrait—his wife as Venus "with a stomacher richly set with diamonds and her two little ones as Cupids by her side, while I, in my gown and band, was to present her with books on the Whistonian controversy" (Ch. 16). When he attempted to draw their "life picture," the family was at tea

---

[9] See, for example, Hogarth's portrait of the Graham family in the Tate Gallery. Of these paintings in general Mario Praz writes: "In the conversation piece the environment is depicted with an attention to detail no less scrupulous than we find practised in the portrayal of the sitters, and this gives to the picture a *Stimmung,* an intimate feeling which is not shared to an appreciable degree by the group scene, isolated or presented against a summarily indicated background as it is" (*Conversation Pieces,* p. 56).

—engaged, in other words, in ordinary domestic activity: "On these occasions, our two little ones always read for us. . . . Sometimes, to give variety to our amusements, the girls sung to the guitar; and while they thus formed a little concert, my wife and I would stroll down the sloping field that was embellished with bluebells and centaury, talk of our children with rapture, and enjoy the breeze that wafted both health and harmony" (Ch. 5).

These painterly details appear in strikingly similar ways in the nineteenth-century domestic novel. One of the best and most popular domestic novelists, Charlotte Yonge, writing almost a century later than Goldsmith, places her family in nature with more individualized detail but the same painter's eye for a "conversation piece"—light, sky, a landscape background with laboring farmers, a foreground peopled with her characters, each engaged in some typical action or inaction:

"It was a glorious day in June, the sky of pure deep dazzling blue, the sunshine glowing with brightness, but with cheerful freshness in the air that took away all sultriness, the sun tending westward in his long day's career, and casting welcome shadows from the tall firs and horse-chestnuts that shaded the lawn. A long rank of haymakers—men and women—proceeded with their rakes, the white shirt-sleeves, straw bonnets, and ruddy faces, radiant in the bath of sunshine, while in the shady end of the field were idler haymakers among the fragrant piles, Charles half lying on grass, with his back against a tall haycock; Mrs. Edmondstone sitting on another, book in hand; Laura sketching the busy scene, the sun glancing through the chequered shade on her glossy curls; Philip stretched out at full length, hat and neck-tie off, luxuriating in the cool repose after a dusty walk from Broadstone; and a little way off, Amabel and Charlotte, pretending to make hay, but really building nests with it, throwing it at each other, and playing as heartily as the heat would allow" (*The Heir of Redclyffe*, ch. 7).

The happiest family in all of George Eliot's fiction, the Garths, are painted in similar activity: "He found the family group, dogs and cats included, under the great apple-tree in the orchard." While one son reads aloud from *Ivanhoe*, the younger children frolic in the grass: "Ben, bouncing across the grass with Brownie at his heels, and seeing the kitten dragging the knitting by a lengthening line of wool, shouted and clapped his hands; Brownie barked, the kitten, desperate, jumped on the tea-table and upset the milk, then jumped down again and swept half the cherries with it; and Ben, snatching up the half-knitted sock-top, fitted it over the kitten's head as a new source of madness, while Letty arriving cried out to her mother against this cruelty—it was a history as full of sensation as 'This is the house that Jack built'" (*Middlemarch*, Bk. vi, ch. 57).

The Victorians liked interior domestic scenes even better than outdoor ones. The sense of warmth, intimacy, privacy, and security, is very striking—both in painted family portraits and in literary ones: the group sitting near the fire or around the parlor table, the home their castle (Wemmick even builds a moat around his cottage in *Great Expectations*). There seems to be a special affinity between such cozy interiors and novel-reading itself. In her preface to *Emilia Wyndham* (1846), a kind of apology and justification for novels, Anne Marsh-Caldwell paints an idyllic domestic scene the center of which is a novel:

"It is a beautiful sight, when the winter wind is raving and howling, the snow and sleet falling upon the window-pane,—servants comfortably sitting over the hearth, and horses snugly sheltered in the stables,—to see, instead of a group of young ladies dressed for the incessant succession of evening parties, too often to return home wearied, dissatisfied, unimproved and out of humour—it is a beautiful sight to behold the blazing fire, the happy circle assembled, the embroidery-frames, or the poor-clothes basket, or the drawing materials brought out; and sweet female forms, surrounded with all the attractive neatness which renders the Englishman's home his paradise, gathered round; while the father rests in his arm-chair, and the brother, or, perhaps the mother, or maybe one of the fair creatures themselves, produces to the bright eyes beaming with pleasure the new novel of the day."

Charlotte Yonge's numerous May family (eleven children) crowd into a sitting-room described so faithfully that it needs only a frame to be imagined as a painting: "It was such a room as is often to be found in old country town houses, the two large windows looking out on a broad old-fashioned street, through heavy framework, and panes of glass scratched with various names and initials. The walls were painted blue, the skirting almost a third of the height, and so wide at the top as to form a narrow shelf. The fire-place, constructed in the days when fires were made to give as little heat as possible, was ornamented with blue and white Dutch tiles bearing marvellous representations of Scripture history, and was protected by a very tall green guard; the chairs were much of the same date, solid and heavy, the seats in faded carpet-work . . . but there was a large table in the middle of the room, with three desks on it: a small one, and a light cane chair by each window; and loaded book-cases" (*The Daisy Chain*, Ch. 1).

Here the Mays assemble to share their joys and griefs, cut off from the outside world, intimate, private, and—in spite of their troubles—secure in their sense of family unity: "Ethel, on coming in, found Flora making tea, her father leaning back in his great chair in silence, Richard diligently cutting bread, and Blanche sitting on Mr. Wilmot's knee, chattering fast and confidentially. Flora made Harry dispense the cups, and called everyone to their places; Ethel timidly glanced at her father's face as he rose and came into the light. She thought the lines and hollows were more marked than ever. . ." (Ch. 14).

21

Faithful and circumstantial as all this detail is, mere "photographic" reproduction of life was never the aim of domestic realism. No matter how sharply the novelist observed or how conscientiously he recorded his observations, he was doomed to failure unless he had those other talents for selectivity, arrangement, and characterization that breathe life into fiction. Tired hacks—Mrs. Gore occasionally and Theodore Hook more frequently—puffed out their formula-fabricated three deckers with descriptions remarkable for camera-like fidelity but little else. Theodore Hook in particular had both microscopic and panoramic lenses but rarely used them to artistic purpose. Describing a character dining in a low-class London inn, he counts the spots on the tablecoth: "He then proceeded to exhibit a pewter tea-pot, with a Davenanted spout, a small jug, containing three or four tablespoonsful of a light-blue liquid, professing to be milk, which, with some half-dozen lumps of dingy sugar, recumbent in a basin, and attended thereon by a pair of brown japanned tongs, shared the board with a bit of salt butter, and a French roll, three inches long by two inches in circumference" ("Passion and Principle," in *Sayings and Doings* [1825]).

Hook was very likely one of the novelists George Henry Lewes had in mind when in 1865 he complained about the vogue for "detailism," which purports to be realism but is actually "false art . . . a preference for the Familiar, under the misleading notion of adherence to Nature." The "rage for realism," he warns, is healthy "in as far as it insists on truth," but it becomes unhealthy ". . . in as far as it confounds truth with familiarity, and predominance of unessential details. There are other truths besides coats and waistcoats, pots and pans, drawing-rooms and suburban villas. . . . And the painter who devotes years to a work representing modern life, yet calls for even more attention to a waistcoat than to the face of a philosopher, may exhibit truth of detail which will delight the tailor-mind, but he is

22

defective in artistic truth, because he ought to be representing something higher than waistcoats. . . ."[10]

Some years later, in "The Art of Fiction," Henry James issued a similar warning against the confusion of mere detailism with realism: "It goes without saying that you will not write a good novel unless you possess the sense of reality; but it will be difficult to give you a recipe for calling that sense into being. Humanity is immense, and reality has myriad forms; the most one can affirm is that some of the flowers of fiction have the odour of it, and others have not." The "illusion of life," James continues, "the air of reality," is "the supreme virtue of a novel." If he could not offer the formula for achieving it, he did at least name its main element—"solidity of specification." It is the solidity of detail, not the quantity, that distinguishes great novels of domestic realism from lesser ones. It is the ring of homely truth that we hear in Miss Phoebe, in Mrs. Gaskell's *Wives and Daughters*, describing her excitement at an unexpected visit from an aristocratic lady:

" 'Oh, dear, Molly! If you're not in a hurry to go to bed, let me sit down quietly and tell you all about it; for my heart jumps into my mouth still when I think of how I was caught. She—that is, her ladyship—left the carriage at "The George" and took to her feet to go shopping—just as you or I may have done many a time in our lives. And sister was taking her forty winks; and I was sitting with my gown up above my knees and my feet on the fender, pulling out my grandmother's lace which I'd been washing. The worst has yet to be told. I'd taken off my cap, for I thought it was getting dusk and no would come, and there was I in my black silk skull-cap, when Nancy put her head in, and whispered, "There's a lady downstairs—a real grand one by her talk"; and in there came Lady Harriet, so sweet and pretty in her

[10] *The Principles of Success in Literature*, ed. Fred N. Scott (third ed., New York, 1891), pp. 83-84. These articles were originally published in *The Fortnightly Review* in 1865.

ways, it was some time before I forgot I had never a cap on'" (Ch. 14).

"Solidity of specification" is the power by which the novelist somehow convinces us of the presence of life. We feel it in a single gesture, like Hetty Sorrel's kissing her arms at a moment when, abandoned and contemplating suicide, she finds shelter in a sheepfold: "She reached the opposite gate, and felt her way along its rails, and the rails of the sheepfold, till her hand encountered the pricking of the gorsy wall. Delicious sensation! She had found the shelter; she groped her way, touching the prickly gorse, to the door, and pushed it open. It was an ill-smelling, close place, but warm, and there was straw on the ground: Hetty sank down on the straw with a sense of escape. Tears came—she had never shed tears before since she left Windsor—tears and sobs of hysterical joy that she had still hold of life, that she was still on the familiar earth, with the sheep near her. The very consciousness of her own limbs was a delight to her; she turned up her sleeves, and kissed her arms with the passionate love of life" (*Adam Bede*, Ch. 37).

For George Eliot homely, realistic detail provides the material out of which she constructs the total social and conceptual reality of her novels. It no longer functions for the single purpose of sentimental decoration, but for a complex of purposes. Dutch genre painting, which she so admired, may have inspired those magnificent rustic and family scenes in *Adam Bede* and also individual portraits—the aged Martin Poyser, for example, ". . . his head hanging forward a little, and his elbows pushed backward so as to allow the whole of his fore-arm to rest on the arm of the chair. His blue handkerchief was spread over his knees, as was usual indoors, when it was not hanging over his head; and he sat watching what went forward with the quiet *outward* glance of healthy old age. . ." (Ch. 14). But domestic realism achieves cumulative effects in her work that go far beyond the pictorial. Out of the domestic scene she constructs an entire social order—like the Dodson world in *The Mill on the Floss*:

"There were particular ways of doing everything in that family; particular ways of bleaching the linen, of making the cowslip wine, curing the hams, and keeping the bottled gooseberries; so that no daughter of that house could be indifferent to the privilege of having been born a Dodson, rather than a Gibson or a Watson. . . . In short, there was in this family a peculiar tradition as to what was the right thing in household management and social demeanour, and the only bitter circumstance attending this superiority was a painful inability to approve the condiments or the conduct of families ungoverned by the Dodson tradition" (Bk. I, ch. 6).

For the Dodsons domestic life defines social standing. The manner in which domestic chores are performed, food prepared, linen arranged, is ritualistic and symbolic. It represents their sense of values; indeed, it is their religion: "The religion of the Dodsons consisted in revering whatever was customary and respectable. . . . A Dodson would not be taxed with the omission of anything that was becoming, or that belonged to that eternal fitness of things which was plainly indicated in the practice of the most substantial parishioners, and in the family traditions—such as obedience to parents, faithfulness to kindred, industry, rigid honesty, thrift, the thorough scouring of wooden and copper utensils, the hoarding of coins likely to disappear from the currency, the production of first-rate commodities for the market, and the general preference for whatever was homemade" (Bk. IV, ch. 1).

II

CARRIED to such heights as *The Mill on the Floss*, domestic realism, not surprisingly, finally bridged the gap between the novel and "literature." The prestige and respectability

25

that the novel achieved in the mid-nineteenth century was the result of its identification with truth. Insisting that it was *not* "the highest vocation of the novelist to represent things as they never have been and never will be," that it was *not* the novelist's privilege to "refashion life and character entirely after my own liking," but instead "to give a faithful account of men and things as they have mirrored themselves in my mind . . . as if I were in the witness-box narrating my experience on oath" (*Adam Bede*, Ch. 17), George Eliot swept away the last lingering prejudices against the novel as romance. The novel as testimony to truth, the novelist as witness—with due recognition of his fallibility as an imaginative-creative human being—is perhaps the highest achievement of domestic realism.

The Victorian novel found its direction and its justification in the symbolic gesture of Charlotte Brontë's Lucy Snowe's tearing up the veil and treading on the bolster of the "phantom nun" that proved to be a silly practical joke, in her resolve henceforth to cut "from the homely web of truth," and in that same novelist's defiant announcement to the reader of *Shirley*: "If you think, from this prelude, that anything like a romance is preparing for you, reader, you never were more mistaken. Do you anticipate sentiment, and poetry, and reverie? Do you expect passion, and stimulus, and melodrama? Calm your expectations; reduce them to a lowly standard. Something real, cool, and solid, lies before you; something unromantic as Monday morning, when all who have work wake with the consciousness that they must rise and betake themselves thereto."[11]

---

[11] See also her *The Professor*: "Novelists should never allow themselves to weary of the study of real life. If they observed this duty conscientiously, they would give us fewer pictures chequered with vivid contrasts of light and shade; they would seldom elevate their heroes and heroines to the heights of rapture—still seldomer sink them to the depths of despair . . . the man of regular life and rational mind never despairs" (Ch. 19).

26

A semantic confusion continued to plague both novelists and critics as to the distinction between the *real* and the *true*. Like many other Victorian critics and most of the novelists who were practitioners of domestic realism, Lewes equated them: "Art always aims at the representation of Reality, i.e., of Truth. . . . Realism is thus the basis of all Art, and its antithesis is not Idealism, but Falsism. . . ."[12] Yet the Victorians were also sensitive to the ambiguities of the terms: "Realism is confounded with materialism . . . and is represented as being the art of copying external nature with correctness, when analysis of human character and motives, and the observation of mental phenomena, form the very foundation of the system."[13] But, like Henry James, Lewes knew that he could not offer a formula for creating "a sense of reality": "It is easy for the artist to choose a subject from every-day life, but it is not easy for him to so represent the characters and their actions that they shall be at once life-like and interesting. . . ."[14] Even more sensitive to this distinction was Charlotte Brontë, who, responding with some pique to Lewes' advice "not to stray far from the ground of experience, as I become weak when I enter the region of fiction," reminded him of the perils of literalism: "I feel that this also is true; but, dear Sir, is not the real experience of each individual very limited? And, if a writer dwells upon that solely or principally, is he not in danger of repeating himself, and also of becoming an egotist? Then, too, imagination is a strong, restless faculty, which claims to be heard

[12] "Realism in Art," *Westminster Review*, 70 (October, 1858), p. 493.

[13] "Balzac and his Writings," *ibid.*, 60 (July, 1853), pp. 199-214. See also R. G. Davis, "The Sense of the Real in English Fiction," *Comparative Literature*, 3 (Summer, 1951), pp. 200-17, and Richard Stang, *The Theory of the Novel in England, 1850-1870* (New York, 1959).

[14] "The Novels of Jane Austen," *Blackwood's*, 86 (July, 1859), pp. 99-113. See also Alice R. Kaminsky, *The Literary Criticism of George Henry Lewes* (Lincoln, Neb., 1964).

and exercised: are we to be quite deaf to her cry, and insensate to her struggles?"[15]

The critical debate continues to this day.[16] Realism, as it involves social contexts and social "relevance," has its vigorous defenders; and, as it involves the faithful and accurate reporting of the way men live in society, it is still regarded as the foundation of the conventional modern novel. "The novel then," writes Lionel Trilling, "is a perpetual quest for reality, the field of its research being always the social world." Richard Chase distinguished between the novel and the romance in terms of their differing approaches to reality: "The novel renders reality closely and in comprehensive detail. It takes a group of people and sets them going about the business of life." The chief interest of the novel, according to Northrop Frye, "is in human character as it manifests itself in society." The novel, he suggests, "tends to be extroverted," concerned with external reality: "The novelist deals with personality, with characters wearing their personae or social masks. He needs the framework of a stable society. . . ."

Yet out of these same currents of cool observation and

[15] November 6, 1847, "Shakespeare Head Brontë," II, 233-34. Charlotte Brontë would have found strong support for her argument in an unsigned review, "The Author of *Heartsease* and Modern Schools of Fiction," *Prospective Review*, 10 (no. 40, 1854), pp. 460-82. This writer, weary of the faithful "Daguerre-type process" of realism in Charlotte Yonge's novels, finds in many novels of the day "a want of any deep imaginative power. What we mean is, that instead of *using* their experience as food for their imagination, they chain down their imagination to the exact forms of life to which their experience has accustomed them" (p. 470).

[16] For a summary of the issues see René Wellek and Austin Warren, *Theory of Literature* (Third ed., New York, 1956), Ch. 9, "Literature and Society." Trilling's remarks are in "Manners, Morals and the Novel," in *The Liberal Imagination* (Anchor Books, New York, 1953), p. 205; Chase's in *The American Novel and its Tradition* (New York, 1957), p. 12; Frye's in *The Anatomy of Criticism* (Princeton, 1957), pp. 304-05.

objective reporting—detailism and literalism—there also emerged with Victorian domestic realism a balancing element of introspection and subjectivity. The reviewer of Balzac's work in the *Westminster Review* in 1853 perceived this when he pointed out that romanticism, with its emphasis on "real and natural models" and "the exact imitation of nature," was already building a bridge to realism: "Those who copy from nature, and, above all, from modern nature, and the nature which surrounds them at every instant, were destined to receive from the champions of conventionality the appellation of 'realists,'—this realism being in fact only a continuation or branch of what had before been absurdly styled 'romanticism.' "[17] The difference between this "new" romanticism and the older spirit—gothic nuns and Byronic heroes—was the shifting of attention from the grand, the wild, and the remote to the domestic scene. Inevitably, then, it manifested itself in quieter action and themes—family love, self-examination, devotion and duty to home responsibilities, resignation to disappointment, self-sacrifice in the interests of those we love. Goethe's "bread-and-buttery" Charlotte confesses to Werther that she has outgrown the romantic novels of her youth. In her maturity she prefers those authors "who describe my own situation in life—and the friends who are about me—whose stories touch me with interest because they resemble my own domestic life. . . ."[18] As Ian Watt has suggested, the "primary criterion" of the modern novel—in contrast to the traditionalism of epic and allegory—is "truth to individual experience," the recognition that the individual discovers truth for himself, empirically, through his senses and sensibilities.[19] To the extent, then, that it is concerned with individual ex-

[17] See above, note 13.

[18] *The Sorrows of Young Werther*, tr. Victor Lange (Rinehart Books, New York, 1949), p. 18.

[19] "Realism and the Novel Form," in *The Rise of the Modern Novel* (Berkeley, Calif., 1964), Ch. 1.

perience in the daily activities of living, the novel of domestic realism achieves a kind of truth. The Victorians certainly received it as such.

III

As THE novel moved away from romance—or toward romance in totally new forms with domesticated heroes and "adventures" drawn from everyday life—it became increasingly bourgeois and feminine. The term "novel" had already been identified with "familiar" domestic life in Clara Reeve's often-quoted definition from *The Progress of Romance* in 1785: "The Romance in lofty language, describes what never happened nor is likely to happen. The Novel gives a familiar relation of such things, as pass every day before our eyes."

During the transitional period, as we have noted, Sir Walter Scott adapted his romantic-historical themes to the demands of a new fiction-reading market. In abandoning narrative poetry for the novel he tacitly acknowledged the changing nature of his public. As his contemporary, the once-eminent bluestocking Mrs. Anna Laetitia Barbauld, editor of a fifty-volume collection "The British Novelists" (1810), pointed out in her prefatory essay "On the Origin and Progress of Novel-Writing," poetry "requires in the reader a certain elevation of mind and a practised ear." But novel-reading, she admitted somewhat apologetically, "is the cheapest of pleasures: it is a domestic pleasure." It demands no education beyond literacy and offers no higher reward than amusement. Its natural audience is therefore women and its area the home. Humble as the novel is, however ("A collection of Novels has a better chance of giving pleasure than of gaining respect"), its effects are far-reaching because it touches the reader's feelings and moral sensibilities. Therefore, Mrs. Barbauld argues, the novelist has a higher responsibility than is at first apparent. In the young and impressionable particularly, novels "awaken a sense of finer feelings than the commerce of ordinary life inspires . . . they mix with the natural passions of our nature all that is tender in virtuous affection; all that is estimable in high principle and unshaken constancy; all that grace, delicacy, and sentiment can bestow of touching and attractive."

Thus without elevating the novel to the ranks of great literature, Mrs. Barbauld cautiously reconciles its end—entertainment—with the higher moral purposes of art. She had a powerful ally in Scott, who in the *Quarterly Review* of October 1815 hailed Jane Austen's *Emma* as a fresh new kind of novel, a happy successor to the exhausted romance: "The substitute for these excitements, which had lost much of their poignancy by the repeated and injudicious use of them, was the art of copying from nature as she really exists in the common walks of life, and presenting to the reader, instead of the splendid scenes of an imaginary world, a correct and striking representation of that which is daily taking place around him."

The two most remarkable qualities of this "new novel" were fidelity to the experiences of ordinary living and sensitivity to the feelings and emotions aroused in and produced by ordinary life. When Thackeray's Laura Bell advised Pendennis to write "good kind books with gentle thoughts" (Ch. 66), she was speaking as a woman, not a literary pundit. But her advice was sound. Intuitively she grasped the nature of the market. As early as 1777 the omnipresent Mrs. Hannah More had observed the fitness of women for writing faithfully and feelingly about real life:

"The merit of this kind of writing consists in the *vraisemblance* to real life, as to the events themselves, with a certain elevation in the narrative, which places them, if not above what is natural, yet above what is common. It further consists in the art of interesting the tender feelings by a pathetic representation of those minute, endearing, domestic circumstances, which take captive the soul before it has time to shield itself with an armour of reflection. To amuse

31

rather than to instruct, or to instruct indirectly by short inferences, drawn from a long concatenation of circumstances, is at once the business of this sort of composition, and one of the characteristics of female genius."[20]

Even earlier Rousseau in *Emile* (1762) had discovered from his analysis of the female character her "natural gift" for human insight and sensibility. He was not concerned with her application of this gift to literature. On the contrary, he felt that she could best use it in her home, educating her children. Science, all abstract and speculative knowledge, were beyond her grasp. But if she followed Rousseau's advice by confining her duties to the more practical work of leading and directing men—her husband and her children—in their moral development, she might also obliquely be preparing herself for the career of a novelist: "A woman's thoughts, beyond the range of her immediate duties, should be directed to the study of men, or the acquirement of that agreeable learning whose sole end is the formation of taste. . . . The men will have a better philosophy of the human heart, but she will read more accurately in the heart of men. Women should discover, so to speak, an experimental morality, man should reduce it to a system" (Bk. v).

Critics and novelists alike were no doubt patronizing and condescending in their commendation of women novelists. Until the domestic novel achieved its full stature as literature in the mid-nineteenth century, its practitioners were inevitably looked down upon. Writers like the Brontës assumed masculine pen-names to assure an objective critical reception for their work. Serious men novelists like Bulwer and Disraeli drew their material from high society and political life or from history, following the respected example of Scott. Others, like Charles Kingsley, took up specific reform causes, producing novels of social realism and crusading for political and social change. By the 1840's, however,

[20] *Essays on Various Subjects Principally Designed for Young Ladies* (New ed., Chiswick, 1820), p. xv.

not only were younger men novelists like Dickens and Thackeray turning to domestic subjects, but the established Bulwer launched himself into domestic realism with a family novel, *The Caxtons* (1848-1849), announcing in his preface that his plot has been drawn from "the records of ordinary life . . . a simple Family picture. And thus, in any appeal to the sympathies of the human heart, the common household affections occupy the place of those livelier or larger passions which usually (and not unjustly) arrogate the foreground in Romantic composition."

Bulwer was both a taste-maker and a barometer of changes in popular taste. His success in all the popular fictional forms—historical novels, society novels, crime novels, novels of the supernatural—had been remarkable, but there was a noticeable decline of interest in these as mid-century approached. When in 1855 a young Cambridge student, Fitzjames Stephen, could define the novel as "a fictitious biography," the age of realism had arrived.[21] In the next decade a critic of considerable reputation, E. S. Dallas, repeated that definition and added the final link to domestic realism: "A novel may be described as gossip etherealized, family talk generalised." Dallas noted the anti-romantic and anti-heroic drift of the novel, citing Thackeray as the supreme example of the "new" novelist who, by reducing the heroic proportions of his individual characters, gave them new importance and dignity as human beings. With heroes and heroic action eliminated, the role of women becomes vastly more significant, Dallas observes. "Now all the more important characters seem to be women. Our novelists have suddenly discovered that the feminine character is an unworked mine of wealth. . . . This is all the more natural, seeing that most of our novelists just now seem to belong to the fair sex. But their masculine rivals follow in the same track." The result, inevitably, is "the ascendency of domestic ideas, and the assertion of the individual, not as a hero, but as a

[21] "The Relation of Novels to Life," in *Cambridge Essays* (Cambridge, 1855), pp. 149-50.

33

family man—not as a heroine, but as an angel in the house."[22]

Since the realistic domestic novel allowed little room for lofty philosophizing and profound erudition (all commentators agreed that if novels were to be realistic they must faithfully reproduce ordinary life and speech) or for spectacular scenery and action, it was considered appropriate for women, with their limited education and experience, to be novelists. The "silver-fork" novelist T. H. Lister, reviewing Mrs. Gore's *Women as They Are* in the *Edinburgh Review* in 1830, even conceded their superiority to men in this field:

"There are some things which women do better than men; and of these, perhaps, novel-writing is one. Naturally endowed with greater delicacy of taste and feeling, with a moral sense not blunted and debased by those contaminations to which men are exposed, leading lives rather of observation than of action, with leisure to attend to the minutiae of conduct, and more subtle developements of character, they are peculiarly qualified for the task of exhibiting faithfully and pleasingly the various phases of domestic life, and those varieties which chequer the surface of society."[23]

Women themselves were prompt to admit that they had made a virtue of necessity. Confined to the home circle, like Rousseau's model wife-mother, they cultivated close observation, introspection, analysis. What better training for a novelist's career? Men, boasting of their knowledge of the world, "know mankind only as they appear in one or two particular habits," Mrs. Elizabeth Hamilton wrote in 1808. They are too actively engaged in life to study "that infinite variety which in reality exists. . . ." But women, scrutinizing "little particulars," observe more and better, ". . . as I am persuaded that a single week spent *tête-à-tête* with a per-

[22] *The Gay Science* (London, 1866), ii, Ch. 17, "The Ethical Current."

[23] The review is attributed to Lister in the *Wellesley Index*.

34

son, in their own house, gives a more thorough insight into the mind and disposition than would in years be obtained in the common intercourse of society."[24] Herself a novelist as well as a once-celebrated philosopher and educator, Mrs. Hamilton seems to offer the *raison d'être* of the female-dominated domestic novel. For its "Poetics," its working critical principles, we may look to two other women, novelists and writers of some reputation in their day—Anne Marsh-Caldwell (1791-1874) and Sarah Stickney Ellis (1812-1872), the latter famous for a series of non-fiction books with echo titles: *The Women of England* (1838), *The Daughters of England* (1842), *The Wives of England* (1843), and *The Mothers of England* (1843).

Mrs. Marsh, mother of seven children, wrote eighteen novels of which only one, *Emilia Wyndham,* survives in flickering memory. Harriet Martineau admired her work and wrote an introduction to another of her books, *The Two Old Men's Tales* (1834), for which, she reported in her *Autobiography,* Mrs. Marsh received "high and well deserved fame." Whatever immortality *Emilia Wyndham* has is the result not of the novel itself but of the preface its author wrote for it. The plot concerns an ardent young girl who learns, first from her mother's teaching and then from the experience of life itself, that one's heroism is challenged and displayed not in lofty romantic adventures, but in "the heavy, wearying every-day evils of every-day actual life . . . combining patience, perseverance, endurance, gentleness, and disinterestedness." Significantly, the novel is dedicated to William Wordsworth, "the fine influences" of whose poetry have contributed to the moral life of "countless numbers."

The Preface to *Emilia Wyndham* is an essay on the realistic domestic novel. Mrs. Marsh firmly rejects fables and fantasy: "The novel must not trench upon the confines of either the allegory or the fable; its essential, its indisputable qual-

[24] *Memoirs of the Late Mrs. Elizabeth Hamilton.* By Miss [E. O.] Benger (London, 1818), I, 251-52.

ity is, that it should convey the sense of reality—that the people we read of should be to us as actual beings and persons—that we should believe in them." Credibility is necessary in order that the moral teachings of the novel be effective. We cannot expect readers to believe in the characters of *The Faerie Queene*, she points out; therefore, "the divine poem is uninteresting and cast aside." But we can believe in "the tale of life," where the novelist's object is to connect actions and their consequences. Long before E. M. Forster, Mrs. Marsh urged, "Only connect": "The object, therefore, of the novelist should be, not so much to illustrate a particular moral maxim, as to *point the tale of life*—to bring actions and their consequences, passions, principles, and their results, into that sort of connexion, which, though it certainly and inevitably takes place in actual life, escapes the careless, or, perhaps, undiscerning eye of the reader of the vast volume amid the multiplicity of circumstances in which it is involved. It is for the writer of fiction, without ever over-stepping the bounds of *easy* probability, to bring . . . causes and their consequences into obvious connexion."

When the novel performs this, its proper function, it finds its proper audience in the home. We have already quoted from this preface Mrs. Marsh's depiction of a cozy family scene—a storm raging outside, parents, children, and servants gathered around the fire, eager to hear one of them read aloud from "the new novel of the day." That saccharin-sprinkled vision should not dazzle or becloud our perception of Mrs. Marsh's critical shrewdness. She knew her medium and her audience. Though she emphasized the moral-didactic function of the domestic novel, she also recognized its need to interest and entertain the volatile "fair creatures," the young daughters of the family, every bit as much as its need to meet with the approval of the Englishman and his matron-wife: "What life, what animation, diffuses itself, as the strange tale proceeds! What sighs—what tears—what anxieties—what smiles!—as the storm-tossed traveller over life's restless ocean reaches the desired haven at last. How the honest heart glows with new aspirations after better things to come for its own inner life—as the loveliness of virtuous self-sacrifice, the grandeur of true heroism, the beauty of sweetness, and temper, and gentleness, and love, are displayed as in a living picture!"

A sterner moral critic, yet an equally enthusiastic advocate of the domestic novel, Sarah Stickney (later Mrs. Ellis) prefaced her *Pictures of Private Life* (note that the title suggests both painting and domesticity) in 1833 with a similar "Apology for Fiction," drawing a firm line between that fiction which offers "lawful" and that which offers "unlawful" pleasure. Unlawful is "whatever weakens your reason, impairs the tenderness of your conscience, obscures your sense of God, or takes off the relish of spiritual things." Turning her severe scrutiny to specifics of novel-writing, she rules out such "abuses" as "the delineation of unnatural characters, by the combination of such qualities as never did, and never could exist in one human being; and the placing such creatures of the imagination in scenes and circumstances, where the common sympathies of our nature find no place." She accepts, however, that fiction in which characters are "drawn from the scenes of every-day life, animated with our feelings, weak with our frailties, led into our difficulties, surrounded by our temptations, and altogether involved in a succession of the same causes and effects which influence our lives. . . ."

In such fiction the more exact the descriptive detail the better. The painter who wishes to exhibit to the public "a personification of old age" would not simply paint an old woman in a cottage. To complete his idea he would "place before our eyes" the interior of her house—furniture, spinning wheel, kettle, cat. "Now, though such an old woman . . . never did exist, yet the picture may be true." By analogous means, the novelist evokes a living reality out of imagined details. He has the additional advantage over the painter of being able to add moral teaching to his picture

37

by creating a plot in which virtue may be tested, other characters introduced to demonstrate actions opposed to virtue, all arranged for the purpose "of tracing causes to their effects." In the scale of moral teaching, Mrs. Ellis points out, "some preach virtue, some only practise it, some make a picture of it, and some a poem, and some . . . adorn it in the garb of fiction, that it may ensure a welcome, where it would not otherwise obtain an entrance. . . . Fiction may be compared to a key, which opens many minds that would be closed against a sermon."

The assumption of order and rationality involved in such teaching, in assuming that actions are connected and that effects have causes that may be traced and consequences that may be properly inferred, is basically anti-romantic. The novel of domestic realism was, in fact, born in reaction to romanticism. Yet even as it rejected and negated those qualities of the remote and exotic, the self-indulgent emotionalism that readers associated with romanticism, it cultivated sentimentality, sensibility, idealism, and spirituality —qualities that are themselves incompatible with the hard core of realism as we generally use the term. Domestic realism in the nineteenth-century English novel may be described, then, as an attempt to substitute one kind of romanticism for another, or at best to transcend the coarser everyday reality and see it in a softer, more idealized glow. It was an effort, relatively short-lived but vigorous while it lasted, to persuade the public that there was an alternative to the romantic ideal. In one of her most popular books, *The Daughters of England,* Mrs. Ellis argued that readers could be persuaded to reject the Corsairs of Byron and the Isles of Greece and even the gypsies of Sir Walter Scott for alternative attractions in "the page of actual life." There, "beneath the parental roof, or mixing with the fireside circle by the homely hearth, there are often feelings as deep, and hearts as warm, and experience as richly fraught with interest, as ever glowed in verse, or lived in story" (Ch. 5).

By "story" Mrs. Ellis meant romance. The domestic novel

that was emerging in the early 1840's when she wrote that sentence was of an apparently if not really different order. Within another generation it had become the established and favorite popular literary genre. In 1874 an article titled "The Domestic Novel," published in the magazine *The Argosy*, proclaimed that "novels to-day seem to occupy the same place in literature that the plays of Shakespeare and Ben Jonson and Marlowe held in the Elizabethan era." Attributing their popularity largely to the influence of women readers who had demanded the elimination of the "gross coarseness of language and customs" of the eighteenth-century novel, the writer hails Jane Austen as a forerunner ("Her region, and in it she reigns unequalled, is that of the commonplace") and, among contemporaries, Thackeray ("whose pictures of English life and manners are without rival in their way"), Trollope, Bulwer (for his "most delightful domestic novel *What Will He Do With It?*"), Dickens (with some reservations about his preoccupation with "low life"), and George Eliot (though *Middlemarch* is "rather too transcendental")—"Doubtless a great change has taken place in the last few years. No one now speaks of novels in the same style of indifferent contempt that was the fashion not long ago. . . . Where are we to look, if not to novels, for the truest and most highly finished pictures of English life?"[25]

The Victorian novel was often described in contemporary reviews as a "picture," but by mid-century the term was conceived far more broadly than a mere literal reproduction of scenes and activities of daily life. A better approximation might be the medieval *speculum*, a reflecting mirror, with all the philosophical connotations of speculative, reflective thought. The novelists were commentators on life, not photographers or reporters. Though they drew from the details that today journalism and photography command, to the degree that they were creative artists they also selected, filtered, and arranged their detail to serve their

[25] 18 (July-December, 1874), pp. 291-97.

philosophical, ideological, and aesthetic purposes. Focussed in the English painter's eye as in the English novelist's eye was a small, orderly, regular, and somehow purposeful and logical world. Reverend Primrose's beautifully ordered little family of 1766 was menaced and came perilously near collapse, but Goldsmith's readers up through the mid-nineteenth century could follow the Primroses' misfortunes with serenity, confident that, however miraculously, all would be restored to right. The major and later Victorian novelists were less secure. Working under the demands of "truth," they had to concede occasional defeats and allow for disappointment, frustration, and compromise. But even their most realistically "truthful" novels end with a consoling sense of resignation to some higher meaning and purpose in life. Lucy Snowe accepts and is almost exalted by her lover's death. Pip buries his lost expectations and his love for Estella in solid, constructive work. Young Clive Newcome, frustrated both in love and in his ambitions to be a great painter, learns how to accept life by witnessing his father's humble acceptance of death. Dorothea Brooke will never be a Saint Theresa or an Antigone, but she will find satisfaction in her second marriage, performing useful "unhistoric acts" in an "imperfect social state." When, however, in the second half of the century, the sense of connected experience and purposeful existence was itself challenged, when established institutions and values were exposed to new and often shattering pressures, painters began to see broken images through reflected light, and novelists of artistic integrity, still concerned with "truth," could no longer find their subjects in the enclosed unit of the home, the family, or the small community. Domestic realism, as the early Victorian novelists practiced it, was a sturdy, serviceable genre that left its mark on the fiction of the second half of the century, but as a literary genre it had run its course.

2

Manners, Morals, and Maneuvering Matrons: Mrs. Gore and the Fashionable Novel

Observe that lady, with the sparkling face and Circassian form, who sits ensconced in the deep recesses of that luxurious reading chair, listening to the handsome dandy who hangs over her, as if his words were the inspirations of that poetry which looks from her own eyes; whereas they are only the newest club-engendered scandal, or at best some of the elaborate nothings of fashionable small-talk which he has perchance picked up (without knowing it) from her own last new novel.

—*Chatsworth: The Romance of a Week,*
ch. 10, edited by the author of
"Tremaine," "De Vere," etc. (1844)

I

CHATSWORTH, written by Peter George Patmore, is a collection of tales told by a group of fashionable people visiting at a palatial country estate. A kind of Victorian *Decameron* (the stories are drawn from medieval and Elizabethan sources, including Chaucer's "Franklin's Tale," Shakespeare, Heywood, and Fletcher), its only interest is the literary talk of its *à clef* characters—Sir Proteus Plume ("an intellect fraught with all pure thoughts and noble aspirations"), Lady Penthea ("the Byron of her sex"), Reginald Beltravers ("the most accomplished writer of the most accomplished era of English letters"), Mr. Tressyllian Toms ("a genius and therefore no gentleman"), and Lady Bab Brilliant, who is described in the passage above. Patmore (father of the poet Coventry) was a minor critic and essayist, editor of the *New Monthly Magazine* from 1841 to 1853, and a friend of many of the literary figures of the period, including the first of the "silver-fork" novelists, Robert Plumer Ward, who "edited" *Chatsworth*, and Mrs. Catherine Gore, who published some of her stories in his magazine and inspired the character of Lady Bab.[1]

A dazzling personality, Lady Bab is "the most accomplished writer that her own sex has hitherto produced . . . the Millamant at once of letters and of fashionable life." She unites the wit of Lady Mary Wortley Montagu with the wisdom and accomplishments of Mesdames du Deffand, de Sévigné, and de Staël. Although she is a needling critic and satirist of the fashionable world, she is also its idol. But the full portrait of Lady Bab is not as flattering as its outlines. Mrs. Gore, reading *Chatsworth* at the age of forty-five in a period when her career as the leading society novelist of England was clearly in decline, may have noted with dismay Patmore's somewhat left-handed compliment that she represented her age so well because she was herself so much a product of it: "Lady Bab Brilliant not only did not pretend to be any better than her friends and associates, but in reality *was* no better. She was in truth an epitome, in

[1] See her letter to him (Brussels, n.d.) in the Patmore Letters, Princeton University Library (AM 17317)—"I see by the hand of the immortal Jenkins of the Morning Post that you are the author of 'Chatsworth.' . . ." Robert Plumer Ward, no special admirer of Mrs. Gore's novels ("I never knew so much real talent in seizing the outside of characters, and drawing magic lantern pictures, so entirely fail in creating permanent interest"), refers to her in a letter to Patmore as "your certainly very clever friend, Mrs. Gore" (P. G. Patmore, *My Friends and Acquaintances* [London, 1854], II, 190). Young Coventry Patmore fell in love with Mrs. Gore's daughter Cecilia ("Cissie") when he was only sixteen and spent considerable time with the Gores while they were living in Paris in 1839. Miss Gore, two years his senior, apparently did not return his affections; she married Lord Edward Thynne (J. C. Reid, *The Mind and Art of Coventry Patmore* [London, 1957], p. 19).

herself, of all the fashionable follies and not a few of the fashionable vices (so called but not by her or us) which she had so effectually held up to public contempt and indignation. . . ."

Privately at least Mrs. Gore might have been the first to admit the justice of Patmore's comment. There is a rare candor in her otherwise conventional and clever but superficial novels—not self-revelation (the facts of Mrs. Gore's biography remain obscure to this day), but a no-nonsense, businesslike honesty about revealing the age and her all but complete identification with it.[2] She observes from inside society, and she is obviously inside because she chooses to be. There is no self-consciousness of the would-be or the parvenu in Mrs. Gore, nor any sense of guilt or betrayal of her class. Of middle-class family origin, married to an army officer, she achieved social position by virtue of her personality and her accomplishments as a writer. She worked hard, producing in a lifetime of about sixty years (1799-1860), some two hundred volumes of poetry, drama, and

[2] There is no book-length biography or critical study of Mrs. Gore. A number of her novels are discussed by Matthew Whiting Rosa in his *The Silver-Fork School: Novels of Fashion Preceding Vanity Fair* (New York, 1936), and her work is mentioned briefly in several histories of the English novel. There are brief biographical sketches, contradictory in some details, in *DNB*; in her obituaries in *The Athenaeum*, February 9, 1861; the *Gentleman's Magazine*, 10 March, 1861; and the *Times*, February 4, 1861; and in a manuscript note in the British Museum (Add. Mss. 28, 510). A good summary of the available biographical material is in Verna Dorothy Wittrock's doctoral dissertation, "The Re-Emergence of Realism in the Minor English Domestic Novel, 1824-1850," University of Illinois, 1957. The best source for material on her professional career is the Bentley correspondence at the University of Illinois. There are also some unpublished letters at Princeton and in the Beinecke Library at Yale to which I refer elsewhere in this chapter. For her critical reputation among her contemporaries, the reader should consult R. H. Horne, *A New Spirit of the Age* (1844), and the *New Monthly Magazine*, 49 (January-April, 1837), pp. 434-35, and 95 (June, 1852), pp. 157-68.

fiction, and a family of ten children, of whom only two survived her. Such industry, accompanied from beginning to end with lively good humor, testifies to a remarkable professionalism. Mrs. Gore was one of that hardy breed of Victorian lady novelists like Mrs. Trollope and Mrs. Oliphant whose energy and prolificness stagger the modern imagination. It is easy, but unwise, to dismiss such writers as mere hacks. Because they combined their industry with clear, keen, uncomplicated vision and a talent for describing what they saw, they were important chroniclers of their times.

Mrs. Gore was one of the best of these chroniclers because she not only observed with a sharp eye but she also interpreted. Her novels are social documents, but they are more. She could refer flippantly to her "ormolu railroad" of fashionable novels, but she had a healthy respect for the genre: "I will not attempt a defence of fashionable novels. I leave it to *Grandison, Clarissa, Belinda, Ennui, The Absentee, Vivian Grey,* etc. to plead their cause, and intrench myself in the obstinacy of a woman's opinion that every picture of passing manners, if accurate, is valuable from the drawing-room to the alehouse and that every writer does best who paints the scene more immediately before him."[3] If, like Lady Bab, she shared in the vices of her time, she was all the better prepared to judge them. She defined her function precisely in a novel of 1830, *Women as They Are; or, The Manners of the Day*: "We have perhaps had more than enough of fashionable novels, but as the amber which serves to preserve the ephemeral modes and caprices of the passing day, they have their value." As one of her contemporaries observed, she not only "shows" the gay world, "she shows it up."[4] Against the charge of some of her detractors that she placed too much emphasis on the life of pleasure

[3] Letter to Edward Bulwer-Lytton, published in Michael Sadleir's *Edward and Rosina* (Boston, 1931), p. 276.

[4] "Female Novelists," *New Monthly Magazine*, 95 (June, 1852), p. 158.

and frivolity, the *Edinburgh Review* defended her: "Mrs. Gore's design is to strip off the moral mask of hollow worldliness; she wishes only to unmask hypocrisy."[5] In 1837 another reviewer rated her high above the rank and file of novelists "who possess a certain facility without depth, in dashing off the external features of the fashionable coteries." Not only are her novels among "the best, the most faithful, the ablest transcript of existing English manners and national characteristics," but, more important, he detected in them, "a philosophical substratum . . . which will ensure their perpetuity."[6] This reviewer's prescience is questionable, but a more astute critic, W. M. Thackeray, commented a decade later of another of her books that for all Mrs. Gore's alleged superficiality and worldliness, there is no one who offers a more faithful picture "of Pall-mall in 1840, of the dandies who frequented Crockford's, the dowagers and virgins who resorted to Willis's." He concludes that we are wrong to complain that she offers no moral: "the moral is that which very likely the author intended—that entire weariness, contempt, and dislike which the reader must undergo after this introduction to what is called the world. If it be as here represented, the world is the most hollow, heartless, vulgar, brazen world, and those are luckiest who are out of it."[7]

Mrs. Gore herself, however, was anything but "out of it" even when she was most vigorously engaged in condemning her world. In the few personal glimpses that we have of her, she appears a lively society matron, every inch the "very sumptuous personage, looking like a full-blown rose,"

[5] Review (attributed to T. H. Lister in the *Wellesley Index*, i), of *Women as They Are* in *Edinburgh Review*, 51 (July, 1830), p. 459.

[6] Review of *Stokeshill Place* in *The Court Magazine and Monthly Critic*, 11 (July-December, 1837), pp. 140-41.

[7] Review of *Sketches of English Character*, May 4, 1846, in *Thackeray's Contributions to the Morning Chronicle*, ed. Gordon N. Ray (Urbana, Ill., 1955), pp. 140-42.

as Disraeli remembered her,[8] and very much the kind of fashionable lady she describes in many of her novels. Her busy literary career and her large family seem rather to have stimulated than discouraged party-going, country-house visiting, and a variety of other amusements. Although at periods in her life she expressed her preference for the country, she also relished the delights of what was then called "the world": ". . . the ball was wretchedly thin and par conséquent, wretchedly dull"; "I am just returned from Brussels, where I have been playing at Longchamps and other fooleries." Even in country retirement she had a merry social whirl: "We are Hampshire rustics," she concludes a letter of invitation to her novelist-friend Lady Morgan. But in the same letter she had urged her to visit between the thirteenth and Christmas—"before and after which we have engagements." Another time she protests that she is "too much in love" with her country retreat "to leave it for balls." Nevertheless, she filled the rural air with the bustling of her social life. "I had assembled a very pleasant party of notabilities here to meet you," she wrote Lady Morgan, "and as soon as they are dispersed we set off for Nottinghamshire and have spent a merry Christmas at Lord Scarborough's at Bufford Abbey . . . we shall not be in town again till after Easter. Lord Lincoln and his children are coming next week to stay here, unless his father should die in the interval, as was daily expected when we were in Notts. and we have a variety of country-neighbour balls and hunting breakfasts in prospect—so do not pity our solitude. . . ."[9]

The "world" in which Mrs. Gore lived so strenuously and enthusiastically was the end and ebb tide of the Rake-and-Regency era. She was in fact a latecomer both to that society and to its literary mirror, the fashionable or "silver-

[8] Letter to Sarah Disraeli, February 18, 1832, in W. F. Monypenny and G. E. Buckle, *The Life of Benjamin Disraeli* (rev. ed., New York, 1929), I, 207.

[9] Letters to Lady Morgan, Beinecke Library, Yale University.

fork" novel. This vogue, initiated by Robert Plumer Ward's *Tremaine* (1825) and exploited by Disraeli, Bulwer, Lady Charlotte Bury, and T. H. Lister, reached its heights with *Granby* (1826), *Vivian Grey* (1826), and *Pelham* (1828). Mrs. Gore's first novel of this type was *Women as They Are*, published in 1830, and her best, *Cecil; or The Adventures of a Coxcomb*, was not published until 1841. Her work therefore was as much historical as contemporary. Like many other and greater social satirists and critics, she looked back to a period that could be pinpointed and examined in the fixed state of the past. Although her novels cover the whole first half of the century—many of the later ones taking place in the Victorian age in which they were published—the most characteristic ones focus on that glittering, frivolous, shallow age when, as Thackeray put it, "the present century was in its teens," and the morals of "the First Gentleman in Europe" were so dubious that an upstart adventuress like Becky Sharp Crawley could achieve presentation at court.

Mrs. Gore lacked the judicial wit, objectivity, and urbanity of Thackeray, but she had an eye as coolly critical as his, though her voice was shriller and her tone too much influenced by the *ton* she condemned. Writing her first society novels in the 1830's, in that colorless reign of William IV—a king whose indiscretions even were dull—she looked back somewhat nostalgically to an age when corruption was at least glamorous and at times amusing. Of that age she is a stern but not unfair judge. In *The Cabinet Minister* (1839) she writes, for example, of the last year of the Regency, when old George III lay dying amid public and private calamities—his youngest daughter dead, the Duke of York having "exposed the name of royalty to popular contempt," the Prince of Wales (the "Sardanapalus of Pall Mall") spending money wildly, leading "the most undomestic domestic life in the kingdom," and demonstrating to society everywhere not only that " 'the first gentleman of the age' was likely to rank low among its princes, but that a [financially] distressed prince may come to rank low among gentlemen."

She could appreciate the charms of "the dandy tribe . . . then in its perihelion" under the glittering lights of the ball-room, but she could also view that tribe in the harsher light of day as "men of talent—(for in that dandy clique many a strong mind was suffered to froth itself to waste)—dis-abled by excess even for their own selfish enjoyments—bloated, blasé, fretful, inconsistent—all that, ten years after-wards, assigned a nervous recluse to the Pavillion and the Royal Cottage." The distinction between moralizer and so-cial historian is blurred from time to time or sacrificed to the demands of a particular novel, but the commentary re-mains significant. In *The Money-Lender* (1843), where, as the title suggests, Mrs. Gore exposes the nefarious practices of debt and credit (with, for that period, a curiously sym-pathetic portrait of a Jew), she begins with an outright con-demnation of the moral degeneracy of the whole Regency. Contrasting the England of pre-Waterloo, when men rallied to the defence of their country, with the post-war period, she deplores "an inglorious sloth of national soul and body arising from prolonged peace and prosperity . . . [which] is hatched into existence by the sunshine of aimless pros-perity." Instead of honoring its heroic dead, Regency Eng-land is "overpowered by a Bacchanalian roar, and the senseless giggle of fashionable levity."

Mrs. Gore's sense of humor may have abandoned her temporarily, but her accuracy of observation is unimpeach-able. No honest witness of the age failed to comment on its corruption or to recognize beneath the façade of elegance and refinement an inherent decadence and coarseness. And no feature of the corruption was more striking than the ab-sence of those softer sentimental values that we designate "domestic." It is not that female influence was lacking. On the contrary, as Mrs. Gore's fiction richly illustrates, female domination was a phenomenon of the age. But it was a fe-male, not a feminine, spirit. From Harriet Wilson to Mrs.

Fitzherbert, whose powers derived from sex, to Princess Lieven wielding diplomatic influence, or Lady Holland and Lady Blessington holding their brilliant salons, or finally Queen Caroline, the names redound with scandal; the moral character is questionable if not openly soiled. They were bold, aggressive women. Politically powerful Lady Holland, a divorcée whose home respectable ladies shunned, bore "the reputation of a hard, imperious woman, who always saw the worst side of the characters of those whom she criticized, and was not afraid of expressing her thoughts freely."[10] Charles Greville, one of the best memoirists of the age, described the Duchess of York as a clever, well-informed woman whose "mind is not perhaps the most delicate; she shows no dislike to coarseness of sentiment or language, and I have seen her very amused with jokes, stories, and allusions which would shock a very nice person." The only evidence of the Duchess' softer qualities seems to have been in regard to animals—her dogs of which "she has at least forty of various kinds . . . it is impossible to offend or annoy her more than by ill-using any of her dogs." As for the solid values of family, home, marriage, Greville catches the moral essence of the age: "The Duke and the Duchess live on the best terms; their manner to one another is cordial, and while full of mutual respect and attention, they follow separately their own occupations and amusements without interfering with one another."[11]

One can fix the moment of political reform with a parliamentary act of 1832. Moral reform cannot be assigned a birthdate. The First Reform Bill reflected at least half a century of historical and ideological gestation, beginning with Rousseau and the French Revolution. Similarly, the refining and purifying of manners and morals after the last of

---

[10] *Elizabeth, Lady Holland to her Son, 1821-1845*, ed. by the Earl of Ilchester (London, 1946), p. viii.

[11] *The Greville Memoirs: A Journal of the Reigns of King George IV and King William IV and Queen Victoria*, ed. Henry Reeve (New York, 1875), i, 5-6.

the Georges reflected several generations of action and reaction, from the softening influences of Romanticism and
sensibility in literature to the religious reawakenings of
evangelicalism and, not least, the steadily growing influence
of bourgeois values in home and family life. George IV died
in June 1830, prematurely aged, the feeble shadow of his
once dazzling self. William IV was a dull, blunt, ordinary
man who happened to become a king. Returning to England from a European tour in July 1830, Greville immediately detected changes: "The present King and his proceed-
ings occupy all attention, and nobody thinks any more of
the late King than if he had been dead fifty years, unless it
be to abuse him and rake up all his vices and misdeeds.
Never was elevation like that of King William IV. His life
has been hitherto passed in obscurity and neglect, in miserable poverty, surrounded by a numerous progeny of bastards, without consideration or friends, and he was ridiculous from his grotesque ways and little, meddling curiosity"
(*Memoirs,* I, 357). As a public image William soon became
identified with the stolid, solid citizenry. His bastards were
tolerated, his *hausfrau* Queen Adelaide (of Saxe-Meinin-
gen) was respectable, his political ignorance pardonable
since he was at least wise enough to seek guidance from the
beloved Duke of Wellington. By 1832, Greville reports, the
King had fallen into obscurity and contempt, but he oblig-
ingly died only a few years later, clearing the way for the
symbol of total reform—and female domination—Victoria.

Historians today no longer credit the new queen for the
extraordinary social and moral revolution of Victorianism.
The reform spirit had emerged long before her birth, and
her influence as queen was probably less pervasive than the
makers of generalizations would allow. Moreover, her reign
was long, and the gloomy Widow of Windsor, the matri-
archal royal marriage arranger, the bejewelled Empress of
India, are vastly different images from the fresh, independent young woman of nineteen who came to the throne in
1837. The reputations of her notorious uncles, her ambitious

mother, and the circumstances of her early life were not necessarily influences that would produce a conventional Victorian heroine. Happily for the young queen, she did not have to fear identification in the public mind with the corrupt Hanoverians. The image to which the public looked was Queen Elizabeth. Lady Palmerston's brother Lord Beauvale echoed what must have been widely held opinion when he commented in a letter to her in 1839 on gossip concerning the queen's choice of a husband: "With regard to the Queen, I have often turned my thoughts to a King Consort, but people who know better than me tell me I am wrong, that if the Girl don't want to marry and is going on steadily and decently, it is better to let her alone, that if you rouse the temperament of the Women you never know what they may take to, and that unless She wants it for herself, She will do much better for a year or two to go on as She is. I know the inconveniences of a female Court, the tracasseries, the scandal, the quarreling which infest it and pass into the whole of society, but these are inseparable from it, and were not much less in that of the married Queen Anne than in that of the Virgin Bess."[12]

Within another year, however, all images of the Virgin Queen were erased. Victoria was a wife. As a queen who adored her husband, produced a crop of healthy offspring, and managed her "household" the kingdom with unobtrusive efficiency, she became the ample, deep-reflecting mirror of middle-class English society. When the French statesman Guizot dined at Buckingham Palace in March, 1840, a month after her marriage, he recorded an impression of homely, bourgeois domesticity that numerous other visitors corroborated—conversation "neither animated nor interesting," no mention of politics, the queen on a sofa, her ladies-in-waiting sewing, and Prince Albert playing checkers. When Guizot saw her four years later, he told her that "he was amazed to see four pink-cheeked royal babies

[12] Mabell, Countess of Airlie, *Lady Palmerston and her Times* (New York, 1922), II, 28.

where four years ago he had seen none."[13] Royal domesticity inspired wide popular adulation and imitation. Victoria certainly did not make England a bourgeois family
and home-centered society, nor did she revolutionize manners and morals, but in her royal personage she reflected
the emergence of a new age and brought together all classes
of society within her living symbolic image. One of the most
popular contemporary commentators on that age, Mrs.
Ellis, wrote in the Preface to her *The Daughters of England* (1842):

"It seems to be the peculiar taste of the present day to
write, and to read, on the subject of woman. Some apology
for thus taxing the patience of the public might be necessary, were it not that both honour and justice are due to a
theme, in which a female Sovereign may, without presumption, be supposed to sympathize with her people. Thus,
while the character of the daughter, the wife, and the
mother are so beautifully exemplified in connection with the
dignity of a British Queen, it is the privilege of the hum-
blest, as well as the most exalted of her subjects, to know
that the heart of woman, in all her tenderest and holiest
feelings, is the same beneath the shelter of a cottage, as under the canopy of a throne."

II

THE limited survival value of the "silver-fork" novel lies in
its charting of this subtle and gradual change not only in
the manners and morals of a given period, but in an entire
way of life. Too often it is dismissed as a mere period oddity,
read only for its vestigial traces in Thackeray. To be sure,
there is little or no intrinsic literary art in any novel of this
genre. The best of them are those which are the most typi-

---

[13] The first visit is reported in his *Mémoires pour Servir à l'Histoire
de Mon Temps* (Paris, 1862), v, 10-11, the later visit in Elizabeth
Longford's *Queen Victoria, Born to Succeed* (New York, 1964),
p. 177

cal—therefore, the most mannered and artificial. The worst of them are unreadable. In their lifetime they were bitterly denounced by Carlyle and devastatingly satirized by Thackeray; with such powerful ammunition fired on them, it is small wonder that they failed to survive. Yet no student of the history of the English novel can ignore their importance—first, simply in filling the vacuum of significant fiction between the passing of Jane Austen and Sir Walter Scott until the coming of Dickens and Thackeray; second, in providing a bridge between upper-class romance and middle-class domestic fiction. No student of English social history can ignore their value as records of the transformation of popular ideals, tastes, and values from a court center to a home center, from the standards of the aristocracy to the standards of the bourgeoisie. Numerous as were its stereotypes and exaggerations, the "silver-fork" novel was a precious repository of details—of manners, fashion, furniture, even of food and shops. Because its concern was exclusively a way of life, it recorded almost everything about that way of life. It was the most circumstantial kind of novel that had ever existed, the most prosaic and precise.[14] The very tedium of which the modern reader complains on being confronted with pages of dinner-party menus and conversations, the contents of dressing tables and wardrobes, proves to be the single greatest contribution of these novels. For they prepared the way for the selective domestic realism of George Eliot, Dickens, and Thackeray. As early as 1740 Richardson had enumerated the contents of poor Pamela's wardrobe: a calico nightgown, a pair of stockings, a cotton handkerchief, some "new-bought knit mittens," and

[14] The fashionable novel, Michael Sadleir observed, "set out to portray the ordinary lives of contemporary aristocrats; and the greater the detail in which the gilded leisure, the foreign travel, the informal talk, the houses, rooms, carriages, clothes and aspirations of these enviable folks were set forth, the more acceptable the 'tale' to a public greedy for just such luxurious precision" (*Edward and Rosina*, p. 115).

a flannel coat (Letter xxix). Even earlier, Moll Flanders kept a faithful record of her midwife's charges. But this was dramatic detail, not social documentation. It defined a character or a particular dramatic situation. The documentation of the "silver-fork" novel defined a period of history. When Mrs. Gore's Cecil describes his rooms in the family townhouse in Hanover Square, his particularity becomes a generalization about a way of life. The walls ". . . were hung with a highly glazed white paper matched with highly glazed white furniture; the whole being vivified by a gay pattern of blue convolvulus. Even the carpet exhibited on its pale grey ground, the same design, and the Worcester china was what George Robins would call *en suite*. . . . The furniture was of the darkest rose-wood; the shower-bath white japan. But the triumph of the whole was the dressing table, on whose spotless marble slab stood the crystal and gold belongings of the dressing-box, manufactured for me by Gray. . ." (*Cecil*, I, ch. 4).

When in another novel Mrs. Gore introduces her heroine to London at the height of the "season," she drops her plot temporarily to write an essay of social commentary, full of names of real people and real shops, fascinating in 1830 not only to the upper classes who knew the people and patronized the shops, but to that emulating middle-class reading public at whom she aimed her work: ". . . water-parties, *déjeuners*, concerts, balls, and dinners—proclaimed that 'the season,'—the canicular Spring—was existent in all its fervid force! . . . Tattersall's and the Red House disputed for the mob of cabriolets; Triaud and Dévy for the mob of Britschkas. The elaborate taste of Storr was torn in pieces between the claims of Lord Breloque's gold *nécessaire*, and the Duchess of Delvile's ninety-fifth bracelet. . . . Gunter was taxing his exhausted imagination for the *caramel* novelties of a *fête champêtre*; and half the pillows in Grosvenor Square were rendered sleepless by the anxious indecisions of an approaching *bal costumé*" (*Women as They Are*, I, ch. 7).

In "Lords and Liveries" Thackeray parodied Mrs. Gore's precious, affected vocabulary, her heavy interlarding of French phrases, her name-dropping; but it is significant that he, the most artistic chronicler of this same age, never challenged her honesty and accuracy of observation: "Cruel woman!" he wrote her, of her *Sketches of English Character*, "Why do you take off our likenesses in that way?"[15]

The "intention" of the "silver-fork" novelists was probably no more than to sell books to a public hungry for reading about fashionable life. They were, to a man (and a woman), literary hacks—whether aristocratically born like young Edward Bulwer Lord Lytton, or ambitiously climbing into society like young Disraeli, or exploiting it from some special inside knowledge like Lady Charlotte Bury, or clinging to its outer fringes like Lady Blessington, or simply in need of money for their families like Theodore Hook and Mrs. Gore. Their perceptions about life were therefore probably more accidental and intuitive than the result of careful scrutiny. The value of these perceptions, however, is in no way diminished, for these novelists were conscientious, shrewd, and sophisticated. They recognized, long before the professional psychologists and sociologists did, that a life style reflects human character and often shapes human destiny. The "humours" character of Elizabethan literature, the eccentric and "original" of Smollett and Sterne, the *type*, was transformed in the nineteenth-century realistic novel into the individual whose behavior is *typical*—of a social class. Rich in-depth characterization eluded the "silver-fork" novelist; indeed, he may never have attempted it. We must look ahead to Rawdon Crawley for a Regency buck who has a real heart. Cecil, and some of Mrs. Gore's other characters, have more wit and vitality than many of their contemporaries, but they remain stock figures.

Nevertheless, the "silver-fork" novelist had moved a step closer to the realism of characterization that is so remark-

[15] *Letters and Private Papers of William Makepeace Thackeray*, ed. Gordon N. Ray (Cambridge, Mass., 1944), III, 74.

able in the Victorian novel. His characters are not romantic heroes larger than life. They are, in fact, smaller than life, the trivia and materialism of their fashionable lives reducing them to mere snobs and fops. Cecil's travelling companion on the Continent is none other than Lord Byron, but what a diminished, ineffectual, unheroic figure the exiled Byron is: "I had left him the spoiled child of London—*the* poet and lion of the day—the bridegroom of an heiress, who was also a beauty and a *bel esprit*—and the idol of the whole residue of her sex. He rejoined me, at the close of a little more than a year's separation, a pariah, a banished man, a monster rejected by the caprices of Great Britain" (III, ch. 1). Like the dandy-heroes of the novels, Byron, "the brightest and weakest of mankind," has become the victim not of powerful, warlike foes, but of his own "extreme susceptibility to female domination." He falls prey to what Cecil calls "the surpassing vulgarity of the Betty Finnikin school . . . the Miss Carolina-Wilhelmina-Amelia-Skeggs . . . the Guiccioli-Margarita-Marianna. . . ."[16] Even his death is more pathetic than heroic: "the man who devoted his blood to the cause of Greece, and who was finally bled to death at Missolonghi."

The morality of the "silver-fork" novelists is explicit and simplistic. For all their worldliness, there is not a single novel in which virtue does not triumph and in which the values of simple domestic life are not ultimately confirmed. At their best and most sophisticated, however, these heroes and heroines do not reform conventionally. The moral may have been, as one contemporary observer put it, "to show that under the corsets of a dandy there sometimes beats a

---

[16] Marianna here is a fictitious mistress. Guiccioli needs no identification. Margarita apparently was Lady Blessington, a sister "silver-fork" novelist of tarnished personal reputation; she lived with the celebrated dandy Count d'Orsay and held famous salons at Gore House (with which Mrs. Gore had no relationship by family or otherwise). Mrs. Gore had little regard for her. See Michael Sadleir, *The Strange Life of Lady Blessington* (New York, 1947), pp. 177-79.

heart."[17] Mrs. Gore was far too wise a novelist to switch a sudden moral conversion upon her Cecil. Instead she has him tell his life story in retrospect, relishing its pleasures but also acknowledging his sense of its emptiness, with a rueful awareness that in having failed to achieve true love, marriage, and a family, he has missed something precious. "The only apology admissable for a fashionable novel," Mrs. Gore wrote in the Preface to her *Sketch Book of Fashion,* "is the successful exposure of vices and follies daily and hourly generated by the corruptions of society."

Such an apology would certainly have been echoed by her colleagues. Bulwer, the model of the fashionable young man in both his personal life and in his early career as a novelist, was a sensitive moralist. Modern readers will find his most interesting book not one of his many novels but a work of non-fiction, *England and the English* (1833). Here he shrewdly notes the ambivalence of the whole concept of fashion ("a compound of opposite qualities") and the clashing, contradictory values of his age—its professed morality and its materialism: "In other countries poverty is a misfortune,—with us it is a crime. . . . The favourite word is 'respectability'—and the current meaning of 'respectability' may certainly exclude virtue, but never a decent sufficiency of wealth" (Bk. I, ch. 2). While the middle class pursues serious matters like making money, "the great interest themselves in frivolities." But he also notes the coming changes in society. Writing at what he correctly regarded as the end of the era of the fashionable novel (although Mrs. Gore continued to produce them for another decade), he observes that such novels reflected the aspirations of the "more mediocre classes" to become "quasi-aristocrats." The value of such novels, however, was moral and satirical. They were warnings to the climbers not to emulate the folly of their betters:

"In these works, even to the lightest and most ephemeral, something of the moral spirit of the age betrayed itself . . .

[17] *New Monthly Magazine,* 95 (June, 1852), p. 161.

people eagerly sought for representations of the manners which they aspired to imitate and the circles to which it was not impossible to belong. But as with emulation discontent also was mixed, as many hoped to be called and few found themselves chosen, so a satire on the follies and vices of the great gave additional piquancy to the description of their lives. . . . Read by all classes in every town, in every village, these works . . . could not but engender a mingled indignation and disgust at the parade of frivolity, the ridiculous disdain of truth, nature and mankind . . . these novels exhibited as a picture of aristocratic society" (Bk. IV, ch. 2).

Bulwer had practiced his own theories as early as *Pelham* (1828) in which his young dandy-hero manages to survive the misguidance of his shallow mother, the example of his melancholy Byronic friend whose life ends in tragedy and violence, and his own flippancy, to become, in the final chapter, an exemplary country squire, happily married, and determined to serve God and his nation. In contrast to the happy fate of the tamed Pelham, Disraeli's untamed Vivian Grey creates only havoc and ends in violent death. But Vivian lacks Pelham's high moral purpose. Pelham's motto is circumspect: "Manage yourself well, and you may manage the world." Vivian's is cynical: "A smile for a friend and a sneer for the world is the way to govern mankind." Therein lies all the difference. Disraeli himself repudiated the headstrong Vivian, dismissing the novel (in the 1853 Preface) as a boyish effort, "founded on affectation." In his later *Coningsby* (1844) an aristocratic and fashionable young hero becomes a model of duty and public service for "the new generation." Like Pelham, T. H. Lister's fashionable heroes survive the temptations of the world to settle down in happy domestic life. Granby triumphs over idleness, "the ill-judged indulgence" of a worldly uncle, romantic misunderstandings, the treachery of a villainous cousin, and a near-fatal fever, to end married to his beloved, "amid a large circle of congratulating friends . . . with bright prospects of long-lived happiness, [in] the splendid retirement of Tedsworth." Arlington, similarly subdued, marries an honorable girl and embraces the realities of home and family: "His visionary plans,—the fruit, at one time, of inexperience—at another of mortification, had vanished; and in their place succeeded a more just and sober view of life." Herbert Lacy, a snobbish young dandy, learns to appreciate character apart from birth and social standing, thanks to the influence of a sweet young lady whom he eventually marries.

Oddly enough, it was a woman novelist, Mrs. Gore, who presented the dandy in his most starched, polished and glittering form. Cecil is that paragon of paragons, boasting himself the "archcoxcomb of his coxcombical times"—"It is not every man who can wear a white waistcoat and cravat, without looking either insipid as a boiled chicken, or dingy as a Spanish olive." To the extent that the dandy image is foppish and effeminate, a synthetic creature of a synthetic fashionable society, it is not perhaps remarkable that Cecil is the brainchild of a woman. But what is remarkable is the masculinity of tone of the novel. For all his foppery, Cecil is a far more manly man, more vigorous and vital, than the host of fashionable heroes created by men from Plumer Ward's Tremaine and De Vere (forerunners rather than archetypal dandies) to Vivian Grey and Pelham. Mrs. Gore's contemporary R. H. Horne was deeply impressed with Cecil's masculine impudence, which he attributed in some degree to the assistance of her friend the novelist William Beckford. But Beckford, Horne admits, gave her only some of the erudition, the Latin and Greek epigraphs with which the novel is sprinkled. He could not have given her the zesty, rollicking spirit of Cecil travelling in Germany: "Dear reader!—wert thou ever in Germany? I do not mean, didst thou ever steamboat it up or down the Rhine, or swallow the natural physic of the waters of Baden or Aix-la-Chapelle;—for who hath *not*?—I mean, didst thou ever abide in the soft bosom of a *recht herzliche* German family, —drink of their beer,—smoke of their tobacco,—and chaw metaphysics with them. . . . But I say again, dear reader, wert thou ever in cordial, kind-hearted, boozy, foozy, Deutschland?" (III, ch. 1).

Cecil; or, The Adventures of a Coxcomb was the result of cool calculation and shrewd observation of the literary scene and marketplace. Mrs. Gore kept a careful eye on the promotion and sales of all her books and she was confident, she wrote to her publisher Richard Bentley, that "this book shall make a hit" because "I who live in the world know how much a *Sensation* is wanted by the novel readers. They are sick to surfeiting of James, Cooper, Hook, Trollope, Gore, and Co.—and are sadly in need of a man in an iron mask, or something else to get them wondering."[18]

Including herself in the company of the "surfeited," Mrs. Gore insisted that *Cecil* be published anonymously. But it was not the familiarity of her name that made her insist strongly on anonymity so much as the "sensation" nature of the new book and its distinctly masculine flavor: "But this work is written in a most peculiar style and with a degree of freedom on all subjects, to which my name would do an injury and the book an injury to me. You saw the attack in the Morning Post the other day on The Dowager [a novel by Mrs. Gore, published in 1840]—a book as *demure* as a Charity-girl! Such a one as 'Cecil' (where there is really something to lay hold of) they would cut up in a style to stop the sale of the work. . . . The novel-writing world has been in a state of stagnation, since the death of Boz, and sadly wants a fillip. 'Cecil' is the very work to attract attention. All that would be impertinence from Mrs. Gore, becomes witty sarcasm when attributed one day to Lord Brougham and the next to Lord Gardner. . . . I am in fact

---

[18] There is a large collection of letters from Mrs. Gore to her publisher Bentley at the University of Illinois. All quotations are from these. Some of this correspondence has been published by R. A. Gettmann in *A Victorian Publisher: A Study of the Bentley Papers* (Cambridge, 1960) and by Gordon N. Ray in an article, "The Bentley Papers," *The Library*, 7 (September, 1952), pp. 178-200.

in despair at the necessity of spoiling a capital book, and losing a golden opportunity for a vogue as great as that of 'Pelham' or 'Vivian Grey' and a sale of 2000!—The book affects to be an *autobiography of one of the friends and companions of Lord Byron in Italy.* Judge how absurd for my name to appear on the title page, and destroy the illusion."[19]

For all her calculation, however, Mrs. Gore failed to produce a financial success with *Cecil.* Not that she had been unprepared for disappointment: "With respect to 'Cecil,'" she wrote Bentley shortly after publication of the first edition, "it has enormous success *in society* but I know from experience that this does not make a sale." The book was widely puffed, favorably reviewed, much talked about in literary and social circles, its authorship the subject of lively speculation and gossip.[20] Bulwer, Lady Blessington, R. H. Horne, and a few others in the center of literary life strongly suspected Mrs. Gore, but her hand was not officially acknowledged until the issuance of the book in Bentley's Standard Novels series in 1845.

Cecil was born too late, and, in spite of its sparkle, it went into quick and permanent eclipse. Yet it survived its genre. People stopped reading fashionable novels by 1840, but some few continued to read *Cecil* appreciatively for the next several decades. The modern reader will find it the one consistently interesting and entertaining "silver-fork" novel. For the very reason that its hero is not a sensitive, intellectual romantic but a fatuous, idle, essentially uncomplicated Regency dandy, the novel has verisimilitude and a freshness that others of this genre lack. Matthew W. Rosa, the historian of the "silver-fork" novel, remarks that "Pel-

[19] This letter is published in Ray's article in *The Library*, pp. 192-93.

[20] See Thackeray's comment in a letter to Mrs. Procter, 19 March 1841, ". . . it appears the whole town is talking about my new novel of Cecil. O just punishment of vanity! How I wish I had written it—not for the book's sake but for the filthy money's, which I love better than fame. . . " (*Letters*, II, 13).

ham and Vivian represent their time perfectly because they are contemporaries of their young authors; Mrs. Gore has made alive once more in Cecil's customary indifference to serious matters, the careless life of men like Brummell."[21] Bulwer and Disraeli, in other words, were indulging in the literary luxury of self-romanticizing. Observing all the conventions of the genre, they were nevertheless personal and subjective, and as reader interest in them declined, so did the value of their novels. But Mrs. Gore was writing historical fiction. Because she is *not* Cecil and there is not the slightest element of autobiography or introspection in it, her novel has more objectivity and is therefore more durable than the others.

By its nature dandyism was ephemeral and ambivalent. Like other cultist movements that embrace manners, speech, and styles of clothing—aestheticism, hippy-ism—it was radical, designed to shock and defy by its extremes. Yet because dandies were of the upper classes, the small aristocratic circle around the Prince of Wales, and emphasized exclusivism and snobbery, the movement was also conservative. Confined entirely to the male sex, it was nevertheless effeminate, with its absurd emphasis on clothing and grooming that tended indeed to shift and unbalance the sex roles. Not surprisingly, in most "silver-fork" novels there are women who wield great power, not only in the home and society but in politics and diplomacy. As a movement dandyism reflected the shifting nature of the times, an age of flux that marked England's transition from the past to modern industrial society. England's French Revolution was vicarious. At best there was "the English revolutionette," as one of Mrs. Gore's characters describes the Reform Bill of 1832.[22]

Whatever his limitations of scholarship and intellect (he is rusticated from Oxford), Cecil is an excellent register of

[21] *The Silver-Fork School,* p. 20.
[22] *Memoirs of a Peeress* (1837; re-issued 1859), Ch. 29.

the changing times. Writing in the 1830's he deplores, in elegant language, the widening urbanization and the effects of industrialization. In his lifetime he has seen the demolition of the landmarks of Regency glory—Carlton House, Ranelagh, Vauxhall: "The suburbs, too, like a lady's hoop, have extended so widely as to treble the dimensions of the body they enclose. The lungs of London are compressed by the enlargement of the circumjacent membranes; and the atmosphere assigned her is not only less clear and salubrious, but her breathing pores are stopped up, and air-vessels abridged. Her gardens are built over. Paddington-fields smoke, like a cigar-divan, from thousands of ignominious issues. . . . The tree in St. Paul's Churchyard will soon be the only green thing left to exalt the imaginations of our sparrows by the rustling of its leaves; for lo! the builders have passed like a swarm of locusts over the land and left all barren" (i, ch. 3). Society has changed. There is everywhere a seriousness and earnestness that the playboy Cecil deplores: "People in general were more agreeable. Knowledge did not pretend to be useful. Society, now so blue, was *couleur de rose.*"

Mrs. Gore was a stern judge of Regency immorality, but she had the historian's objectivity and enough candor to credit dandyism with its charms. Along with her foppish hero she shares a sense of the drabness of contemporary Victorian life in contrast to the color of the Regency. Cecil himself, from the retrospect of the 1840's, comments defensively that "the Brummell school," though apparently effeminate, conceited, and frivolous, were actually vigorous, hearty men, less dangerous to society than "the rufflers of more recent times . . . their victims were sought and found in their own order of society. It is not always that the scum floating on the surface of a great capital, is of so innoxious a nature. Theirs was the foam of champagne, not the frothing of coculus indicus" (i, ch. 5). In a mock epic that she published in 1843 (possibly in collaboration with W. Harrison Ainsworth),[23] *Modern Chivalry, or A New Orlando Furioso,* she laments the taming and toning down of the times: "O ye infinitely little!—O ye Lilliputian worthies!—O ye Pindars of monthly magazines, who have harnessed Parnassus to a pony carriage! . . . Society has become a vast platitude. . . . The happy medium of dulness envelops and environs every object."

More seriously and bitterly, she observed in a very late novel, *Progress and Prejudice* (1854), that the young men of "our times," who write "maudlin" histories and "flaccid romances" and patronizingly "favour Mechanics' Institutes and provincial Athenaeums with a view of their white gloves, embroidered shirts, and fiddle-faddle philosophy," are little improvement over the Regency fine gentlemen: "The dandies fought well at Waterloo,—established the sportsmanship of Melton—and have budded the old crab-stock of John Bull with fruit of excellent flavour" (i, ch. 5).

One must allow, of course, for the querulousness of old age. Mrs. Gore of 1854 had less humor than Mrs. Gore of a decade earlier. In general, however, her attitude toward the Regency was fair-minded, and her survey of its rise and fall reads convincingly. *Cecil* is the model, but elsewhere in her fiction there are equally sound and urbane comments on the era. One of the best of these is in *Preferment; or, My Uncle the Earl,* published in 1840, a year before *Cecil.* In *Preferment* an aging roué, a bachelor uncle who might have served as a prototype of Thackeray's Major Pendennis, personifies the decline of "the temple of fine gentlemanism reared under the auspices of Carlton House." Of his fellow dandies, now all fading into old age, she reflects:

"Some were in exile—some in the grave;—some at Calais

[23] According to the British Museum Catalogue it was "Edited by W. H. Ainsworth." He was the editor of the *New Monthly Magazine* in which it had first appeared. There is no author attribution on the title page, but the Preface is signed C.F.G. and the work is most likely hers. It was illustrated by George Cruikshank, who illustrated several other of her novels.

—some at Coventry;—some married to *divorcees* and estranged from female society,—some to country heiresses, and lost to male. George Robins [the auctioneer] had disposed of the paraphernalia of a dozen or so, whose place remembered them no longer,—whose snuffboxes were dispersed among the curiosity shops,—whose travelling carriages had been bought cheap by retired haberdashers,—whose names were forgotten amid their daily haunts and ancient neighbourhood, except in the defaulter-lists of the clubs. Some were shewing their withered faces and knocking knees at Paris,—some at Florence,—some at Naples,—some concealing them in more obscure retreats. But of the illustrious group in which he had emerged from obscurity in the days when George IV was regent, and Regent Street, Swallow Street,—scarcely a trace remained to keep up tradition of the good old times" (ɪ, ch. 5).

Cecil's fate is not nearly so bleak. He declines into old age, of course, but also into wealth and the peerage. In the sequel, *Cecil, a Peer* (1841), he finds ample consolation: "I possess an excellent cook, an excellent breed of deer, an excellent cellar of wine, . . . My evenings are as bright as the noondays of other men!" (ɪɪɪ, ch. 12). His saving grace is a sense of humor and a sublime ego that console him even for the grey hairs and widening waistline of middle age. They also carry him unscarred over a series of adventures, romantic and military, that would have seared the memory of a romantic hero. In his family life Cecil survives the discovery of his illegitimacy, the death (through an accident in which he is innocently but compromisingly involved) of a favorite nephew and later of a beloved brother, and the scorn of his presumed father. In his romantic life he wins the hearts of and then loses innumerable charming women. In the Peninsular War he fights heroically. But nothing ever really touches him.

Mrs. Gore's extraordinary achievement in this novel is her creation of a consummate egoist who tells his own story with scarcely a lapse in consistency of character or tone.

She sustains her point of view. Although there are lon-gueurs in *Cecil* and particularly in its sequel *Cecil, a Peer*, there is no false note. All the more remarkable is the fact that her shallow, self-satisfied narrator also manages to con-demn himself and his society without realizing it. *Cecil* has the moral earnestness of a pulpit sermon with the compen-sating grace of humor. The self-revealing narrator reviews his life with no brooding guilt, no motivation of confession, but simply with the delight of talking about himself: "I had fitted up my second chamber as a sort of study,—a study of anything but books; for I neither was, nor pretend to be, a reading man. But I studied there something more valuable in the perusal than printed paper. I studied my Self.—I stud-ied the past" (II, ch. 1).

Still, he is not the introspective Byronic egoist—or, if he is, he is of the school of Don Juan, not Harold and Manfred. His nervous sensibilities are those of the dandy, of the senses and the stomach, not the soul: "My sense of smell is at all times painfully acute"—"What barbarisms in Portland stone!"—"More than once on returning to England after long sojourn in France, I have sustained a serious illness from the crudity of the tough meats and parboiled vegeta-bles." He destroys innocent young women but not by rape —only out of neglect, sheer fatuousness and pique.

Cecil's wit is so ebullient that at times it exhausts the reader. The breathless haste of narration—the dashes of punctuation, the helter-skelter of smart London talk, French phrases, Latin and Greek epigrams—would be tedi-ous if it were not so natural an expression of the personality of this narrator. He slows down a little in middle age, apologizing in *Cecil, a Peer* that "I cannot expect the cir-cumstantiality of Cecil at forty, to be like the circumstan-tiality of Cecil at twenty-one" (II, ch. 3). But even his slow-er pace strikes sparks. And at twenty-one he is nothing less than spectacular: "Standing five feet seven in my pumps and five feet ten in my boots, with a trifling hint of the Piping Faun softening the severity of my Roman nose and finely chiselled mouth, I should, perhaps, have passed for effeminate, but that the sentimental school was just then in the ascendant" (I, ch. 1).

Cecil's superb ego gives him a uniqueness among dandy-heroes. Capable only of the emotion of self-love, he is spared the conflicts of his peers—Pelham, Vivian Grey, Arlington, Granby—who suffer varying degrees of passion, pride, romantic love. Like most of them he is a dandy by birth, rich, distinguished from infancy by natural elegance and good looks. Like Pelham and the others, he is molded by women—first, a worldly, fashionable mother, then an equally worldly older woman, often in these novels the mother's friend, usually a widow or married to an elderly husband, who introduces the youth to the arts of flirtation and seduction. The mothers of both Cecil and Pelham are unfaithful to their husbands. Lady Pelham is saved from a scandalous elopement only when she stops to retrieve her china monster and her pet dog. The servants notify her husband, who promptly curses them for their interference. Her matronly counsel to her son includes such advice as: "Remember, my dear, that in all the friends you make at present, you look to the advantage you can derive from them hereafter"; and, "Nothing, my dear son, is like a *liaison* (quite innocent, of course) with a woman of celebrity in the world. In marriage a man lowers a woman to his own rank; in an *affaire de coeur* he raises himself to hers." Fortunately for Pelham's moral character his mother has little permanent influence on him, and the worldly woman who fascinates him is a virtuous widow, Lady Roseville, who "possessed great sensibility and even romance of temper, strong passions and still stronger imagination."

Cecil is uncontaminated by imagination and romantic sensibilities. His mother, who confesses on her deathbed that he is not his legal father's son, had been a beauty. As she ages, she preserves that beauty on her dressing table: "The *flaçons* which formerly contained *bouquet de Florence* or *verveine*, now held the lights and shades of her

67

ladyship's complexion. Blue veins were sealed in one packet, and a rising blush was corked up in a crystal phial. Eyebrows—eyelashes—lips—cheeks—chin—an ivory forehead and a pearly row of teeth,—all were indebted for their irresistibilities to a certain Pandora's box of a dressing-case, furnished by Thévenot, which sent forth Lady Ormington, full-armed for conquest, like the goddess that emerged from the brain of the father of the gods" (i, ch. 1). Her maternal guidance is exactly the sort that Cecil can follow: "What was the use of college?—I should only become a brute of a fox-hunter! . . . *She* wished me to go straight into the Guards. . . . The humiliation of maternity would be less galling, if she had a son in the Guards. In the Guards, I should be on the spot to swear at her chairmen when drunk, or her coachman if disorderly" (i, ch. 1). Cecil's other female mentor is the fascinating widow Lady Harriet Vandeleur, "coquette,—jilt,—flirt,—angel," who rises at noon, spends the next four hours at her dressing table, and emerges at last to dazzle her circle of "old *roués*—men of forty" with her beauty and wit.

It is little wonder that Cecil, so endowed and so tutored, makes coxcombery an art. It is more wonder that he retains our interest and even, grudgingly, our respect. For Cecil's ultimate moral thrust is all the more powerful in the light of his consistency of character. He ages gracefully, sobered but not chastened by witnessing the lives of his friends and family. He watches the dandies sink into lethargy and despair while his noble-spirited elder brother marries and lives a happy, useful life with a devoted wife: "It requires a great mind to enter into the greatness of moderation," he observes, marveling at them: "domestic, without nauseating others by a display of their domesticity" (ii, ch. 4). Meanwhile Cecil falls in and out of love, skates dangerously on the thin ice of his bachelorhood, but concludes, in the spirit of what the later nineteenth century called "the superfluous man": "The longer we float along the stream of life, the better we understand the fable of the vessel of iron and the vessel of clay; and if incompetent to convert our fragile materials into sterner stuff, the further we recede from contact with the hard and powerful, the better" (III, ch. 6).

He ends, therefore, a philosopher of sorts, extolling a surprising but not incongruous doctrine of moderation. His princely model George IV sinks into gouty twilight: "His constitution was already deeply shaken.—He was ill. He was nervous. His defeats were beginning. Like Louis XIV in the decline of his years and fortunes, he began to fear that Providence was ungrateful for his support" (*Cecil, a Peer,* I, ch. 8). An aging Cecil watches William IV usher in a strange new era, restoring the office of queen to the nation by having an acknowledged if not particularly honored wife and children (ten healthy illegitimate ones and two legitimate ones who died in infancy). Visiting the palace gardens, Cecil notes with amazement "a joyous train of nurses and children disporting on the sunny slopes. . . . I could scarcely believe myself at court." It is a "female court," domestic and home-like. At the end of his audience, the King invites Cecil to "take my mutton with him," and on the whole Cecil approves "the manifestation of these domestic affections which, by uniting the sovereign and his subjects in a more intimate union, diminished the isolation of the throne." Finally, Cecil watches with what is, for him, deep emotion, the coronation of young Victoria: "Never shall I forget the influence exercised over my feelings by the first expansion of the pure virgin voice,—when from the throne the new Sovereign addressed herself to the peers of her realm.—No theatrical appeal to their devotion.—All was calm,—dignified,—and right royal" (I, ch. 11). The domestic star was in the ascendant.

III

CECIL is not Mrs. Gore's only fictional chronicler of historical and social change. His female counterpart is a rich, sixty-seven-year-old widow who, in the mid-1830's, reviews her colorful life—"now sitting with my cat on my knee and my silver hairs gathered under my dowager coif"—in *Memoirs of a Peeress* (1837), edited by Lady Charlotte Bury (who wrote only a brief prefatory note to the book). The Peeress' view, like Cecil's, is reflective and moralizing. While she vigorously condemns the corruption and immorality of her youth when the Prince of Wales was lord of mis-rule at Carlton House and Brighton, she also shares Cecil's distaste for the materialism and vulgarity of the emerging middle classes, seeing the present as a period when "all is imitation—all echo—all tautology . . . the aristocracy of rank stands grimacing like a posture-master on its pedestal, in order that its illegitimate brother, the aristocracy of wealth, may try to prove affinity by aping every contortion, and out-vaulting every leap" (ch. 4).

The insights of this lady differ slightly from Cecil's because her point of view is feminine, and she believes that the female is a better gauge of the times than the male: "From the days of Alcibiades, however, to those of Brummell, fine gentlemen have existed, like excrescences on the oak, the disease and not the product of the age. It is rather from women, the matrons of the times, I would draw deductions of its morality" (ch. 4). The power of the female in the year of Victoria's coronation was neither more nor less impressive than it had been for at least a generation. Even when there had been no queen on the throne, the social and political influence of women was widely acknowledged. Introducing a beautiful heroine, Constance Vernon, in his novel *Godolphin* in 1833, Bulwer described the last half century as the most brilliant England had ever known —Byron in his zenith, Madame de Staël in London: "Never had a young and ambitious woman—a beauty and a genius —a finer moment for the commencement of her power. It was Constance's early and bold resolution to push to the utmost—even to exaggeration—a power existing in all polished states, but now mostly in this—the power of fashion" (ch. 23).

In the scandalous last years of the Georges, as we have noted, backstairs and boudoir politics and diplomacy flourished. Lady Charlotte Bury, who had been a confidante of Queen Caroline and a witness at her sensational divorce trial, began her *Diary of a Lady-in-Waiting* with the worldly observation that forms of government may change, but "courts are courts still, and have been so from the earliest times. Intrigues, jealousies, heart-burnings, lies, dissimulation, thrive in them as mushrooms in a hot-bed." From the Continent England imported formidably influential women —Madame de Staël, Princess Esterhazy, Princess Lieven. The latter was wife of the Russian ambassador and mistress of Metternich and of Guizot. Of her sudden recall to Russia in 1834 the *Times* wrote, ". . . this earthquake in the diplomatic world" was caused by "her Highness's appetite for meddling in politics and assuming the direction of every Cabinet in Europe."[24] Native-born Englishwomen were also powerful. Greville's *Memoirs* for the 1820's are full of references to politically sophisticated and influential women— Lady Bathurst explaining to him the subleties of the coming parliamentary elections, Mrs. Arbuthnot and Lady Jersey interpreting the complex moves in the struggle for Catholic emancipation. Lady Holland was expert in political wheeler-dealerism, and at her intimate dinner parties the course of English history was often charted. Lady Melbourne, Caroline Lamb's mother-in-law, quietly advised many politicians and won Byron's wholehearted admiration: "The best friend I ever had in my life and the cleverest of women."[25] He once told Lady Blessington, "No man dislikes being lectured by a woman, provided she be not his mother, sister, wife, or mistress; first, it implies that she takes an interest in him, and, secondly, that she does not think him irreclaimable."[26] Bulwer was less gently domi-

[24] H. Montgomery Hyde, *Princess Lieven* (London, 1938), p. 211.
[25] David Cecil, *Melbourne* (New York, 1954), pp. 115-16.
[26] *Lady Blessington's Conversations with Lord Byron,* ed. Ernest J. Lovell, Jr. (Princeton, N.J., 1969), p. 121.

nated both by his grandmother, who insisted that her maiden name of Lytton be added to the family name and was remembered by him as "a woman of that high spirit which fully enjoys the blessings of liberty and independence," and by his mother-in-law, whom Disraeli remembered, at a dinner party, as "not so pleasant, something between Jeremy Bentham and Meg Merrilies, very clever but awfully revolutionary. She poured forth all her systems upon my novitiate ear and while she advocated the rights of woman, Bulwer abused system mongers and the sex. . . ."[27]

Mrs. Gore's fictional Lady Danvers, who, in 1830, attempts to save the toppling government of her Prime Minister brother, might have had many real life models: "She had heard the first scarcely audible growl of distant thunder which menaced his popularity: she had seen the speck in the horizon, which promised to become an overwhelming storm; and devoting herself in the first instance to the task of appeasing its violence by the operation of many a secret engine, by artful flatteries to opposing spirits, and unsuspected bribery in meaner, but less efficient quarters, she had succeeded for a time in retarding the crisis" (*Women as They Are,* I, ch. 8). Lady Danvers is so skillful and subtle in her maneuvering that her brother is unaware "that many a decision of the cabinet had been partly instigated by the invisible ascendency of Honoria Danvers." But her power is eventually dissipated. Becoming greedy for even more power and political influence, "she had sacrificed her domestic affections, her peace of mind, her time, her health, her ease, her trust in the mercy of God!" Her fate is appropriately tragic—scandal, social ostracism, and finally suicide.

Maria Edgeworth offers a similar portrait of a politically influential society matron, Lady Davenant, in *Helen* (1834), who advises the young heroine: "Let me observe to you,

27 Sadleir, *Edward and Rosina,* p. 140. For Bulwer's recollections of his grandmother, see Edward Robert Lord Lytton, *Life, Letters and Literary Remains of Lord Lytton* (London, 1883), I, 29.

that the position of women in society is somewhat different from what it was a hundred years ago, or as it was sixty, or I will say thirty years since. Women are now so highly cultivated, and political subjects are at present of so much importance, of such high interest, to all human creatures who live together in society, you can hardly expect, Helen, that you, as a rational being, can go through the world as it now is without forming any opinion on points of public importance. You cannot, I conceive, satisfy yourself with the common namby-pamby little missy phrase, 'ladies have nothing to do with politics'" (Ch. 28). Lady Davenant, however, has a happier fate than Mrs. Gore's Lady Danvers. Although she neglects her daughter's education, with potentially dangerous consequences, she is nevertheless tactful and wise enough to submerge her own hunger for power in her unselfish devotion to her husband, and she warns her young protegée: "Female influence must, will, and ought to exist on political subjects as on all others; but this influence should always be domestic, not public—the customs of society have so ruled it" (Ch. 28).

It is on the scale of middle-class not aristocratic life that this emergent "female domination," both in fact and in fiction, carries its heaviest weight. And it is here that Mrs. Gore serves as an especially sensitive register of the shifting values and attitudes. While in *Cecil* she assumed the masculine pose with remarkable facility, her natural voice and her natural audience were feminine. If she consciously followed any literary tradition, it was not the "great bow-wow strain" of Sir Walter Scott (though she was enough of a hack to turn out a number of historical romances) but the quieter tones of Jane Austen. On one occasion she pointedly acknowledged imitation, writing in her Preface to *Pin Money* (1831): "Exhibiting an attempt to transfer the familiar narrative of Miss Austin [sic] to a higher sphere of society, it is, in fact, a Novel of the simplest kind, addressed by a woman to readers of her own sex."

The guiding spirit hovering over Mrs. Gore's novels is

73

Mrs. Bennet and the five unmarried daughters of *Pride and Prejudice*. Matrimony and maternity are the household goddesses. The maneuvering and calculation involved in marriage-making are the raw materials of her plots. But Mrs. Gore was a transitional figure in social history as well as in fiction. In 1830 the young heroine of her *Women as They Are* reluctantly enters into a loveless marriage with a highly eligible nobleman. Her father tells her that it is entirely proper that she should *not* love him: ". . . nor can I imagine anything more indelicate in the mind of a young lady, who considers passion a necessary guide in her choice of an alliance." Fortunately for this heroine and her husband, she learns, after many misunderstandings, to love him. Their ultimate fate is conventionally sentimental. Fashionable society is spurned for home, children, managing the family estates, and serving the country. The domestic virtues triumph, as indeed they do in all Mrs. Gore's novels— even in *Cecil*. They triumph more often in spite of than thanks to the machinations of ambitious, social-climbing mothers.

The mother, nevertheless, is the figure of chief attention in these novels. Heroines tend to be cut from the same virginal white muslin, but matrons are of stronger fiber and are more interesting. This may be partly because they reflect a very real influence in nineteenth-century society. They had a job to do—marrying off their children—and as fictional characters are often more vividly realized when we see them at work, so even in the hands of lesser novelists maneuvering mothers come to life as they practice their vocation. History as well as fiction records the powerful influence of the matron-dowager in English society. The fates of landed families hung on the possession and prosperity of their land. Marriage was therefore an investment of the highest importance. Class lines and barriers were, of course, also significant, but it was the marriage "portion" that often decided matters. Lawyers were the ultimate managers of marriage, at least among the very rich, but all the preliminary negotiations were the responsibility of the matrons like the formidable Lady Patronesses of Almack's, who selected partners, often from birth, arranged assemblies and balls where the young people might meet, and decided on the suitability of matches. Marianne Spencer Stanhope (Mrs. Hudson) opens her novel *Almack's* (1827) with a dedication to these ladies:

> *To that most distinguished and despotic*
> *Conclave*
> *Composed of their High Mightinesses*
> *The Ladies Patronesses of Balls at Almack's,*
> *The Rulers of Fashion, the Arbiters of Taste,*
> *The Leaders of Ton, and the Makers of Manners*
> *Whose sovereign sway over "the world" of London has*
> *long been established on the firmest basis,*
> *Whose decrees are laws, and from whose judgment*
> *there is no appeal. . . .*

The gentry and the middle class imitated the aristocracy. In spite of the remarkable fluidity of social classes in nineteenth-century England there was—as so many novels testify—a rigid adherence to the theory if not the practice of arranged marriage. A mother in Mrs. Gore's *Pin Money* (the phrase refers to a girl's jointure, arranged before marriage) observes casually of her future son-in-law: "Oh, I suppose Sir Brooke's lawyers will settle all that, while the carriage is building and the wedding clothes in hand." In his study of English landed society, F.M.L. Thompson notes many examples of such marriages, the details all faithfully preserved in the legal records of counties and shires. He points out that "negotiations of some delicacy might be called for," but that the final disposition was rarely made by force. Even a century earlier Richardson had warned parents against the tyranny of the Harlowes. "Choice, nevertheless, was understood to be limited to the circle of the acceptable," Thompson points out.[28]

That circle was most often drawn by the mother, the bro-

[28] *English Landed Society in the Nineteenth Century* (London, 1963), p. 103.

ker in the marriage market. "The maneuvering mother" was thus both a domestic and a social power to be reckoned with. She was perhaps a necessary evil, but as the nineteenth century progressed, she began to look more evil than necessary. Lady Charlotte Bury, in a novel called *The Manœuvring Mother* (1842), portrays a cold-blooded woman who, having from the cradle arranged the marriage of her four daughters, regards her newborn fifth daughter with disgust: "Well, Sir John," she tells her husband, "shake hands, love: but we need not congratulate each other. I did hope a son might have repaid me for all this annoyance, but here is another wretched girl, and the little animal looks determined to live" (Ch. 1). In *England and the English* Bulwer described the uniquely English system—"a marketing peculiar to ourselves in Europe and only rivalled by the slave-merchants of the East"—and cited as evidence the novels of Mrs. Gore: "We are a match-making nation; the lively novels of Mrs. Gore have given a just and unexaggerated picture of the intrigues, the maneuvres, the plotting and the counter-plotting that make the staple of matronly ambition" (Bk. ii, ch. 1).

Recognized as the expert on fictional marriage-maneuvering, Mrs. Gore was also its severest judge. Fortunately, satire and cynicism brighten some of her treatments of the theme. A character flippantly dismisses a love match, swiftly terminated when the girl proves penniless: "But pa thought a *ménage sans six sous* would not prove *sans souci* and therefore refused his consent" (*Mothers and Daughters*, ii, ch. 1); writing of the nieces of a powerful politician: "The Miss Lovedens were handsome, portionless, expensive girls, whom no one ventured to marry till it was discovered that they were cards to be played as well as women to be admired; when lo! a clever young lawyer of the Tory party became, by a *coup d'état* the husband of the eldest sister, a Welsh judge, and the honourable member for Fleechem!" (*The Cabinet Minister*, i, ch. 4). But the overall view is grimly condemning. Like Bulwer, Mrs. Gore had measured her country's customs against the rest of the world. Widely travelled, a long-time resident of France and Belgium, she considered the English marriage market a national disgrace. In comparison, the French system of business-like, family-arranged marriages was civilized and humane. The English, however, educate their daughters only to be marketable commodities. A French visitor comments critically:

"You bring them into society—allow them to converse, and dance with, and pass whole hours leaning upon the arm of a comparative stranger, in order that they may put forth their attractions, and allure some man of importance into the snare. You initiate them into all those arguments of sordid interest by which the pure mind of youth should be wholly untainted; you give them permission to choose for themselves at an age when their own judgment cannot but prove a dangerous pilot; yet when their choice is made, you deign to sanction it only so far as your mature worldly wisdom may suggest. And this you call disinterestedness and delicacy in the affairs of the heart!" (*Mothers and Daughters,* III, ch. 14.)

One can trace a developing note of moral outrage in Mrs. Gore. In her early society novels, maneuvering mothers are silly shallow Mrs. Bennets. As she moves on into the 1830's, these mothers wield increasingly harmful influence until, in the novel that might be considered the last word on the managing matron—*Mrs. Armytage; or, Female Domination* (1836)—she attempts domestic tragedy. In an early short story, "The Flirt of Ten Seasons" (published in *The Fair of May Fair,* 1832), a scheming matron overreaches, pushes her beautiful daughter so hard that she frightens away eligible suitors. Her code is simple: "Marrying imprudently implied . . . marrying for love instead of money—for good qualities instead of good estates"; her tactics are aggressive; her daughter, left aging and unmarried, becomes a casualty in her wars.

The same theme gets more extended treatment in *Mothers and Daughters* (1831). The ambitious mother here, widowed Lady Maria Willingham, "was a person who, with indifferent features, had always managed to be called pretty; with very moderate abilities, had maintained the reputation of being extremely clever; and with a narrow selfish heart, was continually cited as the most excellent woman in the world" (i, ch. 1). She educates her two older daughters for their careers of husband-hunting. From childhood they hear nothing but the slogans of fashionable society—"excellent connection—good match—leader of ton —jointure and settlements." They grow up into beautiful but coldly calculating young women:

" 'With a little management on your parts, and vigilance on mine, there is every probability that you will both make excellent matches.'

" 'Thanks to your generalship, mama' " (i, ch. 6).

Overreaching again, this mother frightens away suitors, breaks up love matches, forces her daughters to flirt, thereby tarnishing their reputations. They fade early, become weary and embittered: ". . . they had danced with aching hearts at many a ball, and twined the garland of pleasure around brows throbbing with the consciousness of degradation" (ii, ch. 6). Meanwhile, their younger sister, whom the mother had neglected, grows up sweet, simple, unaffected, and makes a brilliant marriage. Mrs. Gore concludes her moral tale with less purple prose and more homely sentiment. A wise older woman, commenting on the unhappy fates of these girls, observes that, after all, an essential element is love: "for the sentiment of love, if not indispensable to the happiness of wedded life, bestows a charm upon human existence such as no moral or worldly advantage can impart."

The English modern novel may well have begun when novelists switched their attention from match-making to love-making. Mrs. Gore herself never made the plunge and never wrote what could be called a romantic love story, although her novels of the 1840's and 1850's adhere to all the popular literary conventions. As her career progressed she tended to emphasize other facets of human relationships—most especially family love. The domineering mother who wrecks the lives of her children by selfishly imposing her will upon them becomes a larger, more serious figure than the mere match-maker, and other problems enter the scene —the consequences of mismatched and incompatible marriages, adultery, guilt, the rebellion and bitterness of the victimized children. *Mrs. Armytage; or, Female Domination* was in its day a widely read and influential novel. It achieved the dubious distinction of becoming evidence in a notorious murder trial in Paris in 1847—a blood-stained copy having been found on the bed of the murdered Duchess of Praslin.[29] But Mrs. Armytage is not a simple match-maker. She is a despot, a woman who rules with a ruling passion. From childhood, when an indulgent father gave her freedom to manage his home and estates, through marriage when, left a young widow, she dominated her household and family, she has yielded power to no one. Her gentle daughter submits to her will and thereby loses the man she loves. She declines in health and dies. The complaisant son manages to break away long enough to marry

[29] "The book was a favourite one with that ill-fated lady; and a volume of it being found on her bed, stained with her blood, and subsequently deposited in evidence at the trial, it acquired remarkable notoriety on the continent. At home it has enjoyed the applause of divers and distinguished readers—among them, a lord-chancellor—peers, like Lord Holland, without stint—wits, like Jekyll and Luttrell, of vast dinner-table influence—and novelists, like Beckford and Bulwer Lytton, of ungainsayable credit and renown" (*New Monthly Magazine*, 95 [June, 1852], p. 164). Apparently, however, the novel was not a financial success. In an undated letter to the Rev. Mr. Harness, written to acknowledge his letter complimenting her on the novel, she said that her bookseller had informed her "that Mrs. A. 'is a failure.'" She also repudiated "the vulgar second title of 'Female Domination' which implies a lesson I did not intend to teach" and was "chosen by the publisher." This letter is in the possession of Professor Gordon N. Ray and I am grateful to him for allowing me to quote from it.

a girl of his own choice, but he meekly accepts his mother's authority even after learning that the family estate is legally his, not hers. Mrs. Armytage's downfall comes after a bitter quarrel with her son. She leaves her home, travels restlessly on the Continent, and finally dies after a long painful illness. In suffering she at last learns humility: ". . . she was only subjected to the common lot of humanity . . . heretofore she had presumed to hold herself exempted from the vulgar destiny of mankind."

The somber moral of this tale is inevitable and heavy-handed, and the novel as a whole, while lively and interesting, is not an artistically significant book. But the character study of a proud, iron-willed matron is unusually complex. Neither a heroine nor a villainess, Mrs. Armytage dominates her novel as a self-tormenting, self-destroying woman of good will, a mother whose ruling passions are misguided. For all its trappings of high fashion, this is a domestic novel, a family tragedy. Mrs. Gore constructs it carefully, introducing several other families with mothers who affect the destinies of their children too—for bad when, like Mrs. Armytage's friend the Duchess of Spalding, they rear them for shallow lives in society—"She taught the little creatures to plan, to plot, to deceive, to equivocate, to lie; and the young lords consequently grew up into *roués*, and the young ladies into women of fashion" (i, ch. 18); for good when they are like the easygoing Mrs. Jack Baltimore, who adores her gambler husband and her ten children, "whose necessities encroached so largely on her luxuries" (i, ch. 4). Mrs. Armytage is not a monster. She would have her children love her, but her pride and coldness of manner erect barriers. On one occasion she makes a speech presenting valuable gifts to her daughter and daughter-in-law: "There was something chilling in the preconcerted formality of this address. The gift, instead of assuming the interest of a token of affection, appeared rather to be a legal act of donation" (ii, ch. 7). Her son feels constraint in her presence: "He dared not be natural. He was afraid of saying too much, or too little; of implying something capable of giving umbrage to her susceptible temper. She was so little accustomed to forget the legislatress in the mother, that he dared not exhibit half so warmly as he could have wished, the tenderness of a son" (III, ch. 1).

Mrs. Gore's novels offer significant comment on the rapidly changing relationships of parents and children in mid-nineteenth-century England. Looking backward, Cecil notes, among the many transformations of "modern times," a new attitude toward children. In his childhood, fashionable mothers had as little as possible to do with their children who were strictly isolated in the nursery and seldom displayed. But now: "The cockade generation of succeeding times is far better off in the world. The cockade generation of today is at a premium. One might fancy all the little boys one meets were heirs apparent, and all the little girls, countesses in embryo. For them the Tyrian murrey swimmeth. They are not only clothed in purple and fine linen, Flanders lace and oriental cashmeres, but we hear of nursery governesses, nursery footmen, the children's carriage, the children's pair of horses; and, Turkey being brought down from her stilts, the only despotism extant in Europe is the nurseryarchy of Great Britain" (I, ch. 1).

The more typical eighteenth-century attitude is reflected in a debate between several aristocratic ladies in *Women as They Are*, where one quotes Hannah More to the effect that "this is the golden age of children . . . they are made the first objects of the present day." To this another comments: "And why? Because the excellent counsels of Hannah More, and others, have rendered mothers *too* tender of their happiness, *too* exclusively devoted to domestic management."

Just how accurate a register of her times Mrs. Gore was is suggested in Michael Sadleir's account of how Bulwer-Lytton and his young wife put their babies out to wet-nurse. The older child, Emily, spent only about twelve months of her first three years of life with her parents. Sadleir writes that they were both "infected by the rather vulgar flippancy toward child-bearing, parental responsibility and propagation generally which . . . was regarded as chic by the bright young people of the eighteen twenties."[30] Within the next quarter century, however, there was a dramatic reversal of attitudes. From flippancy and indifference the parental role, especially the mother's, became serious, even at times solemn. In Mrs. Gore's novels of the 1840's and 1850's children are more sharply characterized and individualized. They have become integral parts of the family unit.

Charting the emotions of parental and filial love, the sensitive areas of frustration, loneliness, misunderstanding, wounded feelings, Mrs. Gore explored new territory in the fashionable novel. Bulwer, Lister, Disraeli, and other "silver-fork" novelists had domesticated their rakes and roués to provide conventional happy endings or had punished them for proper moral ones. But she moved beyond her contemporaries by settling her characters firmly into domesticity, not merely writing them off in a nebulous future of home, estate-management, and heir-production. Indeed, her power to create a firm reality in her fiction, even out of the flimsy artificial society she portrayed, was acknowledged by her more perceptive readers. Bulwer, as we have noted, used her novels for social documentation in his *England and the English*. Charlotte Brontë, reading an 1850 reissue of Mrs. Gore's novel of 1834, *The Hamiltons; or, Official Life in 1830*, was so struck with its lively re-creation of a remote Regency society that she wrote its author to express her pleasure: ". . . I found in its pages not the echo of another mind—the pale reflection of a reflection—but the result of original observation, and faithful delineation from

[30] *Edward and Rosina*, pp. 150-51. One might note, incidentally, how Thackeray uses attitudes toward children in his contrasting characterizations in *Vanity Fair* of Amelia, the saintly loving mother with her pre-Victorian sentimentality, and the typically Regency Becky, who ignores her young son and has no sentimentality whatever about motherhood.

actual life. Such a book informs while it interests. I knew nothing of the circles you describe before I read 'The Hamiltons' but I feel I know something of them now."[31]

Mrs. Gore's most distinguished novelist-disciple was Thackeray, who met her on her own fictional ground. He overshadowed her; he satirized and parodied her mannerisms in "Lords and Liveries," one of his *Punch's Prize Novelists* pieces. But he also respected her profoundly. He too read *The Hamiltons* in 1850 and, like Charlotte Brontë, was moved to write her in its praise: "And I think some critics who carped at some writers for talking too much about fine company ought to hold their tongues. If you live with great folks, why should you not describe their manners? There is nothing in the least strained in these descriptions as I now think—and believe it was only a secret envy & black malignity of disposition w[h] made me say in former times this author is talking too much about grand people, this author is of the silver fork school, this author uses too much French &c. There's none in this book to speak, perhaps that's why you sent it to me you malicious woman. . . ."[32]

It took a significant novel to provoke a retraction like this from Thackeray. *The Hamiltons* is such a novel because as early as 1834 it recognized the subtleties and complexities of ordinary family relationships. Although its characters move in aristocratic and political circles, its main interests are domestic and parochial—a family dominated by a proud Tory father whose personal and political fortunes collapse in the new wave of liberalism and reform. The parallels between *The Hamiltons* and *Vanity Fair* are coincidental but remarkable. In both there are pairs of foils— a sweetly innocent heroine and a worldly woman who seduces the other's husband; a "playboy" hero who betrays

[31] *The Brontës: Their Lives, Friendships and Correspondence* (Shakespeare Head Brontë, Oxford, 1932), III, 150. In 1856 Mrs. Gore dedicated her novel *A Life's Lessons* to Charlotte Brontë's memory.

[32] *Letters*, II, 724-25.

his wife and dies in a duel; and a stolid family friend who patiently woos and wins the now widowed heroine. In both novels the corrupt scene of the last days of the Georges is the background, and the destinies of the characters are to a degree affected by political developments.

Since Thackeray apparently did not discover *The Hamiltons* until 1850 he could not have been influenced by it in *Vanity Fair*. But he was yet to write his *familienroman The Newcomes* and his major historical novels *Henry Esmond* and *The Virginians*. In Mrs. Gore he found if not inspiration at least examples of writing that revitalized the past with humor, sympathy, and objectivity. Like Mrs. Gore, Thackeray justly valued the amber that preserves "the ephemeral modes and caprices of the passing day." Those vestiges of the decadent Regency that Mrs. Gore preserved turn up fresh in Thackeray. Her maneuvering mothers (and mothers-in-law) survive in his cannibalistic Old Campaigner and Lady Kew in *The Newcomes*. Her worldly dowagers remembering their glamorous pasts are ghostly grandmothers of the Baroness Bernstein in *The Virginians*. Her heartless scheming young women who get their way yet somehow convince us of the futility of their lives are reborn in Becky Sharp, Blanche Amory of *Pendennis*, and Beatrix Esmond. Her superannuated dandies turned into feeble roués come wheezing back in Major Pendennis, and her young coxcombs and bucks are reincarnated in the youthful Pendennis and his friend Harry Foker.

Mrs. Gore, like her younger friend and colleague, wrote with a sense of moral urgency but with none of the smug self-righteousness of the reformers and evangelicals. They shared a cynicism and a cool detachment toward their venal characters at the same time that they were able to identify themselves imaginatively with them. Thus they maintained simultaneously authorial distance and intimacy. Without hypocrisy or disturbing ambivalence, they delighted in the very things that they condemned—the frivolity of fashionable society, the beauty of good clothes and fine ornaments, the savor of rich food and rare old wine. "Objects, titles, splendour," Barbara Hardy observes of Thackeray's art, are set "in the perspective of history, and some of the most solid-seeming grandeur of Vanity Fair is discredited at the same time as it is inventoried."[33]

At the end of her long career, Mrs. Gore was eulogized not as a witty, sophisticated society novelist, but as a sensible woman who taught, the *Times* wrote in her obituary, "the homespun, useful lesson of contentment."[34] It is perhaps sad that so much sparkle should in the end be dimmed for the comforting but dull glow of the family fireside. But her fate is, after all, neither more nor less melancholy to contemplate than the changing scene of London itself. Cecil, we recall, deplored the pulling down of Carlton House and the passing of the pleasure gardens of Ranelagh and Vauxhall. What would he, or his creator, have said to the ultimate irony—the building, on the very site of Gore House where Lady Blessington and the supreme dandy Count d'Orsay held their famous salons, of the Royal Albert Hall?

"O tempora—o mores!"—or, in the words of Thackeray's Charles Yellowplush: "O trumpery! O morris, as Homer says."

[33] *The Exposure of Luxury: Radical Themes in Thackeray* (London, 1972), p. 108.
[34] Quoted in *Gentleman's Magazine*, 10 (March, 1861), p. 346.

3

The Education of the Heart:
Maria Edgeworth and some Sister-Teachers

What we feel, and see, and hear, and read, affects our con-
duct from the moment when we begin, till the moment
when we cease to think. It has, therefore, been my daugh-
ter's aim to promote, by all her writings, the progress of
education, from the cradle to the grave.

—Richard Lovell Edgeworth,
Preface to Maria Edgeworth's
Tales of Fashionable Life (1809)

I

THE tone of Richard Edgeworth's pronouncement on his daughter's literary career is forbidding. It promises the most dreary didacticism, heavy doses of evangelical piety and moralizing. Our reaction, however, tells us more about our own preconceptions and prejudices than it does about early nineteenth-century literature. Just as revealing perhaps is an offhand comment by Maria Edgeworth one day in 1815 when the family was reading *O'Donnell*, a novel by Lady Morgan. At a certain episode in which a character makes a sudden appearance, Mr. Edgeworth remarked, "This is quite improbable." To which Maria responded, "Never mind the improbability, let us go on with the entertainment."[1]

As any reader of Maria Edgeworth knows, her didactic

---

[1] *The Life and Letters of Maria Edgeworth*, ed. Augustus J. C. Hare (Boston, 1893), II, 609 (hereafter referred to as *Life and Letters*).

imperative had a healthy balance of modesty, humor, and good sense. The gift of exalting and purifying the soul was beyond Maria, but she found ready consolation "that there is much, though not such glorious use, in my own lesser manner and department." The general public, she reasoned, did not need to be warned against the great passions and temptations so much as against "the lesser faults" that lead on to the greater ones.[2] Her mission, therefore, was to demonstrate these as vividly as possible. Education was indeed the purpose of Maria's work, as her father had proclaimed; but, beyond the Horatian dictum of sweetening the pill, Maria sought to make the lessons simple, accessible, memorable, and delightful. Jane Austen, shuddering at the austerities of Hannah More's novel *Coelebs in Search of a Wife* —"I do not like the Evangelicals"—had nothing but enthusiasm for Maria's fiction: "I have made up my mind to like no Novels really, but Miss Edgeworth's, yours [Anna Austen] and my own."[3] Sir Walter Scott, who signed himself in a letter to her as "the sincere admirer of your genius," heartily commended both her common sense and her "rich humor."[4] "Vastly improving and moral, and yet quite sufficiently interesting"—this description of Miss Edgeworth's tales is Mrs. Gaskell's in 1864, but it sums up admirably the views of an earlier generation for whom education and entertainment were not the incompatible partners that they have become for us.[5]

In eighteenth- and nineteenth-century England education was a home industry. The nursery served double function as the schoolroom in middle- and even upper-class homes.

[2] *Ibid.*, pp. 606-07.

[3] *Letters to her Sister Cassandra and Others,* ed. R. W. Chapman (Oxford, 1952), pp. 256, 405. See also Jane Austen's citation of Maria Edgeworth's *Belinda,* along with Fanny Burney's *Cecilia* and *Camilla,* in *Northanger Abbey* (Ch. 5) as works "in which the greatest powers of the mind are displayed."

[4] Grace A. Oliver, *A Study of Maria Edgeworth* (Boston, 1882), pp. 332, 431.

[5] The comment is Lady Harriet's, in *Wives and Daughters,* Ch. 14.

The ever-busy and overcrowded nursery of Richard Lovell Edgeworth's home provided a veritable laboratory for educational theorists and practical teachers. Four times married (his last wife was two years younger than his oldest daughter Maria), he had twenty-two children, most of whom survived beyond infancy long enough at least to fill the seats in the family schoolroom.[6] The ready audience thus provided—with a stream of younger children to be taught and of older children to assist in the teaching—was the raw material for educational experiment. They were observed; their baby talk and responses to their lessons were conscientiously recorded (the third Mrs. Edgeworth kept notes on her children's development that Richard and Maria later published in their famous book *Practical Education*). They also had to be amused, for the senior Edgeworth was a hearty, openspirited man with no puritanical-Calvinistic-evangelical obsessions about the spiritual values of pain and suffering. It appears to have been an uncommonly happy family. Babies sickened and wives died, but Richard was never discouraged in his pursuit of domestic felicity. On the occasion of his third marriage, he wrote: "Nothing is more erroneous than the common belief, that a man, who has lived in the greatest happiness with one wife, will be the most averse to take another. On the contrary, the loss of happiness, which he feels when he loses her, necessarily urges him to endeavour to be again placed in a situation, which had constituted his former felicity."[7]

The domestic center of the Edgeworth family was firmly based. Late in her life Maria somewhat diffidently rejected an offer to write a biographical preface for a collected edi-

[6] According to the *DNB*, Richard Edgeworth had nineteen children. In fact he had twenty-two, of whom two died in their first year, one lived two years, and another three. For records of the family line see Maria Edgeworth's *Letters from England, 1813-1844*, ed. Christina Colvin (Oxford, 1971), p. xl, and Marilyn Butler, *Maria Edgeworth, a Literary Biography* (Oxford, 1972), p. 489.

[7] *Memoirs of Richard Lovell Edgeworth*, ed. Maria Edgeworth (London, 1820), i, ch. 16.

tion of her novels: "As a woman, my life, wholly domestic, can offer nothing of interest to the public."[8] Though a domestic life, it was also a crowded lively one, full of travel, friendships with the leading literary and political figures of the age—the Duke and Duchess of Wellington (she was an Irish neighbor and distant relative, Kitty Pakenham, of the Longford family), Sir Walter Scott, Byron, Mme. Récamier, Benjamin Constant—and active participation in the cause of social reform for the poor, especially for the starving Irish peasantry.[9] If Maria Edgeworth believed that nothing in her life would interest the public, she was nevertheless for eighty-two years deeply and busily engaged in living privately. She had early learned that "the happiness of life depends more upon a succession of small enjoyments, than upon great pleasures."[10] It was the chief lesson that she taught in her fiction. Guided, sometimes perhaps misguided, by her enthusiastic and opinionated father, she wrote for a severely critical public, her family: "The sympathy with numbers, the mixture of the younger with the elder parts of the family in one and the same literary interest, was, in every point of view, advantageous."[11]

She did her writing at a little desk that her father had made for her, in the library, surrounded but undisturbed by her large family. Two years before his death, Mr. Edgeworth inscribed that desk: "On this humble desk were written all the numerous works of my daughter, Maria Edgeworth, in the common sitting-room of my family. In these works, which were chiefly written to please me, she has never attacked the personal character of any human being or interfered with the opinions of any sect or party, religious or political; while endeavouring to inform and in-

[8] *Life and Letters*, I, Preface.

[9] See Michael Hurst, *Maria Edgeworth and the Public Scene* (Coral Gables, Fla., 1969).

[10] *Practical Education*, Ch. 9. All quotations from this work are from *Works of Maria Edgeworth* (Boston, 1823), II.

[11] *Memoirs of Richard Lovell Edgeworth*, II, ch. 16.

struct others, she improved and amused her own mind, and gratified her heart, which I do believe is better than her head—R.L.E."[12]

Maria would certainly have been flattered by her father's somewhat ambiguous conclusion. Her head was good; she had no doubts as to her intellectual powers and achievements—good enough at least for the eminently practical and pragmatic purposes to which she lent it. To creative powers and literary ambitions Maria gave little thought. She wrote rapidly and spontaneously. Her father often reproached her "for trusting too much to my hasty glances, *aperçus*, as he called them, of character or truths."[13] Even her "adult" tales of fashionable life, including her full-length novel *Belinda* (1801) with its portraits of rakish and corrupt high society, were primarily "illustrations of moral lessons preached to the fashionable world."[14] Their theme invariably was the effects of early education upon the later lives of the characters. It was the heart that mattered: "With respect to what is commonly called the education of the heart," she and her father wrote in the Preface to *Practical Education*, "we have endeavoured to suggest the easiest means of inducing useful and agreeable habits, well regulated sympathy, and benevolent affections."

The phrase goes back far into the eighteenth century, and by the early nineteenth century it was a familiar slogan among educators. In 1799 Hannah More introduced her "Thoughts on the Cultivation of the Heart and Temper in the Education of Daughters" as "a few short remarks on that part of the subject of education, which I would call the education of the heart." Much attention, she observed, has

[12] *A Memoir of Maria Edgeworth, With a Selection from her Letters by the Late Mrs. Edgeworth.* Edited by her Children. (Privately printed, London, 1867; this is known as the British Museum Memoir), III, 265-66.

[13] *Life and Letters*, II, 607.

[14] Matthew W. Rosa, *The Silver-Fork School: Novels of Fashion Preceding Vanity Fair* (New York, 1936), p. 10.

been given to "female education," but "too little regard is paid to the dispositions of the mind . . . the indications of the temper are not properly cherished, nor the affections of the heart sufficiently regulated."[15] A sister-educator and philosopher, almost as celebrated in her time as Mrs. More, Mrs. Elizabeth Hamilton, similarly distinguished between the two branches of education, "the Culture of the Heart and of the Understanding." In her *Letters on the Elementary Principles of Education* (1801), addressed to female readers, she urged that careful attention be given to maintaining the proper balance: "To expose the absurdity of making mere personal accomplishments the exclusive object of attention, is an easy task; but it is, perhaps, an error little less fatal in the consequences, to direct attention *solely* to the cultivation of the understanding, while we neglect the heart" (Letter i).

This concern for the cultivation of the "heart" reflects the generally softening influences of romanticism upon the dominant rationalism of the eighteenth century. For Keats it was a symbol of the whole human condition: "I will call the *world* a School instituted for the purpose of teaching little children to read—I will call the *human heart* the *horn book* used in that School—and I will call the *Child able to read, The Soul* made for that *school* and its *hornbook.* . . . Not merely is the Heart a Hornbook, It is the Minds Bible, it is the Minds experience, it is the teat from which the Mind of intelligence sucks its identity."[16]

Significant changes were taking place in the nature of society itself and in the nature of the family. Maria Edgeworth sharply noted these shifts, pointing out for example in *Castle Rackrent* that her hard-drinking, high-living Irish landlords "are characters which could no more be met with at present in Ireland, than Squire Western or Parson Trul-

---

[15] *Works of Hannah More* (New York, 1835), ii, 370.

[16] Letter to George and Georgiana Keats (#159), 21 April 1819, in *Letters of John Keats, 1814-1821,* ed. Hyder E. Rollins (Cambridge, Mass., 1958), ii, 102-03. Keats's italics.

liber in England." In *The Absentee* she describes an English country gentleman—"not meaning, by that expression, a mere eating, drinking, hunting, shooting, ignorant country squire, of the old race, which is now nearly extinct; but a cultivated, enlightened, independent English country gentleman—the happiest, perhaps, of human beings" (Ch. 4). One of her best novels, *Ormond*, is quite frankly an Irish *Tom Jones*, suitably refined and feminized. While Fielding's hero requires the epic length of eighteen books before settling down, Maria's Ormond repents his follies as early as the third chapter ("From this period of his life, in consequence of the great and painful impression which had been suddenly made on his mind . . . we may date the commencement of our hero's reformation and improvement") and spends the rest of the novel getting educated.

By the beginning of the nineteenth century in England education had become a way of life. It was no longer regarded simply as a stage or a series of systematic steps by which a child moved out of ignorance into knowledge. Rather, it was a development, a growth that paralleled physical growth and then continued beyond it through the entire spiritual existence of the mature adult. One of the most frequent metaphors in writings about education was the garden. Words like "seed," "plant," "cultivation," "growth," "flowering," and images of weeded gardens, trimmed shrubbery, and propped or trained vines recur. The eighteenth-century garden is domestic, a cultivated piece of family property, not a tamed wilderness. Candide cultivating his own garden, however ironical Voltaire's original intention, was symbolically representative of the eighteenth-century view of the rational life—a settling down to cope with the problems closest at hand. The closest and most urgent problem for most families was the child. His education was the duty and—in the more exalted terms in which it was often described—the divine mission of the parents and most particularly of the mother.

At the beginning of the century Locke's recommendations

on practical, rational education were favorably received though not universally practiced; these included cultivating the body as well as the mind of the child, forming good habits as early as possible, establishing patterns of pleasurable association with learning rather than fear and intimidation, "accommodating the educational program to the child, not the child to the program."[17] Locke's principal essay on education was directed to a father educating a son for life as an English country gentleman. But by mid-century Rousseau had made the philosophical leap across the classes and the sexes. *Emile* is addressed to women: "Tender, anxious mother, I appeal to you. . . . The earliest education is most important and it undoubtedly is woman's work. If the author of nature had meant to assign it to men he would have given them milk to feed the child. Address your treatises on education to the women, for not only are they able to watch over it more closely than men, not only is their influence always predominant in education, its success concerns them more nearly. . . (Bk. i).[18]

Education in the home, by the mother, most nearly ap-

[17] *The Educational Writings of John Locke*, ed. James L. Axtell (Cambridge, 1968), p. 52.

[18] Translated by Barbara Foxley, Everyman ed., 1911. In exalting the role of the mother in education Rousseau found many enthusiastic disciples (including the famous Swiss educator Pestalozzi). One of these was Louis Aimé-Martin, whose *De l'Education des mères de famille ou la civilisation du genre humain par les femmes* (1834) suggests its emphases by its title. Abridged and translated into English in 1839 as *Woman's Mission* (published in America in 1843 as *The Education of Mothers*), the book was widely read. George Eliot recommended it to Maria Lewis in a letter of 17 September 1840 as "the most philosophical and masterly on the subject I ever read or glanced over" (*Letters*, ed. Gordon S. Haight, i, 66). Martin, writing in the stormy days of the monarchist revolutions of the 1830's, saw as France's only hope a spiritual rebirth of the nation, promoted and guided by the mothers of families: "I appeal to mothers for the moralization of the family and of the country. Their true mission is the religious developement of infancy and youth. It is upon maternal love that the future destiny of the human race depends. . ." (Introduction).

93

proaches the state of nature itself, the ideal. Julie, "La Nouvelle Héloïse," painfully learns to control her passion (her love for her tutor Saint-Preux) and rule herself by the law of nature—duty to her mate (i.e. her lawful husband) and her children. Nature, according to Rousseau, is not instinctive animality and sexual appetite. Rather, it is tranquil and harmonious order, the subduing of one's fevered passions to a serene self-control. For Julie this means the role of wife and mother freely chosen over mistress of the man she unlawfully loves: "Le rang d'épouse et de mère m'élève l'âme et me soutiens contre les remords d'un autre état" (4th Part, Letter 1). Under the guidance of her husband she devotes herself to the moral education of her children, following the instincts of her nature, gradually shaping and directing but never forcing them from childhood ignorance into mature wisdom.

Rousseau had defined education as "the art of forming men" and had alluded to the familiar garden: "Plants are shaped by culture, man by education" (*Emile*, Bk. 1). But the first shapers and gardeners are women. Whether viewed in the mildly pagan aspect of Rousseau's Romanticism or in the more severely Christian aspect of Hannah More's evangelicalism, their mission is the same, exalted and divine. Mrs. (a courtesy title, she never married) More's hero Coelebs seeks a wife in the image of Milton's Eve, whose perfection was "To study household good, / And good work in her husband to promote." Presumably she had prelapsarian Eve in mind: "The domestic arrangements of such a woman as filled the capacious mind of the poet, resembles, if I may say it without profaneness, those of Providence, whose underagent she is. Her wisdom is seen in its effects. Indeed, it is rather felt than seen. It is sensibly acknowledged in the peace, the happiness, the virtue of the component parts, in the order, regularity and beauty of the whole system of which she is the moving spring" (Ch. 1).

In the long run, in England at least, Hannah More's

"homely" approach to education prevailed over Rousseau's more ardent idealism, but these were not essentially irreconcilable. Perhaps because of its French and revolutionary associations, Rousseau's influence tended to operate on the more extreme and eccentric education theorists. Richard Edgeworth was a disciple in his youth and educated his first son in complete Rousseauistic freedom. In Chapter 10 of his *Memoirs*, Edgeworth recalls that he once took the child to visit Rousseau. The philosopher judged him "a boy of abilities" but was somewhat disturbed to note that he showed a partiality for things English, remarking excitedly on the English horses and carriages that passed them. This, Rousseau felt, was "a propensity to party prejudice, which will be a great blemish in his character." The boy grew up as bold and free and good-tempered as Emile himself, but with "an invincible dislike to control." He ran away from home, joined the navy, and later settled in the rebellious former colony of North Carolina. An even more extreme theoretician was Edgeworth's close friend Thomas Day, author of the famous children's book *The History of Sandford and Merton* (1783-1789), who abandoned Rousseau to launch his own program for the education of an ideal wife. Day's experiments with the upbringing of young women were ludicrous; his theory of permissiveness, as he extended it to the training of young horses, caused his death when he was thrown by a colt.

Eventually Richard Edgeworth soured on Rousseau and shifted his emphasis from the "negative education" of simply yielding in the free course of nature to a controlled, rational "practical education." Maria reflected this same disenchantment in her novel *Belinda*, in which the hero Clarence Hervey educates a young girl of obscure origins to become an "ideal" wife. Over-indulging in romantic sensibility she falls in love with a young man simply from his portrait and re-christens herself Virginia St. Pierre under the influence of Bernardin de St. Pierre's famous novel *Paul et Virginie*. Hervey's mistake was a literal interpretation of

Rousseau: "this eloquent writer's sense made its full impression upon Clarence's understanding, and his declamations produced more than their just effect upon an imagination naturally ardent" (Ch. 26).

So much for theory. *Practical Education* was indeed an appropriate title for Richard and Maria Edgeworth's first book, published in 1798—actually a family collaboration to which Richard contributed the chapters on grammar and classical literature, geography, arithmetic, geometry and mechanics; son Lovell (who had studied at Edinburgh under the moral philosopher Dugald Stewart) the chapter on chemistry; Mrs. Elizabeth Edgeworth the notes for the chapter on obedience. The remainder of the book—a very considerable portion—is Maria's, and the spirit of the book and its simple, forthright style are hers. The principal emphases are also hers: detailed observations of children in the process of learning, lively anecdotes describing their spontaneous reactions to questions and problems, their games and toys. The method might be criticized, she acknowledged, for its apparent triviality and lack of "elevation of style," but it is actually part of a large pragmatic approach, directly derived from the empirical Locke, that assumes that education works best when it is immediately involved with the hearts of children. They learn better when they are happy and allowed to proceed at a natural, easy pace: "Far from making childhood a state of continual penance, restraint, and misery, we wish that it should be made a state of uniform happiness; that parents and preceptors should treat their pupils with as much equality and kindness as the improving reason of children justifies" (Ch. 25).

The ideal schoolroom is the real home; the ideal teacher is a parent, especially the mother; the ideal method is gradual and developmental; and the curriculum is practical, pragmatic, tending to the cultivation of the moral development of the child rather than to his academic training. As the Edgeworths conclude their book, they sum up with a description of the *total* experience of education and development that in fictional terms would approximate a *Bildungsroman*: "The views of children should be extended to their future advantage, and they should consider childhood as a part of their existence, not as a certain number of years which must be passed over before they can enjoy any of the pleasures of life, before they can enjoy any of the privileges of grown up people."

Viewed practically and empirically, education becomes a series of connected experiences, of tests and trials in which the growing child expands, moving constantly forward and upward. The work of the Edgeworths contains, in sum, the material of the fictional plot as well as the material for a handbook of education. In her Chapter 24, "On Prudence and Economy," Maria might almost be outlining the plot of a *Bildungsroman*: "Instead of deciding always for our young pupils, we should early accustom them to choose for themselves about every trifle which is interesting to childhood: if they choose wisely they should enjoy the natural reward of their prudence; and if they decide rashly, they should be suffered to feel the consequences of their own error." Only a year later, in 1799, Hannah More echoed that idea in her *Strictures on the Modern System of Female Education*: "The best effects of a careful education are often very remote; they are to be discovered in future scenes, and exhibited in as yet untried connections. Every event of life will be putting the heart into fresh situations, and making new demands on its prudence, its firmness, its integrity, or its forbearance" (Ch. 3).

The relationship between educational theory and fictional practice was very close in the early nineteenth century. As increasingly education came to be regarded as child-centered and therefore a function of the home and the mother, the novel became domestic and female-dominated, although men novelists and readers as much as women were concerned and fascinated with the subject. All the little Jane Eyres and David Copperfields and Maggie Tullivers and Richard Feverels were pupils in the schoolroom of the "education of the heart," for which Maria Edgeworth and her sister-novelists like Susan Ferrier and Jane Austen were supplying curricula and texts.

II

THE domestic novel-of-education emerged to meet a specific need. Some time around 1817 the talented and witty Scotch spinster Susan Ferrier, as yet an unpublished novelist, wrote impatiently to her friend Lady Charlotte Bury that she was "labouring very hard" at Maria Edgeworth's novel *Patronage* but finding it "the greatest lump of cold Lead I ever attempted to swallow. . . . I cannot discover a particle of imagination, taste, wit, or sensibility; and without these qualities I never could feel much pleasure in any book." The trouble, she confessed to her friend, is that she must always "prefer a romance to a novel." The mere setting down of details of everyday life is dull and drab, like the Dutch painter, "who chooses for his subject turnips, fraus, and tables, [and] is only the copyist of inferior objects." Longing to live, through her reading at least, "in the enchanted regions of romance," Susan rejected instruction for amusement.[19] In the same spirit she had written her friend Miss Clavering in 1809 that, whatever his good intentions, Mrs. More's Coelebs as a man "is insupportable," and along with Miss Edgeworth's "good ladies and grateful little girls should be returned to their gilt boards, and as for sentimental weavers and moralising glovers, I recommend them as penny ware for the pedlar."[20]

Iconoclastic as Miss Ferrier sounds, for 1809 at least, she

[19] Lady Charlotte Bury, *The Diary of a Lady in Waiting* (London and New York, 1908), II, 176. The letter is undated but assigned to this period although it may have been written a few years later; see *Memoir and Correspondence of Susan Ferrier, 1782-1854*, ed. John A. Doyle (London, 1898), p. 243, n. 2.

[20] *Memoir and Correspondence*, p. 65.

was actually much in tune with her times. If occasionally she became surfeited with heavy moralizing, she was equally suspicious of the frenzies and passions of romances. Byron, Mrs. Radcliffe, Maturin, and Mackenzie were her secret favorites, to be confessed laughingly and somewhat guiltily in letters to her intimate friends. But in her more rational and sober moments, of which there seem to have been a considerable number, she scorned the melodramatic and sensational and opted for the conventional course: "The only good purpose of a book," she wrote, "is to inculcate morality." When Miss Clavering proposed that they collaborate on a novel of "the horrible and the astonishing," Susan firmly rejected the idea: "I *will not* enter into any of your raw head and bloody bone schemes. I would not even *read* a Book that had a Spectre in it, and as for committing a mysterious and most foul murder, I declare I'd rather take a dose of asafoetida." Miss Clavering altered her plans and proposed a less lurid plot, but Susan still complained that "it wants a *moral.*"[21]

Ultimately that novel, *Marriage*, was written almost entirely by Susan with only one interpolation (Ch. 14, "The History of Mrs. Douglas") by Miss Clavering. Published in 1818 it proved enormously popular, successful enough to rank Miss Ferrier with Jane Austen and Maria Edgeworth as writers who, in Sir Walter Scott's words, "have all given portraits of real society far superior to any thing man, vain man, has produced of the like nature."[22] What these ladies had in common, however, was less the fashionable novel of society than the novel of education. For Susan Ferrier, professing impatience with the moralizing and didacticism of much of the fiction of her day yet compelled by her training and disposition to defend the moral purposes of fiction, the education novel was an ideal solution and compromise. On the one hand it offered the appealing romantic ingredients of youthful characters involved in trials and prob-

[21] *Ibid.*, pp. 87, 75. Her italics.
[22] Oliver, p. 215.

lems deriving from their innocence, their ignorance or their inexperience—mystery (in *The Inheritance* the heroine Gertrude learns of a deep secret involving her birth and true identity); suspense (Will the shipwrecked hero in *Destiny* make himself known to the family who think him dead? Will Gertrude in *The Inheritance* choose the attractive fortune hunter or the stolid and sterling suitor? Will the more beautiful but frivolous rival outdistance the more virtuous heroine of *Destiny*?). On the other hand, by showing the rewards of virtue, patience, and prudence, the education novel served its moral purpose. Furthermore, it drew realistically but also poetically upon the physical and social scene in which the characters grow up and develop morally. While not a regionalist in the manner of Sir Walter Scott, Susan Ferrier made capital of the landscape and local color of Scotland and of the peculiar national characteristics of the Scots. She delighted her nineteenth-century readers with eighteenth-century humours types—eccentrics and "originals" like cranky but lovable Uncle Adam Ramsay and rattle-brained spinster Miss Pratt of *The Inheritance*; the outspoken aunts Miss Jacky, Miss Nicky, and Miss Grizzy of *Marriage*; the hot-tempered, arrogant Highland chief Glenroy; and the coarse-grained clergyman Reverend Duncan McDow of *Destiny*.

Like Maria Edgeworth, Susan Ferrier is today read mainly for her "local color." But in their day, as we noted in Scott's tribute, these novelists were appreciated for more than mere regionalism. Scotland and Ireland were educational laboratories offering scenes and social situations that tested and marked the developing natures of the leading characters. In Maria Edgeworth's *The Absentee* and in her "Ennui," young noblemen dangerously tempted by the dissipations of London life return to Ireland to mature in responsible work on their country estates. In all three of Susan Ferrier's novels, characters show their real natures— and the quality of their early education—by the way in which they respond to the Scottish landscape. The silly young Lady Juliana of *Marriage* is miserable in the rugged atmosphere of her husband's Highland home. She leaves him to return to London and fashionable Mayfair society. The baby daughter she takes with her and brings up in the effete South becomes as shallow as her mother. The daughter she leaves behind to grow up under more sober tutelage in Scotland is sensitive and noble-spirited. The nervous, guilt-ridden Mrs. St. Clair of *The Inheritance* is uncomfortable and unhappy in the awe-inspiring scenery of the Scottish Highlands, but her supposed daughter Gertrude responds with ecstasy and Wordsworthian fervor to both "the plaintive murmur of the wood pigeon" and the majestic mountains with "a vague poetical feeling of love and gratitude to Heaven [that] caused her to raise her eyes, swimming in tearful rapture, to the Giver of all good" (Ch. 2). And in *Destiny* the moral superiority of simple Edith over her stepsister, the beautiful Florinda, is demonstrated succinctly in a passage in which Edith responds enthusiastically to "the firs and heather of my own native land," while Florinda rhapsodizes over her memories of moonlight in Naples.

Susan Ferrier's more perceptive readers recognized that Scotland was a moral testing-ground. The shrewd critic of *Blackwood's Magazine* "Christopher North" (John Wilson) observed in 1831 that the unique feature of her novels was their portrait of the ultimate breaking down of the Highland character: "Sir Walter Scott had fixed the enamel of genius over the last fitful gleams of their half-savage chivalry; but a humbler and sadder scene—the scene of lucre-banished clans—of chieftains dwindling into imitation-squires—and of chiefs content to barter the recollections of a thousand years for a few gaudy seasons of Almack's and Crockford's—the euthanasia of kilted aldermen and steamboat *pibrochs* was reserved for Miss Ferrier."[23] A tougher realism apparently existed in her work than Susan Ferrier

[23] "A Dialogue on Modern Novels," *Blackwood's Magazine*, 30 (September, 1831), p. 533.

herself recognized. Yet North also detected in her "a fund of romance," a heavy weight of the pathetic and sentimental (and one might add, the didactic) that overburdened her frail novels.

Susan Ferrier was less successful than either Maria Edge-worth or Jane Austen in balancing her hardcore social realism with her sentimentality and didacticism. Miss Edge-worth really did not try to achieve a balance. Miss Austen had the art to conceal her efforts. But in Miss Ferrier there are only great lumps of moralizing thinly disguised as part of the hero's or heroine's adventures in growing to maturity. Her first novel *Marriage* might more accurately have been titled "Education," for its theme is the effect of childhood conditioning and training upon character. Planning the novel, she wrote to her would-be collaborator Miss Clavering that it was to be a warning to all young ladies against runaway marriage: "I expect it will be the first book every wise matron will put into the hand of her daughter."[24] The consequences of faulty education have an ominous continuity from generation to generation. We begin with the poorly educated Lady Juliana: "Educated for the sole purpose of forming a brilliant establishment, of catching the eye and captivating the senses, the cultivation of her mind, or the correction of her temper, had formed no part of the system by which that aim was to be accomplished. Under the auspices of a fashionable mother, and an obsequious governess, the froward petulance of childhood, fostered and strengthened by indulgence and submission, had gradually ripened into that selfishness and caprice which now, in youth, formed the prominent features of her character. . . . The mind of Lady Juliana was consequently the sport of every passion that by turns assailed it" (Ch. 1). She marries capriciously, deserts her husband, taking away one of her twin daughters whom she in turn mis-educates, putting her in the hands of French and Italian governesses, neglecting the Bible and religious instruction, and produc-

[24] *Memoir and Correspondence*, p. 76.

ing a young lady "as heartless and ambitious as she was beautiful and accomplished—but the surface was covered with flowers and who would have thought of analysing the soil?" (Ch. 28).[25] Predictably this girl makes a bad though socially advantageous marriage, then leaves her husband to live in sin and disgrace with another man.

The neglected twin Mary, however, falls fortunately into the care of a family friend, Mrs. Douglas, who had herself been well educated by a governess of "strong understanding and enlarged mind, [who] early instilled into her a deep sense of religion." Accordingly, she becomes a fine woman, happily married, devoted to the interests of her husband, their model farm, and little Mary. Like the Edgeworths, she is a "practical" educator, though more religiously oriented than they. She is natural, easy, unaffected, less concerned with instilling "accomplishments" in the little girl than in simply guiding her toward a good life: "her example, like a kindly dew, was shedding its silent influence on the embryo blossoms of her pupil's heart." Mary flowers and blooms—sensitive, loving, virtuous, and fully deserving of the happy marriage that she ultimately makes.

In Susan's "middle" novel *The Inheritance* (1824), the heroine's education gets relatively less attention since she comes fully grown upon the scene and her background must be obscured for the purposes of the mystery-plot. Mainly Gertrude must be untainted by the woman who pretends to be her mother: "Mrs. St. Clair had spared no pains to render her daughter as great an adept in dissimulation as she was herself; but all her endeavours had proved unsuccessful, and Miss St. Clair remained pretty much as nature had formed her—a mixture of wheat and tares, flowers

[25] See Miss Clavering's comment on the progress of the novel: "I like the idea of the twin daughter being worse than her mother—she ought to be full of whimsies, and have engrafted on her mother's character more *firmness* and *stamina*, which in that style of education will not fail of completing the badness of her disposition. . ." (*Memoir and Correspondence*, pp. 116-17; her italics).

and weeds" (Ch. 2). But her last novel *Destiny* (1831) is heavy with educational theory. The motherless heroine is fortunate enough to come under the influence of another of these model matrons like Mrs. Douglas. Mrs. Malcolm is the mother of a large family and the wife of a gentleman-farmer who shares her views implicitly. Like the Edgeworths, the fictional Malcolms are opposed to public schools and strongly favor home education (in a footnote Susan Ferrier cites Mrs. Barbauld's "admirable Essay on Education" to support this position). Their large brood grows up uncontaminated by snobbery, affectation, or academic pedantry: "Their minds were kept free from sordid passions and vulgar prejudices, while all the nobler qualities of their nature were strengthened and improved by the constant exercise of the mind's best attributes" (Ch. 7).

Only a practicing novelist like Miss Ferrier, confronting the problems of reconciling didacticism with readability, could have quite so warmly appreciated the genius of Jane Austen, who gracefully accomplished what Miss Ferrier so laboriously attempted: "I have been reading 'Emma,' which is excellent; there is no story whatever, and the heroine is no better than other people; but the characters are all so true to life and the style so piquant, that it does not require the adventitious aids of mystery and adventure."[26] Elsewhere she paid her the even higher compliment of imitation, beginning *The Inheritance* with an unmistakable echo of the opening sentence of *Pride and Prejudice*: "It is a truth universally acknowledged that there is no passion so deeply rooted in human nature as that of pride." But the links among the three leading women novelists of this first quarter of the nineteenth century were more solid than graceful compliments and imitation, more even than the strikingly similar circumstances of their personal lives—all three spinsters of upper-class families, devoted to their parents (Susan and Maria to their fathers, Jane to her ailing mother) and nephews and nieces. They were also women

[26] *Ibid.*, p. 128.

of rare wit and intelligence, responding with sensitivity to the changing ideas of their time, to new concepts of the purpose of life itself, to a recognition of the importance and inevitability of social change and personal growth. They were keenly aware of new approaches to teaching and learning, new knowledge of how man (and woman) learns, how he adapts himself to the realities of daily existence even while he strives to transcend reality and achieve spiritual fulfillment.

These women were gifted too with common sense and the kind of redeeming humor that spared them the pretentiousness and solemnity of many of their sister- and brother-novelists. At heart probably as sensitive, introspective, and romantic as any creative artist, they found the richest source of expression in the circumstances of life both as they literally knew it and as they hopefully envisioned its possibilities. Education—the cultivation of the mind and the heart—was the instrument of social reform and of personal self-government that was most accessible to them. When Emma spends an apparently fruitless few minutes surveying the drab provincial "traffic" of a Highbury street —"the butcher with his tray, a tidy old woman travelling homewards from shop with her full basket, two curs quarreling over a dirty bone, and a string of dawdling children round the baker's little bow-window eyeing the gingerbread"—she is not bored. "A mind lively and at ease," Jane Austen adds approvingly, "can do with seeing nothing, and can see nothing that does not answer" (II, ch. 9). Susan Ferrier's heroine in *The Inheritance* has not yet learned that lesson so well. Trapped for a short visit in a provincial town, she sees little to appeal to her sensibilities. But her creator, though her personal tastes were for romances, as we have noted, nevertheless found lively interest in this homely scene:

"At the next house a great washing was going on; maidservants, with pinned-up sleeves, crimson arms, and loose caps, came occasionally to the door to discharge tubs full of soap-suds, while a roaring infant was dandled at the window by a little dirty dog-eared-looking minx, with her hair *en papillote*. On the other side of the knitting lady nothing was visible to the naked eye; but the sound of an old cracked jingling spinnet was heard unceasingly practising Barbadoes' Bells and Nancy Dawson. Below was a shop, and over the half-door leant the shopmaster, with a long, sharp, raw nose, looking as anxiously as ever did Sister Anne to see if there was anybody coming. Now and then the street was enlivened with the clank of a pair of pattens; at another time a spattered cow was driven reluctantly along, lowing most plaintively. There was also an occasional cart shaking the houses in its progress, as it rumbled over the rugged pavement. A hoarse, shrieking ballad-singer made an attempt to collect an audience. . . . But his only listeners were a boy going to school and a servant-girl bound on a message which required despatch" (Ch. 41).

Observing this scene, Gertrude is engaged in a course of unconcious self-education. She is learning—as Emma had learned—to answer, to respond, to discipline her nervous sensibilities, to educate her heart. To the extent that she learns this lesson, she will be a *better* as well as a wiser woman.

The moral superiority of Fanny Price to charming but shallow Mary Crawford is defined by Jane Austen in *Mansfield Park* with a similar test. Fanny finds pleasure and interest in simple life. She responds to an English garden with genuine delight: "One cannot fix one's eyes on the commonest natural production without finding food for a rambling fancy." Mary responds with more wit but less wisdom: "To say the truth . . . I am something like the famous Doge at the court of Lewis XIV; and may declare that I see no wonder in this shrubbery equal to seeing myself in it" (II, ch. 4). But Fanny too has many lessons to learn.[27] Her heart is

[27] *Mansfield Park* is a model of the "Christian didactic" novel and Fanny of the "Christian heroine." See Robert A. Colby, *Fiction with a Purpose* (Bloomington, Ind., 1967), pp. 95-103.

good, but it requires education so that she can make wise choices and judgments—learning how to control her pride, her self-pity and feelings of inferiority, even her jealousy. She makes "good resolutions on the side of self-government" but she also needs a tutor, Edmund Bertram, who "recommended the books which charmed her leisure hours . . . encouraged her taste, and corrected her judgment" (i, ch. 2). Where parental control is lacking (Mary and Henry Crawford) or delegated through absence or indifference to governesses (Sir Thomas and Lady Bertram), children suffer and pay the price in their adult life. As Elizabeth Bennet warns her witty but irresponsible father about Lydia's weaknesses: "If you, my dear father, will not take the trouble of checking her exuberant spirits, and of teaching her that her present pursuits are not to be the business of her life, she will soon be beyond the reach of amendment" (*Pride and Prejudice*, ii, ch. 18).

The education of the heart comes from within, but all these novelist-educators knew that it must be carefully nurtured and directed by sympathetic teachers—ideally mothers or mother-figures. When these are lacking, others are supplied—helpful older sisters (Elizabeth Bennet Darcy and Jane Bennet Bingley will steer their young sister Kitty to a happier fate than Lydia's; Fanny Price assumes the responsibility for educating her younger sister Susan), friendly older women (Mrs. Douglas and Mrs. Malcolm in Susan Ferrier's novels, Lady Davenant in Maria Edgeworth's *Helen*, somewhat negatively Lady Russell in Jane Austen's *Persuasion*), even sympathetic male friends who sometimes evolve into lovers (Edmund Bertram, Mr. Knightley in *Emma*). A few young heroines are their own teachers, learning instinctively, thanks to the fundamental soundness of their hearts—Elizabeth and Jane Bennet, Susan Ferrier's Gertrude, Maria Edgeworth's Belinda. This last young lady, to be sure, has the guidance by good example of one friend —Lady Anne Percival, a model matron whose happy home and child-centered existence Belinda observes with pleasure and profit. She also has one bad example in another friend, Lady Delacour, whose desperate excesses almost destroy her. Seemingly Belinda is self-educated. Her friend Lady Anne remarks: "Miss Portman is in a dangerous situation . . . but some young people learn prudence by being placed in dangerous situations, as some young horses, I have heard Mr. Percival say, learn to be sure-footed by being left to pick their own way on bad roads" (Ch. 8). Nevertheless, as Miss Edgeworth finally sums it up, Belinda needed "the assistance of Lady Anne and Sir Percival [with which] she established in her own understanding the exact boundaries between right and wrong upon many subjects" (Ch. 17). In early nineteenth-century society, it appears, everyone played some educational role—as pupil, as professional teacher, as parent raising children, as surrogate parent, or as a model or case history for demonstrating lessons of good or bad conduct.

III

IN THE sharply contrasting characters of Fanny Price and Mary Crawford, Jane Austen was observing a distinction familiar to all educators and novel-readers of the age—the debate of Nature versus Art. Fundamentally a concept of aesthetics, it served by extension as a kind of symbol in popular literature—a device for almost instant characterization (as in *Mansfield Park*) and for establishing a motif or theme.[28] In Mrs. Inchbald's novel *Nature and Art* (1796),

[28] The use of the Nature vs. Art theme in *Pride and Prejudice* is pointed out by Samuel Kliger: "The concentration, in fact, in the small plot on singing, letter-writing, the enjoyment of mountainous sublimity, the appreciation of gardening, carries out Jane Austen's carefully premeditated plan for increasing the availability of the art-nature antithesis for the love plot or basic situation of the novel. In other words, the art-nature antithesis is abstracted into a symbolism adequate to cover the adventures and misadventures which keep Elizabeth and Darcy apart in mutual repulsion at the beginning of the tale and bring them together at the end" ("Jane Austen's *Pride and*

for example, the life histories of two brothers and their sons follow different courses, as one boy—kind, honest, "natural," actually raised in the wilderness due to an accident of fate—returns to civilization to right the wrongs committed by his cousin, who is the selfish, affected, "unnatural" product of an upper-class education. This is not a matter of Noble Savage versus Civilized Man, for the hero of *Nature and Art*, having spent his early years in an African jungle, comes to adulthood in the same environment as his morally weak cousin. Rather, it is a psychological distinction, based, however, on acquired and cultivated traits rather than inherited ones. In the eighteenth-century view, Nature was not necessarily antithetical to civilization. Rousseau, as we have noted, understood Nature to be the guiding principle of order and harmony by which rational man rules himself. Even earlier—since the time of Racine at least—the concept of the natural was, as Erich Auerbach has observed, "identified with a well-developed and well-educated type of human being, decorous in conduct and able to adjust with ease to the most exacting situations of social living; just as today we sometimes praise the naturalness of a person of great culture. To call something natural was almost tantamount to calling it reasonable and seemly."[29]

In her far better and more celebrated novel *A Simple Story* (1791), Mrs. Inchbald wrote, "Education is called second nature" (Ch. 15). This novel, which Maria Edgeworth greatly admired, has as its stated theme the importance of "A Proper Education" and traces, with considerable psychological insight, the unhappy life of a society heiress whose upbringing has been frivolous. The result is a charming, accomplished young woman, but one who lacks the strength of character necessary for a prudent life. At

---

Prejudice in the Eighteenth Century Mode," *University of Toronto Quarterly*, 16 (1945-1946), pp. 361-62.

[29] *Mimesis, The Representation of Reality in Western Literature,* tr. Willard R. Trask (Princeton, N.J., 1953), p. 389.

eighteen she emerges from boarding school (significantly she has not been educated at home) "with merely such sentiments of religion as young ladies of fashion mostly imbibe. Her little heart employed in all the endless pursuits of personal accomplishments, had left her mind without one ornament, except those which Nature gave, and even they were not wholly preserved from the ravages made by its rival, *Art*" (Ch. 1).

Maria Edgeworth read *A Simple Story* at least four times and was so delighted that she wrote its author a fan letter. What most impressed her in the novel was the reality of the characters. As a practicing novelist herself, she studied Mrs. Inchbald's technique to learn how she had achieved her remarkable effects. Maria's discoveries about literary realism and point of view anticipate later nineteenth-century critical theories to a surprising degree:

"I never once recollected the author whilst I was reading it; never said or thought, *'That's a fine sentiment,'* or *'That is well expressed,'* or, *'That is well invented.'* I believed it all to be real, and was affected as I should be by the real scenes, if they had passed before my eyes; it is truly deep and pathetic . . . it is by leaving more than most other writers to the imagination that you succeed so eminently in affecting it. By the force that is necessary to repress feeling, we judge of the intensity of the feeling; and you always contrive to give us, by intelligible but simple signs, the measure of this force. Writers of inferior genius waste their words *describing* feelings, in making those who pretend to be agitated by passion describe that passion, and talk of the *rending of their hearts*, etc.—a gross blunder! . . . for the heart cannot feel, and describe its own feelings at the same moment."[30]

What appears therefore to the modern reader as a purely theoretical debate—the shaping influence of Nature versus Art in the education of the young—proved in fact to be a launching point for domestic realism in the English novel.

[30] Oliver, p. 240. Maria's italics.

To show the gradual but ever-widening effects of a system of education upon a young person demanded a leisurely, closely observed, and penetrating study of individual character. The personality could no longer be simply presented, as in seventeenth and eighteenth-century character drawing, where individuals were modeled on universal types. If the new theories of education were to be practiced in actual life, then in fiction that was true to life, the character must be unfolded, developed, and discovered before the reader's eyes. The omniscient narrator must recede to the background, for the reader is now less interested in seeing what the character is (something the author tells us) than in discovering how and why the character became what he is (something the reader will learn for himself).

Re-definitions were in order and Maria Edgeworth was ready to offer them. "All the gestures and attitudes of Anastasia are those of taste and sentiment" she wrote in an early short novel, *Leonora* (1806): "Leonora's are simply those of nature" (Letter XI). Needless to say, Leonora is the heroine. Cultivated taste, sentiment, imagination—these are the elements of Art, and in measure and due proportion they are admirable qualities. Art, indeed, like Nature must be seen in its several aspects. Mrs. Inchbald's dichotomy had suggested only the *artifice-artificial* element, which in excess produces affectation, superciliousness, and even immorality. But Maria's prudent Caroline, in *Letters for Literary Ladies* (written about 1794, published 1799), corrects her friend Julia's assertion that Art spoils a woman's graces and corrupts her heart: "You have with great address availed yourself of the *two* ideas connected with the word *art*; first as opposed to simplicity it implies artifice, and next, as opposed to ignorance, it comprehends all the improvements of science, which, leading us to search for general causes, rewards us with a dominion over their dependent effects:—that which instructs how to pursue the objects which we may have in view, with the greatest probability of success" (Letter II).

111

Understood as "skill" or "accomplishments," Art retained a favorable connotation. But it became increasingly suspect as the bourgeois ideal prevailed in the nineteenth century.[31] There is a recurring theme of contrast, usually running parallel with the Fanny Price / Mary Crawford type of response to nature, in which the "natural" heroine, though highly endowed with prudence, taste, and sensibility, is relatively deficient in the fashionable arts of music, drawing, dancing, and light conversation at which her more sophisticated rival is expert. A lively debate emerged on Nature versus Art in female education. In fiction the cards were immediately stacked in Nature's favor. But in life, as the Edgeworths realistically acknowledge, accomplishments had their uses too. For the leisured woman they were a resource against ennui; they were thought "to increase a young lady's chances in the matrimonial lottery"; they kept her occupied and contented at home and therefore out of the way of "the miseries of dissipation." Provided that they "enliven and embellish domestic life," then, accomplishments have a place in the education of a young woman. But they are to be merely tolerated and only barely cultivated. "Men of superior sense and characters," Maria writes, are not impressed by "superficial accomplishments" when they are choosing wives. The overly accomplished girl in fact risks a dreary fate—which, as Maria describes it, is the plot outline for numerous "silver-fork" novels including at least half-a-dozen of Mrs. Gore's: "How many accomplished belles run the usual round of dissipation in all public places of exhibition, tire the public eye, and, after a season or two,

---

[31] Even in her youthful parodies Jane Austen scored the bourgeois nature of "accomplishments." In "Jack and Alice," a young lady from North Wales, daughter of a tailor, boasts of her first-rate masters, "who taught me all the accomplishments requisite for one of my sex and rank. Under their instructions I learned Dancing, Music, Drawing & various Languages, by which means I became more accomplished than any other Taylor's Daughter in Wales" ("Volume the First," in *The Works of Jane Austen*, ed. R. W. Chapman [Oxford, 1954], vi, 20).

112

fade and are forgotten! How many accomplished belles are there who, having gained the object of their own, or of their mother's ambition, find themselves doomed to misery for life!" (*Practical Education,* Ch. 20, "On Female Accomplishments, Masters, and Governesses"). Less solemnly but no less seriously Jane Austen offers the example of Mary Bennet, who has compensated for her plainness by cultivating bookish knowledge and skill at the piano. Proud to be described as "the most accomplished girl in the neighbourhood," she finds that her fate is spinsterhood: "Mary had neither genius nor taste, and though vanity had given her application, it had given her likewise a pedantic air and conceited manner" (*Pride and Prejudice,* I, ch. 6).

This disparagement of Art was inevitable as long as the fundamental purpose of female education remained domestic. From the mere murmurings of discontent and aspiration at the beginning of the nineteenth century to the clamor for full civil and legal rights at the end of the century, means varied, but the end was never seriously challenged. Even the radical Mary Wollstonecraft, battling for the rights of women with the rhetoric of the French Revolution ringing in her ears, never asked more for her sex than the kind of education that would enable women to be good wives and mothers if they married or to support themselves decently if they remained unmarried. This was radical enough for an age that read Dr. Fordyce's *Sermons to Young Women* (1765) and Dr. John Gregory's *A Father's Legacy to his Daughter* (1774), which warned women against the "masculine pursuits" of learning and advised them, in the interests of their domestic happiness, to conceal whatever education they had. Egalitarian Mary Wollstonecraft argued for educating women alongside of men as "rational creatures and free citizens, and they will become good wives and mothers; that is—if men do not neglect the duties of husbands and fathers" (*A Vindication of the Rights of Woman,* Ch. 13, "On National Education").

All of Mary Wollstonecraft's writings, fiction and nonfiction, were heavily polemical and tendentious. But her concern with female education and female psychology reflected an attitude toward fiction that was symptomatic of the new trends of domestic realism. In her advertisement to her autobiographical novel *Mary, a Fiction* (1788), she announced a new style of heroine—"a character different from those generally portrayed. This woman is neither a Clarissa, a Lady G-, nor a Sophia. . . ." The heroines of romance who ramble in their self-created imaginative paradises and "the hidden springs" of their souls are discarded for "an artless tale, without episode" in which "the mind of a woman who has thinking powers is displayed. The female organs have been thought too weak for this arduous employment [but] . . . in a fiction such a being may be allowed to exist; whose grandeur is derived from the operations of its own faculties. . . ." This heroine, Mary, is educated painfully out of the experience of life. Her moral growth from innocent girlhood into maturity is finely and carefully outlined. An almost Rousseauistic childhood in nature shapes her character and her sensibilities and prepares her, not for some dreamy Utopia or happy-ever-after of romance, but for a life of hard work and service to others. Nature has made its claim over Art, Realism over Romance.

No tinge of Wollstonecraft-Godwinian radicalism can be suspected in the works of Mrs. Anna Letitia Aikin Barbauld (1743-1825). A devout and conservative teacher and writer of children's books and the biographer of Samuel Richardson, she was celebrated by her contemporaries and several ensuing generations of Victorians for her *Lessons for Children* (1780), which inspired the Edgeworths in their stories for young readers. Maria paid her a graceful tribute in her Chapter 12 on "Books" in *Practical Education*: "The first books which are now usually put into the hands of a child, are Mrs. Barbauld's Lessons; they are by far the best books of the kind that have ever appeared; those only who know the difficulty and the importance of such compositions in

114

education, can sincerely rejoice, that the admirable talents of such a writer have been employed in such a work."[32]

Traditional and orthodox as she was, Mrs. Barbauld's educational thinking was rooted in the same soil as Mary Wollstonecraft's—Locke's empirical Reason blended with Rousseau's regulated Nature. She could therefore argue that fundamentally the educational aspirations of men and women are the same: "Every woman should consider herself as sustaining the general character of a rational being, as well as the more confined one belonging to the female sex; and therefore the motives for acquiring general knowledge and cultivating the taste are nearly the same to both sexes."[33] Nature therefore dictated an education that would prepare a woman for a domestic life. Insofar as they enhanced her qualities as companion for her husband and teacher for her children, the "accomplishments"—especially French, history, and natural history—were recommended. Carried to the level of academic learning, however, they were dangerous. When Mrs. Elizabeth Montagu proposed to her once that she establish a "Literary Academy for Ladies . . . where they are to be taught in a regular systematic manner the various branches of science," she rejected the idea as "better calculated to form such characters as the '*Précieuses*' or the '*Femmes Savantes*' of Molière, than good wives or agreeable companions."[34]

The warning was amply demonstrated in early nineteenth-century fiction where blue-stockings were not merely satirized, as they had been earlier, but were now shown as more potentially evil. They are often arrogant young women who intimidate and frighten off suitors or attempt

[32] Almost half a century later Anne Thackeray (later Lady Ritchie) had her first reading lessons "out of her little yellow books" (*A Book of Sibyls* [London, 1883], pp. 1-2).

[33] "On Female Studies," in *Works of Mrs. Barbauld*, ed. Lucy Aikin (New York, 1826), ii, 235-36.

[34] *Ibid.*, i, 19.

to break up the happy marriages of their friends or, worse, are negligent mothers. An especially grim example is in Mrs. Amelia Opie's popular *Adeline Mowbray* (1804). In her youth the heroine's mother had had an expensive but misdirected education: "For her, history, biography, poetry, and discoveries in natural philosophy, had few attractions, while she pored with still unsatisfied delight over abstruse systems of morals and metaphysics or new theories in politics" (Ch. 1). Left a widow of means with an only daughter, she spends her time in "fatal and unproductive studies . . . wrapt in philosophical abstraction," while ignoring her child. Such benign neglect is apparently no worse than the "malign" education that Mrs. Mowbray would have given her daughter had she undertaken it. Adeline manages to grow up sweet and good (she even picks up some lessons in domestic economy and pastry-making from her grandmother). But her mother's failure to give her moral guidance drives the naive girl into a love affair. Following a line of Godwinian iconoclasm, she refuses marriage even when her lover offers it ("Our attachment is sanctioned by reason and virtue . . . but not by the Church"), bears a child, suffers bitterly, and dies in a tearful reconciliation with her contrite mother. Adeline and her mother finally learn from tragic experience the importance of "the education of the heart": "A child's education begins almost from the hour of its birth, and the mother who understands her task, knows that the circumstances which every moment calls forth, are the tools with which she is to work in order to fashion her child's mind and character."

Young women who are introduced in novels as "accomplished" are immediately suspect.[35] Jane Austen might al-

[35] Perhaps the most extended treatment of the subject in fiction is Catherine Sinclair's *Modern Accomplishments; or, The March of Intellect* (Edinburgh, 1836), a novel written "to illustrate the pernicious consequences of an undue prominence in education given to ornamental above useful acquirements."

low superior talents when they are genuine. Jane Fairfax's superiority over Emma at the piano in no way impugns Jane's character, though most readers tend to share Emma's discomfort in her chilly presence. But Mary Crawford's facile grace, her poise and witty conversation, her arts or accomplishments, bespeak a dubious moral character. Poor humble Fanny, a pure product of Nature, measures herself sadly against the glittering Mary. Her heartless cousins Maria and Julia Bertram, encouraged by their aunt Mrs. Norton, mock her ignorance of geography and the chronology of the Roman emperors and kings of England. Their aunt reminds them that because Fanny is poor, "it is not at all necessary that she should be as accomplished as you are" —on which Jane Austen drily muses: "and it is not very wonderful that with all their promising talents and early information, they should be entirely deficient in the less common acquirements of self-knowledge, generosity, and humility" (*Mansfield Park*, I, Ch. 2).

The passage recalls one in Maria Edgeworth's "The Good French Governess" (in *Moral Tales*, 1801) where a precocious little girl boasts of her command of the English kings and the Roman emperors: "A person could make no figure in conversation, you know, amongst well-informed people, if she didn't know these things." The wise governess gently replies, "Certainly not . . . nor could she make a figure amongst well-informed people, by telling them what, as you observed just now, everybody knows." Later in the story we are introduced to Miss Fanshaw, a stiff young lady ("Her person had undergone all the ordinary and extraordinary tortures of back-boards, collars, stocks, dumbbells, etc.") of many accomplishments, whose mother boasts of the enormous expense of her education: "Though firm to her original doctrine, that women had no occasion for learning—in which word of reproach she included all literature—she nevertheless had been convinced, by the unanimous voice of fashion, that accomplishments were *most desirable for young ladies*—desirable, merely because they were fashionable; she did not in the least consider them as sources of independent occupation."

Although the education of the heart is a process of nature, it requires careful human attention. One of the most objectionable features of cultivating the accomplishments was that it was often done at the price of precious time in a girl's life and at a sacrifice of the more important knowledge that she should acquire. To become such a prodigy of accomplishments as Caroline Bingley and Mr. Darcy describe—

" 'Oh! certainly,' cried his faithful assistant, 'no one can be really esteemed accomplished, who does not greatly surpass that is usually met with. A woman must have a thorough knowledge of music, singing, drawing, dancing, and the modern languages, to deserve the word; and besides all this, she must possess a certain something in her air and manner of walking, the tone of her voice, her address and expressions, or the word will be but half deserved.'

" 'All this she must possess,' added Darcy, 'and to all this she must yet add something more substantial in the improvement of her mind by extensive reading.' "—all this strikes sensible Elizabeth Bennet as an absurdity: "I am no longer surprised at your knowing *only* six accomplished women. I rather wonder now at your knowing *any*" (*Pride and Prejudice*, I, ch. 8).

The ideal being unattainable, the issue was to make the best use of time and energy for what could be attained. "If all the accomplishments could be bought at the price of a single virtue, the purchase would be infinitely dear." So Hannah More wrote in her "Thoughts on the Cultivation of the Heart and Temper in the Education of Daughters."[36] The duties and responsibilities of a woman are many. Numerous essays and handbooks were written in the late eighteenth and early nineteenth centuries outlining rigor-

[36] *Works*, II, 370-71.

ous programs of study. Mrs. Chapone's *Letters on the Improvement of the Mind addressed to a Young Lady* (1772) recommended a course heavy with study of Scripture (but not theology), history, geography, literature (Shakespeare, Milton, Addison, Homer and Virgil in translation, and some "heathen mythology" as an aid in understanding poetry), nature (but not natural philosophy), moral philosophy (as exemplified by the essays in *The Spectator* and *The Rambler*), "common arithmetic," some modern languages (classical languages, however, risk the "danger of pedantry and presumption in a woman"), and as much music and drawing "as Genius leads." Mrs. Barbauld and Mrs. More offered virtually the same program, with Mrs. More stressing perhaps more than her sister-teachers the psychological importance of such training as well as its practical value:

"The great uses of study to a woman are to enable her to regulate her own mind, and to be instrumental to the good of others" (*Strictures on Female Education*, Ch. 14). Regulating the mind, self-knowledge, and self-control are favorite themes both in pedagogical literature and in fiction. Popular novels of the period included Mrs. Brunton's *Self-Control* (1811) and *Discipline* (1814) and Mrs. Opie's *Temper* (1812). Except in the case of the most extreme evangelicals who would have outlawed all imaginative literature, or an arch-conservative of early Victorianism like M. A. Stodart, who declared that "A Christian novel-reader is a contradiction in terms" and warned: "On no account whatever, give way to the most pernicious habit of novel reading. Like the use of tobacco, opium, snuff, ardent spirits, and every other bad and ruinous habit, it increases by indulgence"[37]—most female educators tolerated and even encouraged that amount of poetry and fiction which would cultivate the taste and sensibilities without over-exciting the imagination

[37] *Hints on Reading: Addressed to a Young Lady* (London, 1839), p. 32, and *Every Day Duties: Letters to a Young Lady* (London, 1840), p. 122.

and passions. Mrs. Chapone writes: "I would by no means exclude the kind of reading, which young people are naturally most fond of; though I think the greatest care should be taken in the choice of those *fictitious stories,* that so enchant the mind—most of which tend to inflame the passions of youth, whilst the chief purpose of education should be to moderate and restrain them"(*Letters on the Improvement of the Mind,* Letter viii, her italics).

In her celebrated essay "On the Origin and Progress of Novel-Writing" which serves as Preface to her fifty-volume collection "The British Novelists" (1810), Mrs. Barbauld acknowledged that novels are especially influential on the young "in infusing principles and moral feelings." She therefore supports the educational value of carefully selected novels that introduce the young, especially girls, to experiences and people that in their sheltered lives they would never know—"many of whom it is safer to read of than to meet." She endorses in particular "the more severe and homely virtues of prudence and economy [that] have been enforced in the writings of a Burney or an Edgeworth. . . . Where have order, neatness, industry, sobriety, been recommended with more strength than in the agreeable tales of Miss Edgeworth?"

The risks of over-cultivating the imagination and the sensibilities were duly noted. Jane Austen's Marianne Dashwood and Catherine Morland, Maria Edgeworth's "Angelina; ou L'Amie Inconnue" (in *Moral Tales*) are delightful examples of heroines whose minds are at least temporarily inflamed by romantic literature.[38] Hannah More warns that such reading may have even more dire results by encouraging imitation and proliferation: "Such is the frightful facility of this species of composition, that every raw girl, while she reads, is tempted to fancy that she can also write. . . . The glutted imagination soon overflows with the redundance of cheap sentiment and plentiful incident, and by a

[38] See Colby, *Fiction with a Purpose,* pp. 45-52.

sort of arithmetical proportion, is enabled by the perusal of any three novels to produce a fourth. . . ."[39]

It became increasingly difficult for Mrs. More to reconcile the kind of novel that "may be read with safety . . . even with profit" with the kind of novel she saw flourishing around her—translations of French and German romances that celebrate the breaching of the Seventh Commandment ("these soothing pictures of varnished corruption"), imitations of Rousseau who "does not paint an innocent woman ruined, repenting and restored; but, with a far more mischievous refinement, he annihilates the value of chastity, and, with pernicious subtlety, attempts to make his heroine appear more amiable without it."[40]

Mrs. More was not voicing merely conventional prudery. Young women who might read such novels faced awesome responsibilities in their adult domestic lives. On the results of their education depended not only the happiness and well-being of themselves and their families but the future of the nation itself: "On YOU depend, in no small degree, the principles of the whole rising generation. To your direction the daughters are almost exclusively committed; and until a certain age, to YOU also is consigned the mighty privilege of forming the hearts and minds of your infant sons. . . . Your private exertions may at this moment be contributing to the future happiness; your domestic neglect, to the future ruin, of your country" (*Strictures on . . . Female Education*, Ch. 1).[41] What women read is therefore of vital concern to society as a whole, and since they *will* read novels, it becomes an urgent social duty to provide suitable ones.

[39] "Unprofitable Reading," in *Moral Sketches of Prevailing Opinion and Manners, Foreign and Domestic* (*Works*, iv, 138-39).

[40] *Ibid.*

[41] See Aimé-Martin (n. 18 above), who concludes his book with an impassioned appeal: "Young girls, young wives, young mothers, you hold the sceptre; in your souls much more than in the laws of legislators, now repose the futurity of Europe, the world, and the destinies of the human race."

121

IV

THE subtle aesthetic balance between Nature and Art quite eluded Mrs. More and other practical educators. Her own novel *Coelebs in Search of a Wife* celebrates Nature (as the educators understood the term) at the total sacrifice of Art. Maria Edgeworth, however, while as deeply concerned as Mrs. More about the morally questionable side-effects of Art, accomplishments, and excessive sensibility, achieved at least a partially compensating counter-balance, thanks to an educational philosophy that was practical, secular, and firmly grounded in the realities of family life and human psychology. For both sexes, the Edgeworths believed, education is a preparation for life. Hence their emphasis on the home-as-school where a child would constantly test his learning against the challenges of real life in a social environment rather than in the hothouse artificiality of a public (i.e. private) school. He would play with "rational toys," where even in his recreation he would be learning practical skills (the good French governess takes her charges to a rational toy shop, where they buy small tools, seeds for planting in the home garden, miniature models of machines for study). He would read books that portray lifelike characters and problems: "The history of realities, written in an entertaining manner, appears not only better suited to the purposes of education, but also more agreeable to young people than improbable fictions" (*Practical Education*, Ch. 12). The Edgeworths took issue with Dr. Johnson's observation: "Babies do not like to hear stories of babies like themselves . . . they require to have their imaginations raised by tales of giants, and fairies, and enchantments." Children enjoy fairy tales, the Edgeworths concede, but they soon perceive that fairies and giants "are not to be met with in the world." Why not give them "useful knowledge"? They ask, "Why should we vitiate their taste, and spoil their appetite, by suffering them to feed upon sweetmeats?" (Preface to *The Parent's Assistant*, 1796).

For girls especially the reading of highly colored romantic literature is dangerous ("We know, from common experience, the effects which are produced upon the mind by immoderate novel reading"). The Edgeworths did not go to the absurd anti-intellectual extremes of their friend Thomas Day, who was alarmed to learn that young Maria was translating from the French an educational tale of Mme. de Genlis. He warned her, and all her sex, against "imprudent exhibitions" of their learning. In reply, Richard Edgeworth vigorously defended female education: "The mother, who now aspires to be the esteemed and beloved instructress of her children, must have a considerable portion of knowledge." He supported his daughter's freedom to read even as he acknowledged the risks to which it exposed her: "vulgar novels" with their "preposterous notions of love," "the fatal idea," which she might absorb from "the enchanting eloquence of Rousseau," that cunning and coquetry are necessary for attracting a man's heart. Nevertheless, Edgeworth affirmed that he would never proscribe an author but would leave it to his daughter to read, to compare, "and correct her judgment of books by listening to the conversation of persons of sense and experience."[42]

But Maria herself moved cautiously along lines drawn by Mrs. More and her sister-teachers. Though an ardent reader of Mme. de Staël, a translator of Mme. de Genlis, and—if we may judge from the contents of her private library—well acquainted with the writings of Balzac, Rousseau, and Stendhal, she was suspicious of foreign influences.[43] The heroine's mother in *Leonora* warns her against German novels; the villainess reads *Werther* and has been educated in France, where "their systems disdain all the vulgar virtues, intent upon some *beau ideal* of perfection or perfecti-

[42] *Letters for Literary Ladies* (in *Works of Maria Edgeworth*, II, 33).

[43] "A Catalogue of Books belonging to Maria Edgeworth at Edgeworthstown," unpublished MS. in Houghton Library, Harvard University.

bility. They set common sense and common honesty at defiance" (Letter IV).[44] Furthermore, Maria was highly skeptical of sensibility cults and cautioned repeatedly against the indulgence in temper, morbidity, "enthusiasm," and other excesses of Romanticism. Her "sensibility" heroine Julia in *Letters for Literary Ladies* protests: "In vain, dear Caroline, you urge me to *think*: I profess only to *feel*" (Letter I). Not surprisingly, having ignored prudent Caroline's warnings against wasting "that sympathy on fiction which reality so much better deserves," Julia marries impulsively, deserts her husband and child, and dies in repentant misery.

Maria Edgeworth treated the sense-and-sensibility issue more solemnly than Jane Austen did. Where Miss Austen suggests that the difference is one of innate, individual psychology—Elinor and Marianne Dashwood as sisters grew up in the same environment with similar educations—Maria is concerned with the education that can produce the right balance and curb the excesses in every child: ". . . we must cultivate the reasoning powers at the same time that we repress the enthusiasm of fine feeling." The educator must keep his eye steadily on his purpose—the future life of his pupil. Women, "from their situation and duties in society," must be prepared for the "quiet domestic virtues" rather than for grand romantic heroism:

"Sentimental authors, who paint with enchanting colours all the graces and all the virtues in happy union, teach us to expect that this union should be indissoluble. Afterwards, from the natural influence of association, we expect in real life to meet with virtue when we see grace, and we are disappointed, almost disgusted, when we find virtue unadorned. This false association has a double effect upon the

[44] It has been suggested that this heartless coquette, who causes the heroine Leonora such misery, was a portrait of Mme. de Staël. Though they never met, Maria followed her career with avid interest. In this novel Maria may have been refuting Mme. de Staël's liberal views on divorce as expressed in her *Delphine*. See H. W. Hausermann, *The Genevese Background* (London, 1952), pp. 42-46.

conduct of women; it prepares them to be pleased, and it excites them to endeavour to please by adventitious charms, rather than by those qualities which merit esteem. Women, who have been much addicted to common novel-reading, are always acting in imitation of some Jemima, or Almeria, who never existed, and they perpetually mistake plain William and Thomas for '*My Beverly!*' (*Practical Education*, Ch. 10, "Sympathy and Sensibility.")

Introducing her single masterpiece, the short novel *Castle Rackrent* (1800), a broadly comic and earthy picture of the decline of the Irish ruling classes, Maria wrote, "A plain unvarnished tale is preferable to the most highly ornamented narrative." Significantly, *Castle Rackrent* is the only one of her works that is not overtly didactic. Neither directly nor indirectly is it concerned with the teaching of the young, though it serves the oblique educational function of informing "the ignorant English reader" of the customs of "a cruder, older Ireland." As such, however, its goals are realism and good fun. Her humor is not the product of intellectually based wit and word play, but of simple naturalness of expression and honesty of observation. Sir Walter Scott considered her novels "the essence of common sense,"[45] and a reviewer in the *Quarterly Review* in 1814 called her "an anti-sentimental novelist . . . [whose] favourite qualities are prudence, firmness of temper, and that active, vigilant good sense which . . . exercises its influence at every moment."[46] Byron, who met her in 1813, found her "a nice little unassuming 'Jeanie-Deans-looking body,'" impressed as almost everyone who knew her was with her unaffected, no-nonsense manner.[47] "Of all novelists she is the most practical . . . eminently an Utilitarian," wrote the *Edinburgh Review*[48]—a comment almost anticipated by Mme. de Staël's reservation "que Miss Edgeworth était digne de

[45] Oliver, p. 537.

[46] Review of *Patronage* (by Lord Dudley) in *Quarterly Review*, 10 (1811), p. 305.

[47] Oliver, p. 279.   [48] 51 (1830), pp. 447-48.

l'enthousiasme, mais qu'elle s'est perdue dans la triste utilité."[49] Melodrama, sensationalism, gothicism, were entertaining within their limits. Even while she recognized their potential threat to the tender sensibilities of the young, she could appreciate them. She wrote to a cousin in 1792: "Has my aunt seen 'The Romance of the Forest'? It has been the fashionable novel here, everybody read and talked of it; we were much interested in some parts of it. It is something in the style of the 'Castle of Otranto,' and the horrible parts are, we thought, well worked up, but it is very difficult to keep Horror breathless with his mouth wide open through three volumes."[50]

Maria Edgeworth's contribution to the development of the English novel was very modest in substance—a brilliant novella of comic regionalism in *Castle Rackrent* and some satiric vignettes in *The Absentee* and *Ormond*. But one must look beyond substance to spirit—to the intangible but profound influence of her tales for children upon the developing consciousness of the major Victorian novelists. No child growing up and being educated in England during the first half of the nineteenth century is likely to have missed her "Harry and Lucy," "Rosanna," "The Limerick Gloves," "Lame Jervas," or some other of the host of her charming simple stories. These kept Miss Edgeworth's memory alive long after her so-called "fashionable" novels were forgotten. In 1814 the acclaim for her *Patronage* overshadowed *Mansfield Park*, published the same year, but in 1859 George Henry Lewes observed that while Jane Austen's novels are still "very extensively read," Miss Edgeworth "only finds a public for her children's books."[51] It was these that Byron immortalized in *Don Juan*, observing of his hero's strictly correct mother:

[49] A. Heyward, *Selected Essays* (New York, 1879), I, 276.
[50] *Life and Letters*, I, 27.
[51] "The Novels of Jane Austen," *Blackwood's*, 86 (July, 1859), p. 99.

In short, she was a walking calculation,
  Miss Edgeworth's novels stepping from their covers,
Or Mrs. Trimmer's books on education,
  Or "Coelebs' wife" set out in quest of lovers. . . .
                                    (Canto I, 16)

and that Thomas Hood cited in his grisly-comic poem on
the *nouveau riche* "Miss Kilmansegg and her Precious
Leg":

> Instead of stories from Edgeworth's page;
> The true golden loree for our golden age,
>   Or lessons from Barbauld and Trimmer,
> Teaching the worth of Virtue and Health,
> All that she knew was the Virtue of Wealth,
> Provided by vulgar nursery stealth,
>   With a Book of Leaf Gold for a Primer. . . .
>   (ll. 478-84)

But Maria Edgeworth's quickly forgotten *Fashionable
Tales*, and the perishable long novels like *Belinda, Patronage*, and *Helen* were all in their time, however briefly, ac-
claimed and widely read. They are significant because they
broadcast the Edgeworth system of education, popularizing
it with dramatic realism. The reader should not be misled
by titles like *Fashionable Tales*, "Vivian," "Ennui," *Patronage*, into assuming that these were "silver-fork" novels.
While in outline their plots suggest that genre, Miss Edgeworth was not entering the territory of Bulwer, Lister, Disraeli, Mrs. Gore, and Lady Blessington. She visited and
knew the contents of Mayfair townhouses, but the only setting in which she was comfortably at home was the rambling
English or Irish country house with a crowded nursery or
the Irish peasant's hut.[52] Her fashionable novels, therefore,

[52] Matthew W. Rosa attributes her inability to write fashionable
novels to the influence of her father, who always directed her toward
matters of education; see *The Silver-Fork School*, p. 10.

are simply moral-exemplary tales dressed up and peopled with characters who move in high society. Their themes are almost invariably educational—in the broadest sense simply lessons learned, but occasionally and more interestingly, studies of the effects of childhood education and conditioning upon the total life experience. At the beginning of this chapter, we quoted from Richard Edgeworth's Preface to *Fashionable Tales* in which he emphasized his daughter's educational mission. He referred to "this series of moral fiction," and briefly summed up the moral of each one. In her future work, he announced, his daughter would continue "to disseminate, in a familiar form, some of the ideas that are unfolded in 'Essays on Professional Education' [published in 1808 under his name]."

To the extent then that these stories are fictionalized teaching-aids they are of only limited interest. But the "ideas" of education that Richard Edgeworth was unfolding in his essays and Maria in her far more readable tales are of greater interest because they anticipate and reflect so much of the course of the development of the novel itself. Three distinct but interrelated trends of literary realism are to be noted: the anti-romance, the family novel, and a primitive kind of *Bildungsroman*. In Maria's hands the anti-romance more often took the form of a tale seriously cautioning against the tendencies of romantic escapism than the broadly comic burlesque of quixotism where a heroine is so deluded by romance reading that she goes off on foolish adventures herself. Maria's only attempt in this manner is "Angelina; ou L'Amie Inconnue," closely modeled on Charlotte Lennox's *The Female Quixote; or The Adventures of Arabella* (1752). But with their more sober and practical concerns in education the Edgeworths could not give extended treatment to such light-weight literary satire. They were concerned with the serious delusions about mature life that a faulty childhood education could produce. The first of Maria's *Fashionable Tales*, "Ennui, or Memoirs of the Earl of Glenthorn" (written in 1804), is an anti-romance in the fairly literal sense of showing, step by step, how a life of romantic self-indulgence produces the morally debilitating disease of ennui. The still young Earl of Glenthorn, who narrates his own story, looks back at a misspent youth. Orphaned, he had been put into the care of a guardian "who, in hopes of winning my affection, never controlled my wishes, or even my whims; I changed schools and masters as often as I pleased and consequently learned nothing" (Ch. 1). After squandering his fortune in gambling and making a fashionable marriage that ends in divorce, he returns to his family estate in Ireland and begins a gradual process of re-education. The rude awakening from romance to reality comes when the hero discovers that he is not the Earl but a peasant, switched in infancy by his mother whom he had thought his nurse. But even before he makes this Italian-opera type of discovery, he is well on the path to reform. At the end of the story he is a practically educated mature man, a law-student, who has learned to his profit the difference between Romance and Reality. He recites that lesson directly to "novel-readers," rejecting the wonders and changes of fortune for a "plodding" but happy life of "business."

Romantic delusions of all sorts—of feminine innocence (Clarence Hervey with his protegée Virginia St. Pierre in *Belinda*), of social prestige (the "climbing" parents of Lord Colambre in *The Absentee*), of wealth and political power (the Falconer family in *Patronage*)—are all dispelled by proper education. They would never have come into being at all had it not been for faulty education. Since education, good or bad, begins in the home, Maria Edgeworth necessarily wrote family novels. Here, drawing literally from the experience of her own large family and imaginatively from the multiplicity of character types and incidents that family life suggests, she worked experimentally in a new genre that was not to reach full development until much later in the century. Her early novel *Belinda* (1801) makes feeble and generally clumsy efforts to transform the eighteenth-century society novel, with its theme of the young lady's introduction to the fashionable world, into a nineteenth-century family novel. *Belinda* is modeled closely on Fanny Burney's *Evelina*—both heroines of somewhat obscure backgrounds, who come to London, dip their toes genteelly into the muddy waters of high society, but thanks to their good characters are spared total immersion and disaster.

Mr. Edgeworth evidently felt some qualms about the propriety of his daughter's writing a fashionable novel, apologizing in his "Advertisement to *Belinda*, April 20, 1801" that this ". . . is a Moral Tale—the author not wishing to acknowledge a Novel. Were all novels like those of Madame de Crousaz,[53] Mrs. Inchbald, Miss Burney, or Dr. Moore, she would adopt the name of Novel with delight; but so much folly, error, and vice are disseminated in books classed under this denomination, that it is hoped the wish to assume another title will be attributed to feelings that are laudable, and not fastidious."

As a "Moral Tale," *Belinda* proved no better than the genre grimly promises, and Maria herself candidly admitted its failure. Revising it for Mrs. Barbauld's "Collection of British Novelists" in 1810, she wrote, "Belinda is but an uninteresting personage after all; but I cannot mend her in this respect, without making her over again, and, indeed, without making the whole book over again."[54] The problem, she shrewdly recognized, was that a heroine's "goodness" interests a reader "only in proportion to the perils and trials to which it is exposed." Heroines like Clarissa or Miss Milner in Maria's favorite *A Simple Story* by Mrs. Inchbald are often exposed to "perils" or "trials." But "that stick or stone

[53] A footnote to this advertisement identifies Madame de Crousaz as the author of *Caroline de Lechtfeld*. This is an error for *Caroline de Lichtfield*, a French novel published anonymously, written by Mme. de Montolieu. According to Mona Wilson in *Jane Austen and her Contemporaries* (London, 1935), p. 19, Edward Gibbon so admired this novel that he offered to sign his name to it.

[54] Oliver, p. 244.

Belinda," as Maria calls her,[55] merely witnesses the trials of others, like the apparently doomed Lady Delacour, who chooses to throw away her life in dissipation rather than accept what she believes will be inevitable death from breast cancer.

To superimpose an education theme upon the novel, Maria introduces two other sets of characters—Mr. Hervey, with his Thomas Day type of educational experimenting on Miss St. Pierre, and the happy family of Lady Anne Percival, a household drawn directly from Edgeworthstown with a brood of wholesome, healthy children being educated at home by patient, practical, rational parents:

"There was an affectionate confidence, an unconstrained gaiety in this house, which forcibly struck her [Belinda], from its contrast with what she had seen at Lady Delacour's. She perceived that between Mr. Percival and Lady Anne there was a union of interests, occupations, taste, and affection. . . . The elder and younger part of the family were not separated from each other; even the youngest child in the house seemed to form part of the society, to have some share and interest in the general occupations or amusements. The children were treated neither as slaves nor as playthings, but as reasonable creatures. . . . Without force or any factitious excitement, the taste for knowledge, and the habits of application, were induced by example, and confirmed by sympathy. Mr. Percival was a man of science and literature, and his daily pursuits and general conversation were in the happiest manner instructive and interesting to his family" (Ch. 16).

Belinda is a crude experiment in a new kind of domestic novel. Because Maria Edgeworth was totally unable to weave her themes together, she wrote a limping, halting story with a set of lifeless characters. But she knew that if she was to continue to write novels for adults, this was the form in which she must work, and her attempt at it some dozen years later in *Patronage* (1814), though no more suc-

[55] *Life and Letters,* I, 178.

cessful from an artistic point of view, is a better novel of education. Here she made an unequivocal choice to write a family novel. *Patronage* has no single hero or heroine, no single dominating line of plot. That is both its fault and its virtue, for as a family novel with a huge cast of characters, it is unwieldy ("It is so vast a subject that it flounders about in my hands and overpowers me," she wrote during its composition),[56] yet it achieves its purpose surprisingly well. That purpose is to show the Edgeworths' educational theories in practice in two large families—the Percys and the Falconers. Where the influences on the young are rational and morally sound (the Percys), the education is good and the children grow up fully prepared for the trials and triumphs of life. Where the family is corrupted by material ambitions (the Falconers) and seeks advantage for the children through patronage, political maneuvering, and social climbing, there is no proper education and the unhappy results are predictable. As Mr. Percy sums up the moral: "I have secured for my sons what is better than a good patron —a good education" (Ch. 12).

In the salutary atmosphere of the Percy family potentially dangerous traits in the young are corrected early. The light-minded "sensibility" daughter Rosamond is from the outset pointed in the right direction: "Prudence had not, it is true, been a part of Rosamond's character in childhood; but, in the course of her education, a considerable portion of it had been infused, by a very careful and skillful hand" (Ch. 6). That hand, of course, is her mother's, not that of a hired governess or schoolmistress. Mothers carry the major responsibility for the moral character of their children. A daughter of a divorcée, for example, is considered ineligible for a family-approved marriage because she has been educated by her "ill-conducted" mother and "exposed to the influence of her example" (Ch. 4). Similarly, Lord Colambre, the hero of *The Absentee*, refuses to marry Grace

[56] Oliver, p. 251.

Nugent, whom he loves, believing her to be illegitimate; he reasons: "In marrying, a man does not, to be sure, marry his wife's mother, and yet a prudent man, when he begins to think of the daughter would look sharp at the mother; ay, and back to the grandmother too, and along the whole female line of ancestry" (Ch. 15). Happily, Grace proves to be both legitimate and an heiress, but one must still assume that it was her education that somehow determined both her good character and her good fortune.

The negative, destructive influence of mothers is nowhere more tragically demonstrated by Maria Edgeworth than in her short novel "Vivian" (*Tales of Fashionable Life*). Often compared to the fashionable novels of Mrs. Gore, Disraeli, and Bulwer, "Vivian" traces the career of a handsome, wealthy young nobleman who begins life with an adoring mother and every opportunity for brilliant success in the world, but ends unhappily married and compromised in his political career, welcoming death in a duel—"Weakness, weakness of mind! the cause of all my errors." Vivian's "weakness of mind" is a fault that, in the Edgeworth theory, could have been corrected in early childhood with proper education. Instead, his widowed mother spoiled him: "My mother took too much, a great deal too much care of me; she over-educated, over-instructed, over-dosed me with premature lessons of prudence. . . . So I grew up, seeing with her eyes, hearing with her ears, and judging with her understanding, till at length, it was found out, that I had not eyes, ears, or understanding of my own" (Ch. 1). The damage having been done so early, Harrow and later a university education and a good tutor have no power to strengthen Vivian's character. When he comes of age, he takes his seat in Parliament and plunges into society, totally unprepared for adult responsibilities. Irresolute, he drifts from one disaster to another, a kind of early superfluous man like those melancholy romantic anti-heroes of the Russian novels. His violent death seems more one of attrition than of action.

133

Although the hero is an only son, "Vivian" is a family novel because early in the story his destiny becomes involved with the lives of the family of Lord Glistonbury, an unhappy nobleman driven to "dissipation" by a cold and stupid wife. His indifference and her ignorance severely damage the lives of their daughters. She hires a martinet of a governess who makes the elder daughter "stiff, dogmatical, and repulsive," while he engages a bold, imprudent, blue-stockinged governess who indulges and spoils the younger.

The management or mismanagement of a family, which is the responsibility of both parents but more realistically the job of the mother, clearly affects not only the physical but the moral and psychological well-being of the children. Therefore the novel that attempts to deal realistically with the development of character must concentrate on the formation of that character by education. Maria Edgeworth's fiction is hardly distinguished for psychological penetration and character analysis. She is like the eighteenth-century novelists whom we admire mainly for colorful character types—the venal Thady Quirk of *Castle Rackrent*, the roaring Irish patriarch King Corny of *Ormond*, the gauche social-climbing Lady Clonbrony of *The Absentee*. Her eccentrics and "originals" are far more memorable than her conventional young people, who tend at best to be bland, at worst insipid. But she was moving with her times in new directions. Her interest in children, how they learn and develop, was confined mainly to the tales that she wrote for them, while her adult fiction (except *Castle Rackrent*) tended to follow the established conventions. Nevertheless, just as we noted her attempt to impose the new concept of the family novel upon the society novel in *Belinda*, we can also trace the tentative emergence of the *Bildungsroman* in her novels like "Ennui," "Vivian," *Ormond*, and *Harrington*, where young heroes gain wisdom and maturity in the course of "life-education." *Ormond*, her Irish *Tom Jones*, shows a young man triumphing over a bad education.[57] Wild and heavy-drinking (when we first meet him he has just shot a man accidentally), he reforms not in a school-room but in the rugged experience of a visit to a remote Irish island. His tutor, also a hard drinker, is King Corny (according to whose definition, "No man could be called drunk, so long as he could lie upon the ground without holding it" [Ch. 4]), a good man with natural wisdom and honesty. He comes home from a day of hunting to quiz young Ormond on his reading: ". . . now let's hear how you have been getting on with your bookmen—has it been a good day with you today?—was you with Shakespeare—worth all the rest—all the world in him?" No pedant, Corny judges a book by only one criterion: " 'Did it touch the heart or inflame'—if it was poetry—'the imagination?' If it was history, 'was it true?' If it was philosophy, 'was it sound reasoning?' " (Ch. 8). Under such guidance Ormond under-standably becomes a man of high moral principle. Unfortu-nately, we never see the inner man. Disappointed in love, he goes to Paris, where his poise and charm, acquired in rough Irish surroundings, dazzle the court of Louis XV. In the end he returns to Ireland and a happy marriage—"to enjoy the empire which he had gained over himself." He has grown up from Tom Jones into Sir Charles Grandison, an-other favorite book of his youth, and for the reader he re-mains just as lifeless as that paragon.

In only one of her so-called "fashionable" tales, *Harring-ton* (1817), did Maria Edgeworth begin to show those glimmerings of psychological realism toward which the English novel was moving. Her theme here actually in-volves a traumatic experience for the hero—a wildly irra-

[57] See her notes for this novel, "Ormond Objects of this story," where she wrote: *"Prime object.* To shew how a person may re-educate themselves—& cure the faults of natural temper & counteract bad education & unfortunate circumstances" (Butler, *Maria Edge-worth*, p. 236).

tional childhood prejudice that he must painfully outgrow. *Harrington* is an awkwardly conceived novel, written to apologize to her Jewish readers for a number of conventional caricatures of Jews that Maria had written in her earlier tales. A "peace-offering," as Maria described it, the novel has all of the clumsiness of a self-conscious protest that "some of my best friends are Jews." The hero falls in love with a girl who he thinks is Jewish only to discover—in the interests of a happy ending—that she has concealed her mother's Protestant faith, which she practices, in order to test his anti-Semitism. The best of Maria's intentions cannot produce a good novel in *Harrington.* But her concern with the origin, development, and gradual disappearance of her hero's anti-Semitism—which she conceives as a psychological aberration—offers more scope for character analysis than is usual in her work. Like all Edgeworth children, her hero is molded, in this instance warped, by the ignorance or indifference of his parents (in Parliament his father had bitterly opposed a bill for the nationalization of the Jews), by faulty education (as a child he reads many stories that represent Jews as avaricious and treacherous), and by a vicious nursemaid who terrifies him with bedtime tales of a Jewish peddler who will carry him away in his old-clothes bag. A first-person narrative, *Harrington* represents one of the earliest efforts in realistic fiction in which a character explores and reconstructs his own past to try to find out why he has become the man he is. Like Pip or David Copperfield, Harrington digs back into his memory, recalling in vivid detail a single childhood episode which scarred his psyche:

"When I was a little boy of about six years old, I was standing with a maid servant in the balcony of one of the upper rooms of my father's house in London. It was evening of the first day that I had ever been in London, and my senses had been excited and almost exhausted by the quick succession of a vast variety of objects that were new to me.

136

It was dusk, and I was growing sleepy, but my attention was wakened by a fresh wonder. As I stood peeping between the bars of the balcony, I saw star after star of light appear in quick succession, at a certain height and distance, in a regular line, approaching nearer and nearer to me. I twitched the skirt of my maid's gown repeatedly, but she was talking to some acquaintance in the window of a neighbouring house, and she did not attend to me. I pressed my forehead more closely against the bars of the balcony, and strained my eyes more eagerly towards the object of my curiosity. Presently the figure of the lamplighter with his blazing torch in one hand, and his ladder in the other, became visible; and, with as much delight as philosopher ever enjoyed in discovering the cause of a new and grand phenomenon, I watched his operations. I saw him fix and mount his ladder with his little black pot swinging from his arm, and his red smoking torch waving with astonishing velocity, as he ran up and down the ladder. Just when he reached the ground, being then within a few yards of our house, his torch flared on the face and figure of an old man with a long white beard and a dark visage, who holding a great bag slung over one shoulder, walked slowly on straight forwards, repeating in a low, abrupt, mysterious tone, the cry of 'Old Clothes!—Old Clothes!—'Old Clothes!' " (Ch. 1.)

In this remarkable passage of sensitive observation, with its vivid recreation of a child's-eye view, Maria Edgeworth achieved as nowhere else in her work the illusion of psychological reality. But where more generally she herself failed, she made it possible for novelists who followed her to succeed. For in teaching a whole generation of Victorians the importance and the delights of the simple homely experience of educating children, and in demonstrating for them the fundamental elements of that experience—sympathy, patience, concern with the small details of daily living—she was leading the way toward the great domestic novels of the mid-nineteenth century.

137

V

THE novel of education is not a critically valid literary genre because it inevitably overlaps with other more powerful or interesting types. As long as it remained merely the illustrative educational exemplum, the simple tales of Harry and Lucy, Sandford and Merton, etc., it existed independently. But, as Maria Edgeworth's novels illustrate, when educational theory is applied to mature human personality and action, it enters the territory of other fictional types, most especially the family novel and the *Bildungsroman.* If the novel of education, however, tended to become absorbed into other forms, there is no evidence that education ceased to be a subject of fascination to novel-readers and writers alike. The enormous popularity of "school novels" and "governess novels" in the mid-nineteenth century testifies to the fact that with wider public education either in effect or well on its way, literally everyone was interested in the subject and was in some manner involved in it, as pupil, parent, or teacher. Educational theory itself—except as abused or exaggerated by extremists like Mr. Gradgrind of *Hard Times* or Sir Austin Feverel of *The Ordeal of Richard Feverel,* or, in real life, James Mill—seems to have been less interesting to Victorians than actual practice. There was little fundamental controversy or revision in theory; Locke, Rousseau, Kant, Pestalozzi, David Hartley—the major educational theorists and psychologists of the eighteenth century—continued to dominate the thinking of nineteenth-century educators.[58] John Stuart Mill, Herbert Spencer, the Arnolds, Thomas Henry Huxley—much as they

[58] Although both Thomas and Matthew Arnold emphasized the study of the "ancients" in the humanistic-Renaissance tradition, their zeal for duty and social responsibility kept them alert to the importance of practical education for the young of all classes of society. See Sir Joshua Fitch, *Thomas and Matthew Arnold and their Influence on English Education* (New York, 1897), pp. 30-31 and 45-51.

disagreed in philosophy—shared the homely basic beliefs about educating the young child: give him love and security, treat him firmly but gently, guide him empirically and inductively into learning, create the "whole" man by combining his fragmented experiences into patterns of rational and constructive activities. The Edgeworths' *Practical Education* was therefore as timely in 1850 as it had been in 1798 —perhaps appearing somewhat quaint and naive in expression, but hardly outmoded or superseded. The Edgeworths, in fact, thanks to their secular approach to education (for which they had been sharply criticized in their own time), sturdily outlasted the evangelically inspired educational writings of their contemporaries like Mrs. More, Mrs. Barbauld, and Mrs. Chapone.

In the late 1820's Charlotte Yonge's enlightened parents educated their little daughter at home following "the Edgeworth system ... though modified by religion and good sense,"[59] and there is no reason to doubt that numbers of parents did the same. When Charlotte Yonge herself grew up to become an author of many very popular books for young readers, she also became an important influence on Victorian education and kept the Edgeworth system alive and flourishing. In 1868, for example, writing to Emily Davies, a crusader for higher education for women, she reaffirmed the Edgeworth opposition to schools and their advocacy of home training for children: "I am obliged to you for your letter respecting the proposed College for Ladies, but as I have decided objections to bringing large masses of girls together and think that home education under the inspection and encouragement of sensible fathers, or voluntarily continued by the girls themselves, is far more valuable, both intellectually and morally than any external education, I am afraid I cannot assist you.

"I feel with much regret that female education is deficient, but I think the way to meet the evil is by rousing the

[59] Charlotte Yonge, "Autobiography," in *Charlotte Mary Yonge, Her Life and Letters*, ed. Christabel Coleridge (London, 1903), p. 56.

parents to lead their daughters to read, think, and converse. All the most superior women I have known have thus been formed by home influence, and I think that girls in large numbers always hurt one another in manner and tone if in nothing else."[60]

"Home influence," to borrow Charlotte Yonge's phrase, was at once both a practical reality and an educational ideal in Victorian society. In novels about childhood its presence or absence is critical. The institutional schools—whether "public" with their emphasis on classical languages and fun-and-games, or the seminaries like Miss Pinkerton's "academy for young ladies" or Mrs. Lemon's school where daughters of the bourgeoisie like Amelia Sedley and Rosamond Vincy were honed and polished into gentility, or prisonhouses like Lowood and Dotheboys Hall—were intended for the older child, already formed and predestined by early environment in the home. Even then, however, the quality of his school was often measured in terms of its duplication of the values of home influence.

Today our widely accepted notions of English schooling are based on novels that describe early educations strikingly different from the Edgeworth ideal. Almost invariably the child has been deprived of the wholesome happy environment of home. From Charlotte Brontë and Dickens mainly, but also from many other Victorian novelists, we have the image of the pale and persecuted young "victim," "wraith-like," "joyless," often actually sick, hungry, and physically abused, or exposed to depraved and corrupting influences. Nor is this necessarily the impoverished orphan child. Sons of the middle class and rich also suffered—little Paul Dombey, Tom Brown before the enlightened administration of Dr. Thomas Arnold at Rugby, Eric Williams of Frederic W. Farrar's *Eric; or, Little by Little*, who suffers "little comparative danger . . . as long as he continued to be a home boarder," but becomes fatally corrupted when he

[60] Quoted in Georgina Battiscombe, *Charlotte Mary Yonge* (London, 1943), p. 146.

goes to live at Roslyn School. Only in rare instances where a child is tutored in a homelike atmosphere—Philip Wakem and the unappreciating Tom Tulliver at Dr. Stelling's in *The Mill on the Floss* or David Copperfield as a day student at Dr. Strong's school—does he fare well both physically and morally. Significantly, too, the novelists are far less preoccupied with their young heroes' and heroines' academic progress than with their moral and psychological development. It is the education of their hearts, not their heads, that matters.

Thus the Edgeworth influence prevailed in the nineteenth-century novel if it did not always prevail in educational practice. Nowhere is its presence more striking than in the novelist who at first glance seems most at variance with it—Charles Dickens. A romantic at heart, convinced of the ideals of childhood purity and innocence and implacably opposed to utilitarian notions, Dickens was an open foe of "Practical Education." For him the phrase meant at best narrow vocational training and at worst Gradgrindism with its spirit-crushing emphasis on facts, facts, facts. He despised factual and didactic children's literature like Day's *Sandford and Merton*, as Lamb had despised Mrs. Barbauld and Mrs. Trimmer for their attacks on imaginative tales for children.[61] He would have deplored the Edgeworths' description of fairy-tales as mere "sweetmeats" and challenged their suspicions of the "inflammatory" nature of much imaginative literature. Maria's comment in the chapter "Books" in *Practical Education*—"The history of realities, written in an entertaining manner, appears not only better suited to the purposes of education, but also more agreeable to young people than improbable fictions"—sounds like grist for a gradgrinding mill.

Yet essentially Dickens and the Edgeworths were moving in the same direction. They shared a profound distrust of the institutionalized school. Maria Edgeworth's rich young

[61] Philip Collins, *Dickens and Education* (London, 1964), p. 213.

141

Harrington dismisses his life at a public school as "five years
. . . of which I have nothing to relate but that I learned to
whip a top, and to play at ball and marbles, each in their
season; that I acquired in due course the usual quantity of
Greek and Latin; and perpetrated in my time, I presume,
the usual quantity of mischief" (Ch. 3). Dickens' Richard
Carstone profits little from his years studying the classics
at Winchester. Esther Summerson observes that although
his Latin verses may have been beautiful, his teachers might
better have studied him "to find out what his natural bent
was, or where his failings lay, or to adapt any kind of
knowledge to him" (*Bleak House*, Ch. 13).

The child-centered, as opposed to the knowledge-cen-
tered, system of education was at the heart of all their
thinking. The growing minds of the young need nourish-
ment, the stimulation of personal interest, attention, and
affection, every bit as much as they need information. "It is
not sufficient, therefore, in education, to store up knowledge," Maria Edgeworth wrote; "it is essential to arrange
facts so that they shall be ready for use, as materials for the
imagination, or the judgment, to select and combine" (*Practical Education*, Ch. 12).

The bridge between the Edgeworths and Dickens could
have been built by the progressive educational theories of
Friedrich Froebel, whose work was highly praised in Dickens' *Household Words*. Froebel advocated infant schools,
kindergartens, with "education by doing," manual activity,
mild discipline, "a happy family school."[62] More likely, however, the spirit that links Dickens with the Edgeworths was
their faith in the simple education of the heart. It is a poetic
spirit, Rousseauistic and Wordsworthian, rather than a
pedagogic one. The Edgeworths began with Rousseau but,
rejecting his extremes of romanticism, they adapted him to
the necessities and realities of family living. Nevertheless
they retained, and in a sense handed on to Dickens, Char-

[62] John Manning, *Dickens on Education* (Toronto, 1959), pp.
133-34.

lotte Brontë, and others, the notion of natural sympathy in education. They moved education indoors from the lakes, mountains, and forest ranges—where it could hardly, after all, function efficiently for most of society—into the schoolroom. But they firmly resisted all efforts to sterilize, institutionalize, and de-personalize education—as society otherwise seemed to be doing. Keeping it close to the home, the heart, the individual child, the Edgeworths cultivated the child's imagination by stimulating it with what was closest at hand—the activities of daily family life. They stripped away magic, in its glamorous romantic disguises, but they retained the "marvellous," the "surprising," and the "delightful." Writing of Maria's tales in *The Parent's Assistant*, Alice Patterson notes that while her purpose was "to provide an antidote to the desire for overmuch fairy-tales," she did so "by retaining the fairy-tale element in a realistic atmosphere."[63] The little boy hero of "Waste Not, Want Not" saves a string that later loops and winds itself in such a way as to punish a wasteful boy. Other little heroes and heroines —all of them, incidentally, characterized as charmingly real children—save their families in financial crises, trap burglars and swindlers, perform feats of courage of an almost but never quite miraculous nature. Rationality and reality dominate, but in the charmed circle of childish imagination, miracles are miracles.

Dickens' world of childhood, while infinitely more infused with imagination than the Edgeworths', is also, nevertheless, a natural not a supernatural one. Fagin, Mr. Murdstone, Miss Havisham, Magwitch, Sissy Jupe, Boffin—ogres, giants, good and bad fairies—emerge in the light of day as real people, however grotesque some of them are. Similarly, Charlotte Brontë's fairy-tale imagination always settles back into reality. Malevola, who addresses Lucy Snowe to the accompaniment of a peal of thunder and a flash of lightning ("The tale of magic seemed to proceed with due accom-

[63] *The Edgeworths: A Study in Later Eighteenth Century Education* (London, 1914), p. 82.

143

paniment of the elements. The wanderer, decoyed into the enchanted castle, heard rising, outside, the spell-awakened tempest"), is in reality a cranky, disagreeable old lady (*Villette*, Ch. 34). And the steed that comes galloping out of the darkness like the legendary Gytrash slips on the real ice to unseat "only a traveller taking the short cut to Millcote," Mr. Rochester (*Jane Eyre*, Ch. 12). "I have purposely dwelt upon the romantic side of familiar things," Dickens wrote in his 1853 Preface to *Bleak House*. The Edgeworths did not themselves romanticize the familiar, but they advocated an educational system in which the familiar could serve many purposes, not the least of which was the uses of the imagination.

4

The Victorian "Ayenbite of Inwyt": The Evangelical Novel from Charlotte Elizabeth to Charlotte Yonge

No one will ever understand Victorian England who does not appreciate that among highly civilised, in contradistinction to more primitive, countries it is one of the most religious that the world has known.

(R. C. K. Ensor, *England, 1870-1914*)[1]

I

THE English church of the Victorian period was Protestant. Beyond that simple declarative statement it is impossible to make any generalization about Victorian religion that cannot be seriously challenged. The stability, tranquility, and homogeneity so often and so wrongly attributed to the Victorian age was nowhere more vulnerable and tenuous than in matters of religious belief. The half century from 1800 to 1850 that saw the passage of the Catholic Emancipation Act and the First Reform Bill, the flourishing of the Claphamite sect and the Oxford Movement, the evolution of Evangelicalism and Dissent from the status of radical fringe to solid respectability, the emergence of textual criticism and revisionism in biblical study, and open expression of skepticism and even atheism, was a period of religious ferment and turmoil less violent but no less dramatic than the Reformation.

Because religion was so pervasive a part of man's private

[1] (Oxford, 1936), p. 137.

145

and emotional life as well as of his public experience, its extraordinary transformations and challenges in the first half of the nineteenth century figure large in the literature of that period. The deepest and most intimate expressions of religious consciousness were probably reserved for poetry (works like Arnold's "Grande Chartreuse" and Tennyson's "In Memoriam") and spiritual autobiography (Newman's *Apologia*). But the domestic-realistic novel that so faithfully charted the everyday lives and preoccupations of men and women inevitably became a register of these changes. We look to historical records for legislation that affected men's worship, to poetry for expressions of men's emotional responses to religious controversy, but it is the novel that most minutely details and chronicles the religious experience of the living Victorian.

The strongest religious force in nineteenth-century English life was evangelicalism. This term is to be understood in its broadest sense, referring not merely to that school of Protestantism which, by dictionary definition, maintains that "the essence of the Gospel consists in the doctrine of salvation by faith in the atoning work of Christ, and denies that either good works or the sacraments have any saving efficacy," but to the many movements of religious enthusiasm and reform that swept through every Christian denomination. Victorian evangelicalism, as church historian Owen Chadwick describes it, was all but ecumenical in spirit if not in fact:

"Congregationalists and Baptists and Quakers were warmed by its fire. Within the established church was a small but growing group of evangelical clergymen, who attained their summit of influence as Queen Victoria was widowed. But outside the Anglican clergy who called themselves evangelical were high churchmen and converts to Rome whose mind and piety accepted typical insights of evangelical tradition. If we look at the Church of England alone, evangelicals often appear weak and despised. If we look at the religious map of all England, from Brompton

Oratory among Roman Catholics to the simplest Quaker meeting house in Rochdale, we trace at unexpected points the evangelical mind. To many Victorians evangelical doctrine was the authentic voice and the scriptural piety of Protestant Reformation."[2]

We may therefore stretch the designation "evangelical novel" to embrace the extremes from Low Church to High, from Charlotte Elizabeth (Mrs. Tonna), whose passionate anti-Catholicism made her positively regret her missed chance for Protestant martyrdom (as a child inspired by "that magic book" Foxe's *Acts and Monuments*, she asked her father if she might someday hope to become a martyr; "Why, Charlotte," he replied, "if the government ever gives power to the Papists again, as they talk of doing, you may probably live to be a martyr"),[3] to Charlotte Yonge, whose Anglo-Catholicism inspired her to translate the intellectual issues of the Oxford Movement into romances of daily life that enchanted several generations of readers. In between we may include novelists of every variety of sect—Methodist, Presbyterian, Low-Broad-High Church. Even Roman Catholic converts like Lady Georgiana Fullerton and John Henry Newman wrote novels with the same zeal and fervor though for a different faith. And a Jewish novelist, Grace Aguilar, was evangelical, affirming in her Preface to *Home Influence: A Tale for Mothers and Daughters* (1847) that Christian readers need not fear: ". . . as a simple domestic story, the characters in which are all Christians, believing in and practising that religion, all *doctrinal* points have been most carefully avoided, the author seeking only to illustrate the spirit of true piety and the virtues always designated as the Christian virtues hence proceeding. Her sole aim with regard to Religion has been to incite a train of serious and loving thought toward God and man, especially

[2] *The Victorian Church: An Ecclesiastical History of England, Part I* (New York, 1966), p. 5.

[3] *Personal Recollections*, Letter I, in *The Works of Charlotte Elizabeth*, I (New York, 1850).

147

toward those with whom he has linked us in the precious ties of parent and child, brother and sister, master and pupil."

Evangelicalism embraced not only the entire spectrum of Protestant belief but also the widest social scene. It cut across class divisions and barriers that no political revolution could have trampled. Emphasizing practical morality and philanthropy rather than theology, directed primarily to the emotions rather than to reason, it appealed to all ages and to all classes. Humble uneducated men and women went forth to preach the Gospel to the rich and powerful, while aristocratic ladies distributed their bounty, their time and energy, among the poor and lowly. In 1852 the *Home Friend* described as the social ideal "the beautiful feeling which connects the superior with the inferior, and binds the interests and pleasures of both into one."[4] Reacting against the cold formal rationalism of the eighteenth century, the burgundy-drinking, card-playing, fox-hunting clergymen whom Thackeray lampooned in Parson Sampson of *The Virginians*, the evangelicals found inspiration in the piety and enthusiasm of preaching Methodists like John Wesley and George Whitefield. Hymn-singing and tub-thumping sermons invited ridicule (the traveller in *Adam Bede* in 1799 "knew but two types of Methodist—the ecstatic and the bilious")[5] and even, in the early days, open persecution, but the vigorous spirit of evangelicalism could not be sub-

[4] Quoted in Margaret Dalziel's *Popular Fiction 100 Years Ago* (New York, 1957), p. 73.

[5] Ch. 2. Also in *Adam Bede* (Ch. 52), contrasting the eighteenth-century's apathy toward religion with the active religious interests of nineteenth-century men and women, George Eliot describes a contemplative stout gentleman whom she calls "Old Leisure," who "knew nothing of week-day services, and thought none the worse of the Sunday sermon if it allowed him to sleep from the text to the blessing. . . . Do not be severe upon him, and judge him by our modern standard; he never went to Exeter Hall, or heard a popular preacher, or read *Tracts for the Times* or *Sartor Resartus*."

dued. The nineteenth century began with revolution in France, a tired and debauched monarchy in England, a starved and exploited working class both in the farms and in the industrial towns, massive drunkenness, prostitution, and crime. By the middle of the century, social and moral reform had swept England. No historian of the period underestimates the importance of evangelicalism in that reform movement.

Even more effective than the evangelical hymns and sermons in the transmission of this new spirit were tracts. The term, like much of the language of popular religion, is fluid in meaning. To the dairy maid and farm laborer spelling their way through Hannah More's *Cheap Repository Tracts* —cheap in price and in quality of production, illustrated with blurred engravings, plain in language, simple in incident—*tract* meant something vastly different from that series of learned theological essays that emanated from Oxford in the 1830's, expounding the Catholic principles of the Church of England—*Tracts of the Times.* Yet a Victorian who had come of age before 1860 had likely been exposed to both extremes. In childhood he read the writings of Mrs. More, Legh Richmond, Mrs. Sherwood, and other easy-reading, crudely but graphically illustrated stories that set forth so clearly, often luridly, the basic lessons of his faith. He grew up in the 1830's and 1840's reading the learned controversial tracts of the Puseyites. Shocked, inspired, or dismayed (whatever his reaction, certainly not unmoved) by Newman's break with the Church of England, he had by now perhaps outgrown tracts, but he continued to ponder and debate the issues they raised.

By mid-century, in the popular mind at least, tracts had become associated with Low Church and lower-class readership. They were the subject of ridicule and condescension among the sophisticated, who were suspicious of "enthusiasm" and contemptuous of status seekers using religion for purposes of social climbing. Different as they are in tone, there is a fundamental agreement in spirit between Mrs. Frances Trollope's *The Vicar of Wrexhill* (1837), introducing an evangelical clergyman who is a monster of canting hypocrisy, and Anthony Trollope's *Barchester Towers* (1857), with its devastatingly satirical, but far more human characterization of the socially ambitious Mr. Slope. Charlotte Brontë mocked the smug superiority and intolerance of the evangelical Sympson family in *Shirley* (Ch. 26). Mrs. Oliphant recorded their association with the lower classes, with tradesmen who smelled of their merchandise, writing of the Dissenters in *Salem Chapel*: "Greengrocers, dealers in cheese and bacon, milkmen, with some dressmakers of inferior pretensions, and teachers of day-schools of similar humble character, formed the *élite* of the congregation," while George Eliot's proud Reverend Augustus Debarry in *Felix Holt* complains: "The character of the Establishment has suffered enough already through the Evangelicals, with their extempore incoherence and their pipe-smoking piety. Look at Wimple, the man who is vicar of Shuttleton—without his gown and bands, anybody would take him for a grocer in mourning" (Ch. 23).

When not the object of social satire or condescension, the tract-reading, tract-writing, tract-distributing evangelicals were pictured as comic absurdities—Dickens' distraught Mrs. Jellyby wielding her pen on behalf of the natives of Borrioboola Gha and Mrs. Pardiggle, "an inexorable moral Policeman," brandishing her "good book" among the poor "as if it were a constable's staff"; Thackeray's Lady Southdown (her headpiece waving "like an undertaker's tray") dispensing medical advice along with "Fleshpots Broken, or The Converted Cannibal," and "The Washerwoman of Finchley Common"; Wilkie Collins' tract-sowing Miss Drusilla Clack of *The Moonstone*, exiled finally to a colony of genteel but impoverished English Protestant friends in Brittany—"a Patmos amidst the howling ocean of popery that surrounds us." If not comic, the excesses of the evan-

150

gelicals were represented as morbid and sinister. David Copperfield's persecutor Mr. Murdstone is "ferocious" in his evangelical doctrine and freely consigns to perdition all who disagree with him. But in poetic justice Mrs. Chillip observes of his kind, "they undergo a continual punishment; for they are turned inward to feed upon their own hearts, and their own hearts are very bad feeding" (Ch. 59). Mrs. Clennam, who had terrified little Arthur with "a horrible tract which commenced business with the poor child by asking him in its title why he was going to Perdition?" lives in the private hell of her "mystical religion, veiled in gloom and darkness, with lightnings of cursing, vengeance, and destruction" (*Little Dorrit*, I, 3, 5). Another evangelical fanatic, Trollope's Mrs. Bolton, "one of those who regarded all discomfort as meritorious, as in some way adding something to her claim for heaven," bitterly opposes her daughter's marriage and attends the wedding dressed in black, praying only that the girl will not be dragged down to hell along with her bridegroom (*John Caldigate*, Ch. 21).

Among large numbers of the populace, however—the earnestly religious, church workers, educators, social reformers, in middle-class households where parents were seriously concerned with the religious education of their children—evangelicalism remained a solid force and tracts were still a presence. The Religious Tract Society, founded in 1799, had issued over four million tracts by 1807. As late as the 1850's, Owen Chadwick writes: "The distribution of tracts took no account of seasons. They were handed out in pleasure-boats and omnibuses, left open on the tops of hedges, proferred on sticks to galloping horsemen, sent to criminals awaiting the rope, given to cabmen with their fare." Figures on sales are staggering—four million copies of Newman Hall's "Come to Jesus"; another, "The Sinner's Friend," by his father J. V. Hall, sold over 800,000 copies between its first publication in 1821 and 1845. Translated into numberless languages they travelled all over the world.

In Tahiti alone 20,000 copies of "The Sinner's Friend" were distributed.[6] A copy of Legh Richmond's *The Dairyman's Daughter* was seen in the hut of a North American Indian; another was in the possession of the Emperor of Russia; and still another copy was said to have been instrumental in the conversion of a female convict at Botany Bay. As of 1828, eighteen years after its first publication, some two million copies of *The Dairyman's Daughter* were in active circulation.[7] In 1843 the anti-evangelical Lady Eastlake complained in a review of Mrs. Sherwood's seven-volume novel *The Lady of the Manor: Being a Series of Conversations on the Subject of Confirmation intended for the Use of the Middle and Higher Ranks of Young Females* about the proliferation of evangelical literature: "They possess, in fact, a complete and distinct literature of their own, issued by booksellers and publishers of their own—comprising not only every ingenious degree and denomination of religious writing, from the voluminous biography, diary, letters, and remains of a departed member, sold at ten shillings a volume, to the significantly-titled tract, circulated at threepence per dozen, but furnished out with newspapers, magazines, reviews, and every other modern device for the propagation of knowledge or amusement."[8]

On the other side of the coin—or altar—High Church and Anglo-Catholic literature also proliferated. Generally shunning the term "tract" these authors wrote simply "re-

---

[6] *The Victorian Church*, pp. 443, 444, n. 2. See also Louis James, *Fiction for the Working Man* (London, 1963), Ch. 7, for a survey of tract distribution from 1830 to 1850.

[7] T. S. Grimshawe, *A Memoir of the Rev. Legh Richmond, M.A.* (New York, 1830; originally published 1828), p. 166. In *The Victorians and their Reading* (Boston, 1962; originally published 1935), Amy Cruse quotes George Borrow in *Lavengro* (1857), whose publisher suggested that he write "a series of Evangelical tales. . . . Something in the style of *The Dairyman's Daughter . . .* that is the kind of literature, sir, that sells at the present day" (p. 80).

[8] "Evangelical Novels," *Quarterly Review*, 72 (May-September, 1843), p. 28.

ligious stories," but their propagandistic and proselytizing zeal was evangelical. If Lady Eastlake was exercised about the mushrooming of evangelical publications, a reviewer in *Fraser's Magazine* in 1848 was equally, though more good-humoredly, concerned about Anglo-Catholic fiction: "There were the *Lives of the English Saints,* or Littlemore Myths; considerably more fictitious than any of the tales, and worthy to have proceeded from Mr. Newman of the Minerva Press, rather than from his namesake of Oriel. There was a profusion of little books for children and the poor, at prices from a halfpenny upwards; some of them very clever, and better adapted for their purpose than anything that before existed in our language; others intolerably foolish and affected."[9]

Whether we measure the influence of the tracts themselves or, more broadly, the influence of what might be called the "tractarian impulse," it is reasonable to conclude that evangelicalism was a major shaping force in the development of the nineteenth-century English novel.[10] Its effects are apparent both stylistically (in the emergence of a simple prose more akin to Bunyan's and Defoe's than to the major eighteenth-century novelists) and thematically (in a gradual inward-turning of the direction of the novel toward themes of self-examination, guilt and conscience, duty and moral obligation). Evangelicals of all sects firmly rooted religion in the home, in the daily observances and practice of Christianity. "We should never forget, that however great or clever a man may be in the world or society,

[9] "Religious Stories," *Fraser's Magazine,* 38 (July, 1848), p. 154.

[10] See Kathleen Tillotson, *Novels of the Eighteen-Forties* (Oxford, 1961), p. 136: "My argument is that the 'religious novels' of the forties assisted in important changes of emphasis in the novel as a whole. Without making exaggerated claims for individual writers, it is possible to discern a vital connection between their work and that of later and greater novelists." See also Margaret M. Maison, *The Victorian Vision: Studies in the Religious Novel* (New York, 1961), p. 89: "Indeed, the longer type of Evangelical tract, known as the 'tale,' was in fact the forerunner of the Victorian religious novel."

home is the element and trial of a Christian," Harriett Mozley wrote in *The Fairy Bower* (Ch. 46). In their fiction, therefore, they moved steadily forward from polemical and didactic tales toward more natural and realistic narrative. In 1843 a reviewer writing in the High Church *Christian Remembrancer* of a polemical Low Church novel, *The Rector in Search of a Curate* (by "A Churchman"), sarcastically dismissed this "viscid" and "treacly" novel of domestic life as having "sweet glimpses of evangelical domesticities and charming families . . . according to the pious canons, both of the Church and the Minerva Press." He found this family chronicle trite and unreal: "Now this happy circle is a paragon of domestic right-mindedness. It is like one of Holbein's family groups . . . all quiet, all attentive, and all discussing justification by faith only . . . there is not a single yawn; bed-candles are unsought; the cat purrs harmoniously."[11] But in 1860 a writer for this same journal was applauding the domestic-religious novel. He traced its evolution from the stern moralizing of the Puritans and Mrs. Sherwood, where "the tale was a mere bait to catch the unwilling into listening to an enunciation of Calvinistic views or Tractarian doctrine," to the present age of fairy tales and secular novels where children freely read and enjoy books "in the brightest blue and red bindings, and illustrated with delightful woodcuts." Now, he continues, ". . . the good effects of the practice of [faith] is shown in the life and conversation. The inner life of the family is described, not always talking goodness and speaking as if there was always a suspicion that the walls have ears to hear and mouths to tell the little pieces of nonsense that brothers and sisters always do talk when by themselves; but as such boys and girls really do talk and act."[12]

[11] "Low Church Novels, and Tendencies," 6 (November, 1843), pp. 519-21.

[12] "The Moral Character of Story Books," 40 (July-December, 1860), pp. 61-62.

The novel itself had changed, becoming less polemical, less self-consciously evangelical and domestic. But reader attitudes had also changed. Realism, as the young book reviewer for *The Nation* Henry James observed in 1865, had become the fashion. What was most remarkable, he added, is that this development had emerged in England and in America not as in France, where "it is associated with great brilliancy and great immorality," but in "female writers" in the service of religion like Charlotte Yonge, with "a special literature for women and children, to provide books which grown women may read aloud to children without either party being bored."[13]

The crude simplistic evangelical tract may have been more influential ultimately in shaping the English novel than in reforming men's souls. The tracts awakened a mass public to the appeals of narrative. How do people live? How does a starving shepherd feed his family of eight children on six shillings a week, as does the Shepherd of Salisbury Plain in Hannah More's extraordinarily popular tract? Her readers found the answer in specific homely detail: "Though my wife is not able to do any out-of-door work, yet she breeds up her children to such habits of industry, that our little maids, before they are six years old, can first get a half penny, and then a penny, a day by knitting. The boys, who are too little to do hard work, get a trifle by keeping the birds off the corn: for this the farmers will give them a penny or two-pence, and now and then a bit of bread and cheese into the bargain."[14] They dine on a dish of potatoes and a coarse loaf and praise God for His bounty—". . . little fresh-coloured Molly, who had picked the wool from the bushes with so much delight, cried out, 'Father, I wish I was big enough to say grace; I am sure I should say it very heartily to-day, for I was thinking what

[13] "The Schönberg-Cotta Family," in *Notes and Reviews* (Cambridge, Mass., 1921), pp. 77-79.

[14] *The Repository Tales*, in *The Complete Works of Hannah More* (New York, 1835), I, 182.

must *poor* people do who have no salt to their potatoes, but look, our dish is quite full.' "

There is of course a moral and religious lesson to be gleaned from the good shepherd's story, but one wonders if its appeal was not rather in its domestic incident. Surely the dubious reward offered by the visiting stranger at the end of the tale—the setting up of a Sunday school in the parish ("for I am not going to make you rich, but useful") —was less impressive to the young reader than was the catalogue of realistic descriptive details that he could recognize in his own home or easily imagine—the brightly polished old-fashioned candle sticks on the chimney of this impoverished home, the four brown wooden chairs, "which by constant rubbing were become as bright as a looking-glass; an iron pot and kettle; a poor old grate, which scarcely held a handful of coal, and out of which the little fire that had been in it, appeared to have been taken, as soon as it had answered the end for which it had been lighted—that of boiling their potatoes."

Within the tale itself Mrs. More acknowledged her secret —namely that in order to teach effectively one must reach an audience at its level. The visiting benefactor discovers that the simple untutored shepherd is a more successful teacher than he is: ". . . for though his meaning was very good, his language was not always very plain; and though the things he said were not hard to be understood, yet the words were, especially to such as were very ignorant. And he now began to find out, that, if people were ever so wise and good, yet if they had not a simple, agreeable, and familiar way of expressing themselves, some of their plain hearers would not be much the better for them."[15]

Guided by a theory of fiction as practical and pragmatic as this, Hannah More achieved her purposes with stunning success. She had set out to reach the common people, to refute the radical political tracts of the Jacobins, by producing three tracts a month, "at so cheap a rate as to undersell

[15] *Ibid.*, 196.

the revolutionary publications."[16] Selling at from a half penny to one and a half pence, over two million were in circulation within a year of their first publication. One need read only a single paragraph to appreciate their lively appeal. Here is the opening of "Tawny Rachel; or, The Fortune Teller":

"Tawny Rachel was the wife of poaching Giles. There seemed to be a conspiracy in Giles's whole family to maintain themselves by tricks and pilfering. Regular labour and honest industry did not suit their idle habits. They had a sort of genius at finding out every unlawful means to support a vagabond life. Rachel travelled the country with a basket on her arm. She pretended to get her bread by selling laces, cabbage-nets, ballads, and history-books, and used to buy old rags and rabbit-skins. Many honest people trade in these things, and I am sure I do not mean to say a word against honest people, let them trade in what they will. But Rachel only made this traffic a pretence for getting admittance into farmers' kitchens, in order to tell fortunes."[17]

Rachel is a "con" artist of superlative skill. Telling fortunes and interpreting dreams (if her interpretations did not come to pass, "she would get out of that scrape by saying that this sort of dreams went by contraries"), she ingratiates herself into farmhouses where she tricks gullible servant girls and superstitious farmers' wives (one of whom "never made a black pudding without borrowing one of the parson's old wigs to hang in the chimney, firmly believing there were no other means to preserve them from bursting"). Justice finally catches up with Rachel and she is sent off to Botany Bay. The tale ends with a warning to heed the Bible instead of conjurors, but it is Rachel's craft rather than her fate that fascinates the reader. We can understand the cautionary criticism of Dr. Christopher Wordsworth,

[16] Charlotte Yonge, *Hannah More* (Boston, 1890), p. 130.
[17] *Works*, I, 349.

Master of Trinity College, who found Mrs. More's tracts too "novelish and exciting."[18]

Mrs. More's *Cheap Repository Tracts* were not the first tales intended for the religious and moral instruction of the poor. The S.P.C.K. (Society for the Promotion of Christian Knowledge) had distributed Bibles and devotional literature to the "vulgar" since 1699. Her friend Mrs. Sarah Trimmer, author of a favorite of children's literature *The Story of the Robins* (1786), also published *Instructive Tales* and edited *The Family Magazine, or Repository of religious instruction, and rational amusement designed to counteract the pernicious tendency of immoral books which have circulated of late years among the poorer classes of people to the obstruction of their improvement in religion and morals.*[19] But Mrs. More's tracts were cheaper and livelier. In format they resembled the chapbooks, broadsides, and ballads that were the staples of popular literature in the late eighteenth century. It was not easy for a writer as serious as she, until then the author of poetic tragedies, poems in the classical manner, and didactic essays on education, to woo the common reader. Indeed, she had fallen into the popular vogue reluctantly, with a political tract written at the request of Beilby Porteous, the Bishop of London, who "came to me with a dismal countenance and told me I should repent it on my death-bed if I, who knew so much of the habits and sentiments of the lower orders of people, did not write some little thing tending to open their eyes." The "little thing" was a pamphlet, "Village Politics" (1792), an answer to Thomas Paine's *The Rights of Man*. Of it she said apologetically: "It is as vulgar as heart can wish; but it is only designed for the most vulgar class of readers." But the enthusiastic reception of the tract, the praise from the learned and literary as well as its huge sale, convinced her of her powers and duties. The *Cheap Repository Tracts*

[18] Yonge, *Hannah More*, p. 143.
[19] See Peter Coveney, *The Image of Childhood*, rev. ed. (Penguin Books, 1967), ch. 1.

that followed from 1795 to 1798 are believed to have shared with Robert Raikes's Sunday Schools the credit for the remarkable religious and moral reform that took place in the first quarter of the nineteenth century.[20] Although their literary influence is less easily charted, it is significant that they were read for the next half century not only by the vulgar audience for whom they were intended, but by the middle and upper classes as well. Like most of this graphic, simplistic literature, they quickly found their level among children. Here they held their place in family reading comfortably alongside Bunyan, Foxe's *Acts and Monuments,* Thomas Day's *Sandford and Merton,* selections from Dr. Watts's *Hymnology,* the tales of Mrs. Trimmer and of Mrs. Sherwood.

II

WHILE Hannah More portrayed the marginal life of the poor, drawing her domestic detail from the humble working classes, her younger contemporary Mrs. Mary Martha (Butt) Sherwood (1775-1851) drew upon the domestic life of the upper middle classes. Most of her tales and tracts, intended for moral instruction rather than political propaganda, were therefore more immediately suitable for "nursery" consumption. Her semi-fictional biography of a real-life missionary, *The Life of Henry Martyn* (which Janet Dempster of George Eliot's "Janet's Repentance" read with deep interest), *Little Henry and his Bearer Boosy,* and most especially her *History of The Fairchild Family* (1817) were standard reading for Victorian children. A poll of prominent men taken in the year 1900 showed overwhelming agreement among all who had grown up in the 1850's or earlier that *The Fairchild Family* was "a dominant book."[21] Like so many other writers of children's books,

[20] M. G. Jones, *Hannah More* (Cambridge, 1952), p. 134.

[21] F. J. Harvey-Darton, Introduction to *The Life and Times of Mrs. Sherwood* (London, 1910), p. ix.

Mrs. Sherwood drifted into literature from Sunday School teaching. Inspired by Hannah More's activities on behalf of the poor and lowly, she wrote a tale for older girls in her school to be read as a warning against the military men stationed in the neighborhood—*Susan Grey* (1802). This tale, she claimed inaccurately but revealingly, was "remarkable in the annals of literature from its having been the first of its kind—that is, the first narrative allowing of anything like correct writing or refined sentiments expressed without vulgarisms, ever prepared for the poor, and having religion for its object."[22]

Mrs. Sherwood continued teaching after her marriage in 1803 to an army officer, conducting regimental schools in remote regions of India, where she lived for twelve years. She had a ready audience for her children's tales—her own large family and several adopted children as well as her school pupils. Returning to England in 1816 with her husband on half pay, her children to educate, and an invalid mother to support, she now sought more than spiritual rewards for her efforts and produced a staggering number of works (some 350 it has been estimated). Though generally writing for a middle-class public, she also reached a mass audience with tracts or "penny books" produced to fit woodcuts and steel engravings supplied by her publishers. Her unique contribution was her ability to create a continuous narrative for the separate pictures.[23] As evangelical tracts intended for the education of the "vulgar," these graphic and often lurid tales reflected the stark, crude technique of their illustrations. Even the more carefully produced *Fairchild Family* series appalls a modern reader with its gruesome, morbid Calvinistic moralizing. The gentry who put these tales into the hands of young children could hardly have been aware of their potentially horrify-

[22] *Ibid.*, p. 201.
[23] Naomi Royde-Smith, *The State of Mind of Mrs. Sherwood* (London, 1946), p. 104.

ing effects.[24] Mrs. Sherwood herself had had a happy child-hood. She grew up in an enlightened family numbering among their friends Erasmus Darwin and the eminently wholesome-minded Richard Edgeworth. Under the most painful and strenuous conditions of life in India, bearing and losing children, she remained cheerful, and her later years were busy and prosperous. One can therefore account for the grislier elements of her tales only by citing Puritan-Calvinist belief and practice. Allowing for all the individual exceptions—including Mrs. Sherwood's own family history —the fact is that evangelicalism in all its forms stressed punishment and suffering, obedience and humility. Family love was on the one hand sentimentalized into an ideal of sweetness and tenderness, but the other hand was an iron fist for instilling discipline and distributing punishments.

The Fairchild family is a model instance of this paradox. Prosperous and genteel (though not rich), they live in an edenic country scene properly balanced with the concerns of practical everyday domesticity: "Mr. and Mrs. Fairchild lived very far from any town; their house stood in the midst of a garden, which in the summer-time was full of fruit and sweet flowers. Mr. Fairchild kept only two servants, Betty and John; Betty's business was to clean the house, cook the dinner, and milk the cow; and John waited at table, worked in the garden, fed the pig, and took care of the meadow in which the cow grazed."[25] Their three children (ages nine, eight, seven) are educated at home, as the Edgeworths would have approved, with practical instruction and whole-some outdoor activity. The chief emphasis, however, is upon their religious and moral instruction (the Fairchilds

[24] By 1884, however, Miss Royde-Smith writes that at least one English family, her own, had confiscated the book from their nursery "on the ground that it was unsuitable reading for the young" (Dedication).

[25] *The Works of Mrs. Sherwood* (New York, 1834), ii. Page references are to this edition.

"did not wish their dear little children to be handsome, or rich, or powerful in the world; all that they desired for them was the blessing of God"), and the book is a collection of their prayers, hymns, and daily experiences. Father Fairchild misses no opportunity to instruct—a country walk inspires a celebration of glories of God's creation; children's games provide illustrations of the virtues of generosity; their spending of small money gifts teaches them thrift and value; a visit to a humble cottager shows the blessings of pious poverty. But the little Fairchilds are exposed to more terrifying experiences in the course of their education, including a visit to a gibbet in the woods where a murderer's corpse has been exposed. Mrs. Sherwood spares us—and the children—nothing: "It had on a blue coat, a silk handkerchief round the neck, with shoes and stockings, and every other part of the dress still entire; but the face of the corpse was so shocking that the children could not look upon it" (p. 57). Determined to confront his children with the realities of death Father Fairchild takes them on another occasion to see the corpse of the family gardener: "You must see these things one time or another and attend dying people: it is therefore better in early life to become acquainted with such things" (p. 125). This episode concludes with "A Prayer for a Happy Death," which the family recite together.

Reading of the innocent and presumably happy childhood of the Fairchilds, we are struck with the heavy emphasis upon guilt, contrition, confession, and punishment. The children are encouraged to keep journals in which they record their "wicked" thoughts. Little Lucy writes, "When papa was reading and praying, I wanted to be at play; and was tired of the Bible and did not wish to hear it," and in due contrition shows the entry to her mother, who praises her for keeping "an account of what passed in her heart, that she might learn more and more to know and hate her own sinful nature." Her mother recalls that in her own childhood she had sinned by concealing that she had broken a dish. She "reformed" when she saw a dead child lying in its coffin: "I had learned to know the wickedness of my heart and to ask God to help me to be good; and when I had done wrong, I knew whose forgiveness to ask. I took great delight in my Bible, and used to read and pray and sing psalms in my little closet; and I do not think that I ever fell into those great sins which I had been guilty of before—such as lying, stealing, and deceiving my aunts; but still I found my heart full of sin; and till I die, the sins of my heart, and the wicked inclinations of this vile body, will make me unhappy: but blessed be the Lord Jesus Christ, who will in the end give us the victory" (p. 46).

Physical punishments in Mrs. Sherwood are ghastly—a naughty girl, ignoring warnings, plays near a fire and burns to death; a vain young woman is crippled for life in a carriage accident; another frivolous girl catches cold at a ball and the white plumes of her hearse wave in the breeze at precisely the spot where the white plumes of her riding hat had waved a few weeks before. But psychological torment is infinitely more terrible than physical pain. In one tale, "The Stranger at Home," illustrating the theme "that the absence of necessary correction is the severest of all punishments," a bright little girl who had demanded to be educated like her older sisters is punished by total isolation. She is ignored in family conversations, Bible readings, all activities, until, driven desperate by loneliness, she begs her parents to forgive her, "to let me be their servant till they had proved whether I was worthy of being loved again."

Mrs. Sherwood was hardly a subtle psychologist. Her stories simply substitute the black-and-white extremes of nursery-level naughtiness and punishment for moral and criminal sin and harsh social justice. But in their passion for self-examination and self-recrimination, her characters anticipate the psychological novel. Lady Eastlake, reviewing her *Lady of the Manor*, was exasperated by the confessional urge of her "pious auto-anatomists, who, conceiving that all assurance of present goodness consists solely in the excessive sense of previous guilt, find a morbid pleasure in the most extravagant self-condemnation, and persuade themselves that the greater violence they do to nature, the higher homage they pay to religion."[26] Lady Eastlake's anti-evangelical bias, it should be noted, was so strong that it also soured her on "auto-anatomists" like Jane Eyre. Her tastes were probably not representative of the large reading public that welcomed the evangelical-confessional novel.

Mrs. Sherwood's rather considerable literary skill is demonstrated not in her moral tales for children but in her personal writings and in a novel, *Caroline Mordaunt, or The Governess* (1845). Her diary, actually an autobiography, is a long but lively record of a woman thoroughly and happily engaged in life. There is no guilt or self-recrimination here. Gifted with almost total recall, an eye for realistic detail, a delight in gossip, and a genuine interest in people, Mrs. Sherwood writes with the verve of a skilled novelist. Her experiences in India are chronicled with sharp reportorial skill, with no element of pious self-righteousness or self-pity for the hardships she suffered. She is at her best, however, in the home scene, recalling impressions of her childhood—visits, at age fourteen, to a bishop who had returned from India and furnished his home with exotic souvenirs ("with all this profusion of curiosities, conveying to the mind no idea whatever of refinement, but of that peculiar taste which appertains to a tea-garden"[27]). With a sharpness of wit worthy of Jane Austen she sketches a distant French relative who arrived at the family parsonage "with a maid, a lap-dog, and a canary-bird, and boxes heaped upon boxes, till it was impossible to see the persons within [the carriage]."[28]

[26] *Quarterly Review*, 72 (May-September, 1843), p. 33. Lady Eastlake's often quoted attack on *Jane Eyre* titled *"Vanity Fair—and Jane Eyre,"* appeared in *Quarterly Review*, 84 (December, 1848).

[27] From the "Diaries of Captain and Mrs. Sherwood," in *The Life and Times of Mrs. Sherwood*, p. 3.

[28] *Ibid.*, pp. 42-43.

She displays wit also in her novel *Caroline Mordaunt*.[29] Her heroine, the orphan daughter of a clergyman, is brought up by a respectable lady who keeps a boarding school, and she is trained to be a private governess. But she receives no solid religious education. Proud, self-confident, and rebellious, she goes off to a series of governess posts, losing one after another of these because she lacks the humility that true religious faith would have given her. She fails in all her endeavors until, after several years, she is brought back into religion by a pious little pupil who, like Jane Eyre's inspiration Helen Burns, dies in her arms. By now thirty and duly chastened, she marries "the humble rector of the parish" and has six children. In the somewhat turbulent course of her career, however, Caroline has a series of lively adventures, described with real wit and a knack for phrase-turning. One of her employers, for example, is "little more than a bustling housewife,—one who, under the idea of economy, would soon have reduced a man of moderate income to the debtor's place in the nearest jail; but being happily allied to a man of a deep purse, had hitherto effected little by her plans of good management, except to swell his Christmas bills to about double the amount of what they might otherwise have been." (Ch. 3).

Visiting Bath early in her career, Mrs. Sherwood attended a literary salon given by the blue-stocking philosopher Mrs. Elizabeth Hamilton. The guest of honor was the famous Child of Nature, one of those "wild child" waifs discovered in the wilderness and brought into society as objects of wonder and study (she later introduced this episode into *Caroline Mordaunt*). Mrs. Hamilton is best remembered today—if she is remembered at all—for a genre novel of Scottish peasant life, *The Cottagers of Glenburnie* (1808), which Sir Walter Scott admired. In the first

[29] Naomi Royde-Smith rather over-rates "this little masterpiece," comparing it to *Emma* as a portrait of a "self-opinionated young girl who after many mistakes, errors and repentances, is rewarded . . . by marriage to a clergyman" (*State of Mind of Mrs. Sherwood*, p. 51).

half of the nineteenth century, however, her writings on the education of children and the psychology of learning were very influential. Maria Edgeworth had the highest praise for her *Letters on the Elementary Principles of Education* (1801): "In those she not only shows that she has studied the history of the human mind, and that she has made herself acquainted with all that has been written on this subject by the best moral and metaphysical writers, but she adds new value to their knowledge, by rendering it practically useful."[30]

A devout and ardent Christian, Mrs. Hamilton was inspired in her studies by her evangelical zeal. "These volumes," she wrote in the Introduction to her *Popular Essays on the Elementary Principles of the Human Mind* (1812), "which are rather of a religious than a philosophical cast, illustrate principles that perfectly harmonise with the pure precepts of the Gospel." Her most important book was *A Series of Popular Essays Illustrative of Principles Essentially Connected with the Improvement of the Understanding, the Imagination, and the Heart* (2 vols., 1813), the purpose of which was to urge her readers to a serious course of self-improvement by self-examination. The obstacles to human progress, she argued, "are to be found within, and can only be discovered by an actual survey of our common nature: such as may, however, be taken by every person capable of observation and reflection." The results of such a survey, Mrs. Hamilton assures her reader, will prove "that revealed religion offers the only effectual means of improving the human character."

Without writing many novels herself, Mrs. Hamilton laid down the ideological principles of the evangelical-domestic novel. These involve man and God in an intimate relationship in which God shapes individual man's (or the child's) moral growth and development as man obeys and worships Him—thus the evangelical preoccupation with children and

[30] Quoted in Miss [E. O.] Benger, *Memoirs of the Late Mrs. Elizabeth Hamilton* (London, 1818), I, 208.

the family, the influence of the home and especially the mother in the moral development of the Christian. Mrs. Hamilton emphasizes the "benevolent affections . . . the affections of the heart." These begin to emerge in infancy, in the child's response to kindness and to demonstrations of affection. From here secular educators like the Edgeworths move outward in the direction of "practical" learning, preparation for life in society. But from here the evangelicals move inward. The best means "of cultivating and improving the affections equally" is in the Revelation of God, says Mrs. Hamilton, regretting "that philosophers have so seldom availed themselves of the assistance derived from Scripture, in the study of the human mind" (Essay v, "Inquiry into the Means Appointed by Providence for the Development and Cultivation of the Benevolent Affections"). Thus the evangelical Mrs. Hamilton justified the study of psychology for religious ends, and thus the evangelical novelists, clumsy and crude as they often were in their treatment of human character, nevertheless reached surprising depths in psychological characterization.

Citing the authority of John Locke, Mrs. Hamilton acknowledges the limitations of self-examination; we are "shortsighted and very often see one side of a matter . . . we see but in part, and we know but in part." The myopia is induced by our pride, our prejudices, but mainly by "a propensity to magnify the idea of self" (Essay iv). She traces at great length the variations on this phenomenon—family pride, vanity, love of dress, the tendency to romanticize and make oneself the hero or heroine of one's life story, in extreme measure malevolence, the vindictive passions—a veritable catalogue of the themes of fiction. To draw a line between psychological and religious introspection in the nineteenth-century novel would be difficult if not impossible. Indeed it is often difficult to distinguish religious novels from the autobiographies, diaries, and confessionals that proliferated during this period. Kathleen Tillotson writes of the 1840's: "Religious novels enforced, and perhaps even

167

initiated, the growing tendency to introspection in the novel. They are not a backwater, but a tributary of the main stream." She reminds us that contemporaries recognized as characteristic of their age the "diseased habit of analysis," "the ingenious invention of labyrinth meandering into the mazes of the mind," or simply "the dialogue of the mind with itself."[31]

The range of self-examination and introspection was from works of religious profundity like Newman's *Apologia pro Vita Sua* to *The Fairy Bower* by his sister, Mrs. Mozley, explorations of conscience from agonized self-searchings of prominent clergymen down to little girls hiding guilty secrets about broken kitchen jugs or their envy of a play-mate's curly hair. The evangelical impulse manifests itself more strikingly in the *desire* to confess and repent, than in the content of the confession itself.[32] How much of the impulse was the result of inhibitions of strict Protestantism it is hard to say. We have already noted the need for emotional outlets that the various evangelical movements of the late eighteenth and early nineteenth centuries offered— spirited preaching, hymn singing, the Anglican drift toward ritualism, formalism, and church decoration. From the personal witness of the diaries and spiritual autobiographies of the period we may trace this growing introspection developing right out of the home and daily life. The historian James Anthony Froude, whose brother Hurrell played so important a part in the Oxford Movement, testifies to the almost desperate craving he felt for the release offered by evangelicalism. The son of a clergyman, he grew up in a religious but emotionally sterile home. There were daily pray-

---

[31] *Novels of the Eighteen-Forties*, p. 131.

[32] One recalls the rigorously Protestant Lucy Snowe's impulsive visit to the confessional in *Villette* (Ch. 15)—"To take this step could not make me more wretched than I was; it might soothe me"— all the more remarkable because Charlotte Brontë herself once made a confession at the Roman Catholic Cathedral of Ste. Gudule in Brussels (see Shakespeare Head Brontë, I, 304).

ers and Sunday services, but religion was simply a guide to life not a way of life: ". . . we were never worried about our spiritual emotions, and in this respect nothing could have been more excellent than our education. Religion meant essentially 'doing our duty.' It was not to be itself an object of thought, but a guide to action. Life was a journey in which were many temptations and pitfalls. Religion was the lantern by which we could see our way on the dark road. Let the light be thrown on the road and you will see your way. Keep your eyes fixed on the light itself and you will fall into the ditch."[33]

As a young man Froude was unprepared for "the jarring notes," the challenges to his faith of Catholic Emancipation, the Reform Bill, the Oxford Movement. It was not until, fully grown, he met an evangelical clergyman living in Ireland, in whose home the Bible and evangelical doctrine were talked about and practiced, that he became aware of "the presence of a purely spiritual religion, the teaching of the New Testament adopted as a principle of life, and carried into all the details of ordinary thought and action."

Froude attempted to describe his religious experience in two novels—*Shadows of the Clouds* (1847), the first narrative of which, *The Spirit's Trials*, is a thinly disguised autobiography, and the better-known *The Nemesis of Faith* (1849), of which he said, "I cut a hole in my heart and wrote with the blood." But his fiction is far less compelling than the autobiographical notes that he collected but never published. It is in fact remarkable that so much of the evangelical fiction of this period is inferior to the personal writings of the same authors. The qualities that are most striking in these confessionals—candor, immediacy, vividness of detail and incident—are lacking in most of the fiction. Mrs. Sherwood's autobiography is infinitely more delightful than her tales and is a model work of domestic realism. The same observation holds for Legh Richmond,

[33] Waldo Hilary Dunn published excerpts from his unpublished autobiography in *James Anthony Froude* (Oxford, 1961), I, 20, 66.

Charlotte Elizabeth, and Elizabeth Missing Sewell among the evangelicals and for the free-thinking Harriet Martineau (whose *Autobiography* is discussed below in Ch. 5). All of these were writers of fiction, but their best "novels" —that is, their most readable, imaginative, sensitive and emotionally stirring writings—were non-fictional spiritual autobiographies.

One of the most successful of all evangelical tract writers was the Reverend Legh Richmond, whose *The Dairyman's Daughter* (1810) is today unread and all but unreadable. A tale that its author insisted was "founded on fact" (when challenged that his heroine's prose style was too noble for a poor girl, he identified his real-life inspiration and produced her letters to him as evidence), it was written by a clergyman who had been "converted" to the Claphamite movement after reading Wilberforce's *Practical View of Christianity*. Reverend Richmond (1772-1827) shared the romantic sensibilities of his contemporaries like Gray, Wordsworth, and Coleridge, addressing himself to the poor and lowly: "Among such, the sincerity and simplicity of the Christian character appear unencumbered by those obstacles to spirituality of mind and conversation, which too often prove a great hindrance to those who live in the higher ranks." His brief narrative concerns a pious girl who, after a period of frivolity in her youth (a taste for pretty clothes is her only weakness), hears a sermon, reforms, devotes herself to religion and the care of her aging parents until she herself dies—at great length—of consumption. The scene is homely and rural, the characters simple and uneducated. But Reverend Richmond writes in a lofty manner reflecting his eighteenth-century education. Country scenes are painted in the panoramic grand style. The narrator favors mountain views from which he sees ". . . a rich and fruitful valley, filled with corn-fields and pastures . . . the open ocean bounded only by the horizon . . . an expanse of near and remote beauties, which alternately caught the observation, and which harmonised together . . ." (Ch. 2). He seeks seclusion for contemplation: "Many grotesque rocks, with little trickling streams of water occasionally leaping out of them, varied the recluse scenery, and produced a romantic and pleasing effect" (Ch. 3). Even when he moves inside to describe the humble cottage of the dairyman, he sees an idealized interior, a model not a real room: "On each side of the fire-place stood an old oaken chair, where the venerable parents rested their weary limbs after the day's labour was over. On a shelf in one corner lay two Bibles, with a few religious books and tracts. The little room had two windows; a lovely prospect of hills, woods, and fields appeared through one; the other was more than half obscured by the branches of a vine which was trained across it; between its leaves the sun shone, and cast a cheerful light over the whole place."

In striking contrast to the stiff formality of Richmond's tract is the account—a good deal of it in his own voice—of his personal life, *Domestic Portraiture; or, The Successful Application of Religious Principle in the Education of a Family Exemplified in the Memoirs of Three of the Deceased Children of the Rev. Legh Richmond* (1833). Charlotte Brontë wrote to her friend Ellen Nussey that this book "strongly attracted and strangely fascinated my attention. Beg, borrow, or steal it without delay."[34] Reading through the earnest, intimate, pathetic, and ultimately ironic family record of the Richmonds, we can readily understand its appeal for her. The Brontës were also an evangelical family, and their stern clergyman father Patrick would have assented strongly to its sentiments. The father of twelve children, Richmond was deeply concerned with the responsibilities and duties of parenthood and the importance of the home in performing these: "I have long thought," he wrote, "that though a good school is better than a bad home, a good home is the best of schools. . . . It has ever been my

[34] June, 1837 (Shakespeare Head Brontë, i, 159).

171

heart's desire and prayer to give them [his children] a useful, happy, exemplary home; were I to fail here, life would
become a blank to me" (Ch. 2).

The subtitle of Richmond's book is somewhat misleading,
however, for although the religious principles were applied
in generous measure, the results were not entirely successful. Starting from the sternly evangelical premise that "all
children are by nature born in sin, and the children of
wrath; that they inherit from their parents a *carnalness
which is enmity toward God,*" Richmond was forced into
ambivalence. He believed that the home should be the center of a child's existence, that it should be so happy a place
that he would not be tempted to forsake it for outside (and
therefore corrupting) interests. He provided "innocent"
amusements and practical, instructive toys, including pictures, a telescope, a magic lantern "to exhibit phan-
tasmagoria and teach natural history." But his evangelical
principles outlawed "all games of chance, fishing, field
sports, dancing, theatre, oratories and other sources of
gratification, which he thought to be inconsistent with the
spirit of religion." The little Richmonds might have grown
up happily enough without such amusements. More trou-
bling was their father's strange inhibition about communicating directly with them. He confessed to a friend: "I feel
an insurmountable backwardness to close personal conversation with my children; when I begin they are silent, and
it is not long before I feel tongue-tied; yet I cannot be easy
without ascertaining the effect of my instructions, and
hence I have been driven to use my pen, because I could
not open my lips" (Ch. 3).

The Richmond household was therefore run as a kind of
correspondence school from father to children. He wrote
brief, affectionate letters, usually suggesting a religious text
for the day and posing religious questions for the child to
ponder on and reply to in writing. Occasionally these contained homelier matters—"You tremble at the thought of
a school-examination,—but what is this to the examination

before the judgment seat of God?" Reverend Richmond's method of discipline was equally ambivalent and disturbing. He punished mainly by showing the erring child how much pain he was causing his loving parents, thus encouraging in the young the cultivation of introspective tendencies, self-examination, and conscience-pricking. Like the little girl in Mrs. Sherwood's tale "The Stranger at Home" who became a pariah at her own family's hearthside, the Richmond children were punished by being made to feel their guilt inwardly: "From the misconduct of his child, he seemed to reflect on himself, as the author of a corrupt being. He humbled himself before God, and in prayer sought help from above, while he kept the offender at a distance, or separated him from the society of his family, as one unworthy to share in their privileges and affections. No one of his children could long endure this exclusion, or bear with sullen indifference, a countenance which silently expressed the deepest anguish" (Ch. 3).

Remembering the painful experiences of little Jane Eyre locked in the red-room, of David Copperfield cast off by the Murdstones, of the many fictional Victorian children who suffered so bitterly under this kind of solitary confinement, we read *Domestic Portraiture* with compassion. The fates of at least three of the Richmond children would be subjects worthy of the master novelists. Nugent, the eldest, having fallen into bad company in spite of his father's protection, ran away to sea. After a series of harrowing adventures, including two shipwrecks and missing a third ship that went down with the loss of the entire crew of 350 (Richmond credits this escape to the "Grace of God," leaving the reader to wonder where that grace was for the 350 aboard), he died of fever. A younger son, Wilberforce, had a less physically hazardous life, but was torn apart emotionally by a religious struggle.[35] His father intended him

[35] Charlotte Brontë especially recommended to Ellen the "Memoir of Wilberforce"—"that short record of a brief, uneventful life, I shall never forget it; it is beautiful, not on account of the incidents it

173

for the clergy, but—in the way of all flesh of many Victorian fictional characters—"Willy" felt that he lacked the vocation ("I shrink from assuming a profession for which I cannot but know myself most unworthy"). After an agonizing struggle of conscience, the boy died of consumption, leaving his father to muse on his son's "impenetrable reserve; he shrank from personal conversations on religious subjects, though his thoughtful and often depressed countenance exhibited traces of inward conflict, and need of help and comfort" (Ch. 7). Finally, there was a lively and exuberant young daughter who gave her father "much anxiety" because of her volatile temper, a tendency to giggle and to treat religion lightly. She married happily but died in childbirth after a long and painful deathbed scene. *Domestic Portraiture* was, in short, a kind of casebook for Victorian novelists. When so many of them subtitled their domestic novels tales "founded on fact," they might have looked to Legh Richmond for their witness.

III

THESE evangelical autobiographies and confessions were indeed "semi-developed" novels, not, however, as Henry James used the term to describe fiction written for family reading, but as works arising out of the same roots as the realistic domestic novel, using many of the same techniques but never achieving the imaginative release of fiction. The first-person narrator, for example, so successful in the novel from *Moll Flanders* onwards as a device for revealing the inmost nature of a character, gives these non-novels the same illusion of intimacy and immediacy. Here, for example, is a passage from *Personal Recollections*, the autobiography of Charlotte Elizabeth, written of a moment in her life when her unhappy first marriage to George Phelan, an

details, but because of the simple narration it gives of the life and death of a young, talented, and sincere Christian" (*ibid.*, pp. 159-60).

174

army officer, her lonely existence in distant Ireland, and mainly her sense of the absence of God from her life have led her to an "abyss of gloomy despair": "My existence was a feverish dream, of vain pleasures first, and then of agitations and horrors. My mind was a chaos of useless information, my character of unapplied energies, my heart a waste of unclaimed affections, and my hope an enigma of confused speculations. I had plenty to do, yet felt that I was doing nothing, and there was a glowing want within my bosom, a craving after I knew not what; a restless, unsatisfied, unhappy feeling, that seemed in quest of some unknown good." In seclusion and contemplation she resolved ". . . to become a sort of Protestant nun, and to fancy my garden, with its high stone-walls, and little thickets of apple-trees, a convent-enclosure. I also settled it with myself to pray three or four times every day, instead of twice; and with great alacrity entered upon this new routine of devotion" (Letter v).

Charlotte Elizabeth emerges as a real life evangelical Dorothea Brooke suffering her dark night of the soul. She awakened to a new career of crusading in the interests of exploited factory workers. Out of her battles came a novel, *Helen Fleetwood* (1841), more influential in its day than Mrs. Gaskell's *Mary Barton*, and a collection of essays and sketches on the sufferings of the poor, *The Wrongs of Women* (1843-1844). *Helen Fleetwood* is credited with leading the way to the Factory Bill of 1844, which limited the working day of factory women to twelve hours.[36] As a novel it has no merit whatever beyond its good intentions and the graphic pictures it offers of life in the wretched slums of factory towns. Her portraits in "The Little Pin

[36] Wanda Fraikin Neff, *Victorian Working Women: An Historical and Literary Study of Women in British Industries and Professions, 1832-1850,* (New York, 1929), p. 16. See also Ivanka Kovačenić and S. Barbara Kanner, "Blue Book into Novel: The Forgotten Industrial Fiction of Charlotte Elizabeth Tonna," *Nineteenth Century Fiction,* 25 (September, 1970), pp. 152-73.

Headers" of sunken-eyed, hollow-cheeked children working at the home industry of pin-making in cold, dingy rooms, of desperate mothers collapsing in exhaustion from overwork, are domestic realism carried to almost Hogarthian depths. But at least one of her literary contemporaries recognized that Charlotte Elizabeth's real art was in autobiography. This was Harriet Beecher Stowe, who wrote a glowing introduction to her collected works in 1844 and singled out her *Personal Recollections* as a small masterpiece of its genre: "The sketches of her early life and residences, the portraits of her father, mother, grandmother and brother, are given with all the picturesque effect of a romance, and the authoress, whole-hearted, confiding, full of passionate impulses,—full of the thought and motion and excitement which belongs to a strong and ardent mind, is herself no inconsiderable heroine. We know of no piece of autobiography in the English language which can compare with this in richness of feeling and description, and power of exciting interest."

A woman as dedicated to strict evangelical Protestantism as Charlotte Elizabeth understandably shunned novel-writing. Once, when her family was in need of money, she resolved to write novels, confident that "I should probably have succeeded very well, but it pleased God to save me from this snare" (Letter IV). No doubt she associated novels with love-stories and "worldly reading."[37] But romance, in the sense of wild flights of the imagination, day-dreaming, and ardent idealism, was part of Charlotte Elizabeth's very being. Writing as a mature woman devoted to solemn religious and social causes, she confessed to certain excesses of romanticism in her early years: "I acquired the habit of dreamy excursiveness into imaginary scenes and among un-

---

[37] See Joseph E. Baker, *The Novel and the Oxford Movement* (New York, 1965; originally published 1932), p. 11, and Elizabeth Missing Sewell, who defined a "regular novel" as "a story in which love is the essential interest," thereby distinguishing it from the "tale" (*Autobiography*, Ch. 16).

real personages which is alike inimical to rational pursuits, and opposed to spiritual mindedness. . . ." Reading Shakespeare and other works of imaginative literature, "My mind became unnerved, my judgment perverted, my estimate of people and things wholly falsified, and my soul wrapped in the vain solace of unsubstantial enjoyments. . . ."

Her childhood in Norwich, within sight of the great cathedral where little more than two centuries earlier Protestant martyrs had suffered for their faith, inflamed her imagination ("I have recalled the fact of being born just opposite the dark old gateway of that strong building where the glorious martyrs of Mary's day were imprisoned. I have recollected that the house wherein I drew my first breath was visible through the grated window of their prison, and a conspicuous object when its gates unfolded to deliver them to unjust judgment and a cruel death"). A severe childhood illness complicated by even more severe medical treatment ("for certainly I was long kept hovering on the verge of the grave by the barbarous excess to which medical experiments were carried") further heightened her nervous and emotional sensibilities. The strict evangelical teaching that she had from her parents honed her conscience to a razor's edge. Led once into a lie at the instigation of a servant, she suffered agonies until she confessed and joyfully received a beating from her father: "I took the punishment in a most extraordinary spirit; I wished every stroke had been a stab. I wept because the pain was not great enough; and I loved my father at that moment better than even I, who almost idolized him, had ever loved him before. I thanked him, and I thank him still; for I never transgressed in that way again" (Letter 1).

In retrospect, of course, Charlotte Elizabeth reconstructed her childhood with heavy evangelical-didactic emphases. In reality a woman of such exquisitely refined moral sensibilities could never have survived the vigorous, active, at times even physically hazardous, life that she led. Living in Ireland during the rebellions against the English-

Protestants in the 1820's, she demonstrated a toughness—
and a sense of humor—that contrasts strikingly with the almost neurasthenic image she drew of herself in childhood.
But then we remember that many fictional Victorian children survived their emotionally harrowing childhoods with
their sanity intact—Oliver Twist, David Copperfield, Florence Dombey, Esther Summerson, Jane Eyre, Hareton
Earnshaw.

Charlotte Elizabeth not only survived the emotional
rigors of an evangelical childhood but recorded them conscientiously in her *Personal Recollections.* Her contemporaries received the book in the spirit for which it was
intended—as much domestic as religious—a work that, Harriet Beecher Stowe wrote, "the most scrupulous parent may
safely leave on the family center-table, and yet which contains an abundance of interesting matter for the young
members of the family." One might quite appropriately
place on the family table beside it the *Autobiography* of
Elizabeth Missing Sewell (1815-1906). Although Miss
Sewell's Protestantism was as "High" as Charlotte Elizabeth's was "Low," they were equally evangelical. Miss
Sewell was not a social reformer, but she was a far better
novelist, ranking almost with Charlotte Yonge in popularity
and literary esteem.[38] Her *Autobiography,* published posthumously in 1907, was edited by her niece Eleanor L.
Sewell, who remarked in a postscript that her aunt's books
"were never intended for amusement, they are distinctly
didactic and intended to illustrate the truths of the Christian faith as practised in English homes." Thanks to a delicacy of perception and a simplicity of language (the result
perhaps of a lifetime of teaching children), Miss Sewell's
novels were far less formidable and solemn than her niece

[38] "Next to Charlotte Yonge, the greatest Anglo-Catholic novelist
before Shorthouse was Elizabeth Missing Sewell" (Baker, *The Novel
and the Oxford Movement,* p. 116). Margaret M. Maison (*The Victorian Vision,* p. 42) considers her "in many ways" superior to Charlotte Yonge—"she goes deeper into the inner life of her characters."

suggests. Her real charm, however, survives, not surprisingly, in her candid, self-revealing memoirs rather than in her fiction. Like her fellow and sister-evangelicals, she had a passion for confession and self-examination. Hers was a less eventful life than either Mrs. Sherwood's or Charlotte Elizabeth's. A happy though strictly disciplined home life, a large family, a long, busy and useful career of parish work and teaching in girls' schools—this constituted the material of her biography.

The one "dramatic" event of Miss Sewell's life appears to have been the accidental discovery on a bookseller's stall of *Tracts for the Times*. She took it home, read it aloud to her sisters and brothers, and discussed it with her elder brother William, a clergyman (author of a lurid anti-Catholic novel *Hawkstone*) who had been a disciple of Newman's at Oxford. Already deeply religious, she found inspiration now to direct her thinking and activities toward propagating the teachings of the Oxford Movement in fiction for young readers. Her model was Mrs. Sherwood, whose stories "in my childhood had been a great source of Sunday amusement." Under the softening influence of domestic realism, however, she resolved to produce a warmer, more natural, and less didactic kind of story that, in spite of its blandness, retains some interest and appeal even for modern readers. Miss Sewell lacks the vitality of Charlotte Yonge. She uses less dialogue and more generalizing character description. But her intentions are so modest that she disarms us. Like Gray almost a century earlier honoring those who "kept the noiseless tenor of their way" in the "cool, sequestered vale of life," or her contemporary George Eliot, who in the conclusion to *Middlemarch* honored "the number who lived faithfully in a hidden life and rest in unvisited tombs" because "the growing good of the world is partly dependent on unhistoric acts," Miss Sewell celebrated the romance of the unromantic, uneventful domestic life:

"I am not going to write a tale, not at least what is usually so called. A tale is, for the most part, only a vignette, a portion of the great picture of life, having no definite limit, yet containing one prominent object, in which all the interest is concentrated. But this is not a real representation of human experience. For one person whose life has been marked by some very striking event, there are hundreds who pass to their graves with nothing to distinguish the different periods of their probation, but the changes which steal upon them so naturally as scarcely to occasion a momentary surprise. They hope and enjoy, they are disappointed and sad, but no one points to the history of their lives as containing warning or example" (*The Experience of Life*, Ch. 1).

The first-person narrator in this fictional autobiography is a sixty-year-old spinster, one of a large family—"my own history is to be found in the history of others"—who traces that history "less with the view of exciting great interest, than with the desire of describing the lot of hundreds similarly placed, and marking the snares into which we have fallen, and the blessings by which we have been supported."

Home—"the Paradise of my brightest joys and holiest affections"—is the center of her story. A shy and delicate child, she early dedicates herself to quiet service to others, her model being a spinster aunt from whom she learns self-mastery: "Trial in some shape or other has followed me from my youth, but there has been no 'must be miserable.' The must, if I believed it to exist, was of my own creation— a phantom which had only to be rightly confronted, and it vanished." The only "plot" in this uneventful novel involves an envious cousin who causes the narrator some brief unhappiness, and a proposal of marriage from a kindly clergyman whom she refuses sorrowfully because she is the main support of her mother and younger sisters.

Willing service and cheerful submission are the homely domestic equivalents of Anglo-Catholic sainthood in Miss Sewell's fiction. In one of her most popular early novels, *Amy Herbert*, the young heroine finds her model in a meek governess, Miss Morton, ". . . her daily life was one of

wearying mortification and self-denial; and yet Emily Morton had never been heard to utter a single murmur . . . her
heart was a perpetual well-spring of quiet gratitude, which
made the heaviest trials of her life sources of improvement
to herself, and of blessing to those around her."[39] In another
novel, *Gertrude* (1845), the heroine, who has inherited a
fortune, must make a painful choice between fulfilling her
dearest dream of building a church ("an infinite privilege
to make an offer of worldly wealth for the benefit of the
Church of Christ") or coming to the assistance of an extravagant brother and sister-in-law who face disgrace and
bankruptcy. In aiding them she makes a noble sacrifice—
"she had schooled herself into submission."

Hand in hand with self-sacrifice of this kind was the
evangelical rejection of self-indulgence and its correspond-
ing distrust of any source of human pleasure. Hannah More
confessed in her diary: "I feel in finishing my garden that
I have too much anxiety to make it beautiful; that it occupies too much of my attention, and tends to give worldly
thoughts a predominance in my mind."[40] Submission to the
will of God demanded asceticism. Dorothea Brooke, given
to "self-mortification," enjoys horseback riding "in a pagan,
sensuous way," but looks forward to renouncing it. "She
likes giving up," her sister shrewdly observes (*Middlemarch,* i, Ch. 2). Maggie Tulliver, having discovered the

---

[39] ii, ch. 5. A shrewd London publisher in Frank Smedley's *Lewis
Arundel* (1852) advises an aspiring author to try to write a novel
like *Amy Herbert*: "Clever book, *Amy Herbert*, very. So much tenderness in it, ma'am; nothing pays better than judicious tenderness;
the mothers of England like it to read about—the daughters of England like it—the little girls of England like it—and so the husbands
of England are forced to pay for it. If you recollect, ma'am, there's a
pathetic governess in *Amy Herbert* who calls the children 'dearest';
well-imagined character, that. She's sold many copies, has that governess." (Quoted by Amy Cruse in *The Victorians and their Reading,*
p. 60.)

[40] *Memoirs of Hannah More,* ed. William Roberts (New York,
1841), ii, 103.

joys of great literature, renounces them—"for Maggie had turned her back on the vain ambition to share the thoughts of the wise. In her first ardour she flung away the books with a sort of triumph that she had risen above the need for them" (*Mill on the Floss*, IV, Ch. 3).[41] Lucy Snowe wrenches herself from the pleasure of keeping Dr. John's letters and buries them—"long pain had made patience a habit. In the end I closed the eyes of my dead, covered its face, and composed its limbs with great calm" (*Villette*, Ch. 26). Guy Morville, Charlotte Yonge's heir of Redclyffe, feels guilty about planning a honeymoon trip—"he could not see that happiness was a reason for going pleasure hunting"— and consoles himself finally that "for fear we should get too much into the stream of enjoyment, as people abroad forget home duties, let us stick to some fixed time for coming back" (Ch. 29).

Sainthood, self-sacrifice, and martyrdom are thus translated into homely virtues, displayed in the lives of ordinary people. Their pangs and struggles are less dramatic in Miss Sewell's quiet stories than they are in the novels of George Eliot and Charlotte Brontë. But they acquire considerably more interest in her *Autobiography*, a record of an evangelical childhood almost harrowing in intensity. As a child Elizabeth's meek, submissive exterior concealed an inner life of wild fancy, a "morbid and over-strained conscience," as she confessed in her veritable passion for self-recrimination. We must of course allow for a generous measure of exaggeration—not of fact but of feeling—produced in a sensitive child by rigorous evangelical teaching. Her fictional Amy Herbert learns "to look upon what are often considered trifling faults in a child—ill-temper, indolence, vanity, greediness, and similar evil dispositions—as real sins in the eyes of God, which must be checked at the very be-

---

[41] See Bernard J. Paris, *Experiments in Life: George Eliot's Quest for Values* (Detroit, 1965), who observes of the young evangelical Marian Evans, "She practiced asceticism. . . . She felt guilty about her delight in nature" (p. 5).

ginning by all who wish to continue what they were made at their baptism—His children" (I, Ch. 7). In real life little Elizabeth, though deeply religious, had "a very violent temper, and was extremely self-willed." It was difficult for her to separate religious faith from imaginative fancy: "I was always given to strange, scrupulous fancies, and not long before had made myself miserable, after reading about Jephthah's vow, because I imagined that every time the thought of making a vow came into my head I had actually made it, and was bound to keep it. I even went so far as to worry myself with the question whether I was not bound to kill my mother, because I thought I had made a vow that I would" (Ch. 4).

So riddled with guilt was this little girl that she developed a compulsive urge for confession. School was a grim prison run by a strict disciplinarian appropriately named Miss Crooke—a real life Lowood, if not Dotheboys Hall, where a child was punished for lying by being made to stand for hours in a long black gown wearing around her neck a piece of red cloth in the shape of a tongue with the word "Liar" spelled out on it in large white letters, where even to hesitate in reciting a lesson was reckoned a mistake, and where the chilly unheated bedroom, shared by five girls, had its windows blocked up to prevent their looking out. In these wretched surroundings Elizabeth managed to retain enough spirit to inscribe an exercise book with the initials "O.W.," referring to Miss Crooke as "Old Witch" and to conceal the book from her teacher. But as a result she suffered such agonies of conscience that she was driven to a public confession: "My conscience, however, went on working; having once begun to confess, the practice became a necessity, and I begged that I might be allowed to tell every day the things I had done wrong, because I felt so wicked. Miss Crooke treated me at first as a converted penitent, but by degrees she must have become alarmed. My confessions verged on the ludicrous, and the climax must have been reached when having received an order in common with my companions to mention if we saw any black beetles in the schoolroom, I made it a subject of confession that I had seen a black beetle crawl out from under a large bureau, and had not told of it" (Ch. 4).

Within the circumscribed limits of a life like Elizabeth Missing Sewell's the little crises of childhood loomed large and left deep impressions on the adult character. Carried over into her fiction they remain minor, but to the Victorian reader they had profound moral significance. The relatively new emphasis on children as characters, as individuals with developing personalities ripe to be shaped, reflects many emerging nineteenth-century interests—in education, in psychology, in social conditioning. Among these concerns evangelicalism played an important role. Overt didacticism disappears in the major novels of the period, or rather it is absorbed in more artistic and logical form, becoming an integral part of the total developing characterization and theme. An example of a transitional novel, where the evangelical elements are every bit as pronounced as they were in Miss Sewell but the manner is lighter, more subtle and humorous, is the highly esteemed *The Fairy Bower* (1841) by Mrs. Harriett Mozley.

The Fairy Bower is another of those "semi-developed" novels intended for young readers but endearing themselves to older readers by their simplicity and freshness. It is concerned with the education, practical and religious, of children, but instead of writing long didactic essays and speeches expounding her ideas, Mrs. Mozley develops them in a story about a Christmas house party where a group of parents and children are assembled. Mainly she focusses on little Grace Leslie and her widowed mother, a devoted parent-child relationship not unlike the close mother-daughter relationship in Miss Sewell's *Amy Herbert*. To appreciate the difference in spirit between these novels, however, one need only compare any two passages of dialogue. Amy and her mother discourse in a lengthy catechism, the

184

child asking carefully directed questions, the mother reply-
ing in long expositions of the faith. Grace and her mother
chat in easy conversation: " 'Mama,' said the little girl timidly, 'would you be so very kind as to tell me if you think I
did right?'

" 'My dear child,' answered Mrs. Leslie, 'I cannot quite
tell without having been present; young people together are
apt to become rude or forget themselves, and if one can put
a little check upon the rest without being tiresome, it is very
right and proper.'

" 'Ah, mamma,' said Grace, despondingly, 'there is the
difficulty—"without being tiresome" ' " (Ch. 14).

Grace suffers her crisis of conscience as a result of allowing another girl to take credit for designing a bower that is
her work. Once involved in an act of deliberate concealment, she is forced to conceal more to cover up. But the
whole matter is treated with delicacy. Grace is not morbid.
She feels guilty, but "She was not of that weak cast of heart
that would make herself more guilty than she was; nor did
she brood over such things. Hers was healthy habit of mind,
that turned her failings, her pains, and her pleasures, to
some good account, present or future" (Ch. 31). Later,
when the matter has been cleared up, her mother reminds
her gently that "you should therefore take this visit as a
trial, a sort of *rehearsal*, Grace, that you may act properly
when you are on the real stage of life" (Ch. 43).

IV

The Fairy Bower was much admired by a young woman
just beginning her literary career when it was first published—Charlotte Yonge. Many years later she described
it as "a memorable book" that set up "a wave of opinion" on
which her own "little craft" floated. In its time, Miss Yonge
wrote, it had the charm of novelty too, "an attempt rather
to exhibit characters as they really are, than to exhibit

185

moral portraitures for unreserved imitation or avoidance. . . . It introduces young persons to those scenes and situations of life which are their actual sphere and trial."[42]

The gap between tract and family novel was finally and effectively bridged by Charlotte Yonge. Many other women writers worked in this same genre of religious-domestic novel in the mid-nineteenth century. Grace Aguilar's *Home Influence: A Tale for Mothers and Daughters* emphasized the important role of a mother in the religious training of her children. Julia Kavanagh's *Rachel Gray* (1856) recorded the drab life of a pious, self-sacrificing spinster seamstress; George Eliot wrote in *The Leader* (January 5, 1856) that it "professes to show how Christianity exhibits itself as a refining and consoling impulse in the most prosaic stratum of society, the small shopkeeping class." Dinah Mulock Craik, who affirmed that the modern novel was "one of the most important moral agents in the community,"[43] published the highly successful *John Halifax, Gentleman* (1857) about a self-made businessman hero and his family who represents the evangelical ideal of Calvinistic industry combined with Christ-like humility. Even as major a novelist as Mrs. Gaskell wrote much short fiction in the tradition of the simple evangelical tract for *Howitt's Journal* and the *Sunday School Parish Magazine*. A Unitarian, she practiced her religion by emphasizing social reform, by pleading the cause of the oppressed and exploited, with just as much evangelical zeal and considerably more art than Charlotte Elizabeth.[44] But Charlotte Yonge, among all these writers, was the novelist who most gracefully converted the tractarian impulse into novels of family life.

[42] Quoted in Kathleen Tillotson's "Harriett Mozley," in *Mid-Victorian Studies* (London, 1965), p. 42.

[43] "To Novelists—and a Novelist" (a review of *Adam Bede* and *The Mill on the Floss*), in *The Unkind Word and Other Stories* (Leipzig, 1869), I, 296.

[44] Edgar Wright, *Mrs. Gaskell: The Basis for Reassessment* (London, 1965), Ch. 3, "Religion and Purpose."

In "the inner life of the family," a contributor to the *Christian Remembrancer* wrote in 1860, "instead of a disquisition on daily prayer, or confession . . . the good effects of the practice of these things is shown . . . [and] faith is illustrated more by the life of the character described than by mere theological terms."[45] Thus when Mrs. Margaret Oliphant observed, through the mouthpiece of a character in her *Phoebe, Junior* (1876), that "one reads Scott for Scotland . . . and one reads Miss Yonge for the church," she was not praising her contemporary's mastery of theology so much as her skill at portraying a real society, a "new world of excellent Church people, good, noble and true, with all their fads and little foolishnesses, all their habits of mind and speech, their delightful family affection, and human varieties of goodness."[46] Mrs. Oliphant perceived that Charlotte Yonge's hold on her readers was the result of her preoccupation with human-domestic concerns within a broadly Christian framework. Church-building, Sunday-School teaching, missionary and parish work are the activities in which her characters engage, but these are Anglo-Catholic only to the extent that Charlotte set her novels in a particular community, at a particular time. High, Broad, or Low in their church preferences, her readers were concerned with her characters' problems of daily living far more than with their problems of dogma and ritual.

Nevertheless, the dogma and ritual of Anglo-Catholicism filled Charlotte Yonge's personal life as fully as romance and motherhood filled the lives of most women of her generation. From her confirmation at fifteen, she dedicated herself to her religion. Her writing began with and essentially never moved beyond the simple tales she published in the *Monthly Packet* to give religious instruction to school children. The money she made went to support church building

[45] "The Moral Character of Story Books," *Christian Remembrancer*, 40 (July-December, 1860), p. 61.

[46] *The Victorian Age of English Literature* (New York, 1892), pp. 493-94.

and the missionary work of the Society for the Propagation of the Gospel. Her religion was parochial in the most literal sense. She shared her work totally with her parents, publishing only with their consent. Her spiritual guide was the vicar of her home church, John Keble, who brought the Oxford Movement to her own hearthside. Therefore it is hardly surprising that her fiction should be equally parochial and domestic. She describes her most popular novel after *The Heir of Redclyffe* (1853), *The Daisy Chain*, as "a Family Chronicle—a domestic record of home events, large and small, during those years of early life when the character is chiefly formed," a book "of a nondescript class" intended for an audience somewhere in between the nursery and the adult world. Her modest disclaimer was sincere. Charlotte Yonge never aspired to literary greatness and never regarded her talent as more than simply another tool with which to work for the celebration of God. Although she took healthy satisfaction in the stunning success of *The Heir of Redclyffe*, she also confided her fears about "vain-glory" to Keble. He responded comfortingly, "not telling one not to enjoy the praise, and like to hear it talked about," and reminding her of the pleasure that her success brought her mother and father.[47]

Everywhere in Charlotte's life spiritual values were translated into domestic ones, and this habit she quite naturally carried over into her fiction. The highest praise we can render her is that her method was one of religious translation or transference, but not reduction. In her work religion is seen in its simplest, homeliest garb, yet it retains its dignity and profundity. Her talent was slight, her range of thought and experience narrow, her conception of human passion confined mainly to adolescent moods of temper, envy, and sentimental love, but within those limitations she achieved psychologically sound and valid percep-

[47] Letter to Miss Dyson, February 23, 1853, in Christabel Coleridge, *Charlotte Mary Yonge: Her Life and Letters* (London, 1903), p. 192.

tions. Henry James had high regard for her. Although he had described the type of fiction she wrote as "semi-developed novels . . . books which grown women may read aloud to children without either party being bored," he considered *The Heir of Redclyffe* a novel legitimated "by the force of genius." This occurs, however, "only when a first-rate mind takes the matter in hand . . . a mind which . . . is the master and not the slave of its material."[48] Her characters are conditioned by the reality of their family and religious experiences. They react spontaneously and sensitively. Many of them are idealistic, but some are self-serving, selfish, and callow. Villainy—in the conventional fictive sense—rarely figures in her novels. Occasionally, in response to the vogues of the sensational novel, she introduces some episode of melodrama or violence (in *The Trial* there is even a murder), but she dismisses it quickly to get back to the comfortable business of Christian family living. Even her idealism is practical rather than visionary. Her heroine of *The Daisy Chain* refuses marriage not to become a nun in a cloister or a martyr-missionary in some distant jungle but to keep house for her widowed father and to raise her younger brothers and sisters. "Her religion," Joseph E. Baker remarks, "is not mysticism, but church-going raised to the *n*th degree. She does not take us into the world of ideas nor of great events, but of personal domestic feeling."[49]

Circumscribed as a world of "personal domestic feeling" must be—especially for a Victorian spinster who rarely travelled beyond her village of Otterbourne and who devoted her life to parents and church—it is nevertheless a lively

[48] *Notes and Reviews*, p. 78. Not long after writing this review James introduced the novel into his own *Watch and Ward* (1871) as favorite reading of his young heroine Nora: "She had grown in the interval, from the little girl who slept with *The Child's Own Book* under her pillow and dreamed of Prince Avenant, into a lofty maiden who reperused *The Heir of Redclyffe*, and mused upon the loves of the clergy" (Ch. 5).

[49] *The Novel and the Oxford Movement*, p. 111.

and emotionally engaging world. Ethel May, one of a brood of eleven children, growing up from painful, clumsy adolescence into warm maturity, is one of those secular saint-heroines of the sisterhood of Maggie Tulliver and Dorothea Brooke. Her ardent idealism is no less ardent than theirs, only it is confined to the more humble goals of building a village church and establishing a school for some poor children in the neighborhood. Intellectually Ethel aspires as loftily as these others; she reads widely and keeps up with her brother in the study of Latin and Greek. Her sensibilities are keen and delicate, though never exaggerated. She displays a natural guilty conscience when she neglects a younger brother, allowing him almost to set himself on fire while she is engrossed in a book. Awkward, near-sighted, and plain in appearance, she is understandably timid and self-conscious. At the ceremony opening the little school that she helped to establish, she suffers paralyzing embarrassment: "She took hold of Flora's hand, and squeezed it hard, in a fit of shyness, when they came upon the hamlet, and saw the children watching for them; and when they reached the house she would fain have shrunk into nothing; there was a swelling of heart that seemed to overwhelm and stifle her, and the effect of which was to keep her standing unhelpful, when the others were busy bringing in the benches and settling the room" (Pt. I, Ch. 17).

But Ethel May is the focussing center of a larger-scale domestic drama than these merely parochial events would indicate. The novel that begins with a cosy and idyllic domestic scene of family prayer ("It was pleasant to see that large family in the hush and reverence of such teaching, the mother's gentle power preventing the outbreaks of restlessness to which even at such times the wild young spirits were liable") switches suddenly in the third chapter to tragedy. A carriage accident kills the mother, permanently cripples the eldest daughter, leaves the father, who had been the driver, seriously injured and morbidly brooding over his responsibility for the disaster. In an instant this large happy

190

family is bereaved and the problems and duties of adulthood are thrust upon the older children. At a single blow
Ethel's "myriads of fancies" about finding money to build
a church ("She had heard in books, of girls writing poetry,
romance, history—gaining fifties and hundreds. . . . She
would compose, publish, earn money—some day call papa,
show him her hoard, beg him to take it, and never owning
whence it came, raise the building. Spire and chancel, pin-
nacle and buttress rose before her eyes. . . .") are shattered.
Holding her infant sister in transcendent love she quietly
prays: "We have the keeping of you, mama's precious flower, her pearl of truth! Oh, may God guard you to be an un-
stained jewel, till you come back to her again—and a
blooming flower, till you are gathered into the wreath that
never fades—my own sweet poor little motherless Daisy"
(Pt. I, Ch. 4).

A healthy resiliency in the May family—and in their creator Charlotte Yonge—saves the novel from the maudlin
and the morbid. Their Christianity is a working faith that
carries them gropingly but successfully through their increasingly heavy domestic responsibilities. Ethel May
learns "that to embrace a task heartily renders it no longer
irksome," so she sets about nursing her invalid sister Margaret, educating her younger brothers and sisters, cheering
her father, and teaching in the village school. She sacrifices
her own studies as later she sacrifices her one opportunity
to marry; but this is done in such a natural easy manner
that neither she nor the reader broods over the alternatives:
"If there had ever been disappointment about Norman
Ogilvie [her suitor], it had long since faded away. . . . She
had her vocation, in her father, Margaret, the children,
home and Cocksmoor [her school], her mind and affections
were occupied, and she never thought of wishing herself
elsewhere" (Pt. II, Ch. 24).

In Charlotte Yonge's fiction even more strikingly than in
Elizabeth Missing Sewell's, the Church functions both literally and metaphorically. Not only are her characters ac-

tively engaged in religious practice, but that practice assumes symbolic and dramatic significance. Confirmation and the taking of the sacrament mark peaks and climaxes in her stories: Guy's receiving the last rites of the Anglo-Catholic Church in a remote Italian village in *The Heir of Redclyffe*, the final "awakening" of the two misguided young sisters of *The Castle Builders* (1854) in the ceremony of their confirmation, the consecration of the church that marks the climax of *The Daisy Chain*. Church building, especially the restoration of neglected ruins, becomes a goal, a romantic ideal. In *The Daisy Chain* even the form of the new church memorializes the ill-fated lovers of the story, Alan Ernescliffe and Margaret May: its timbered roof is shaped like the ribs of a ship because Alan had been a sailor, and Margaret's pearl engagement ring is placed around the stem of the chalice.

Charlotte Yonge's special genius, which distinguishes her charming and still readable novels from the run of evangelical fiction, was her ability to integrate her material. Where Miss Sewell, Grace Aguilar, and Julia Kavanagh stop their narratives cold for their moralizing and have their simple homely characters speak the formal rhetoric of the pulpit, Charlotte writes sprightly, natural dialogue, keeps her story going briskly at all times, invents fitting occasions for the introduction of religious solemnities and then carefully balances these with lighter incidents. Knowing instinctively when to open windows for fresh air, she weaves her moralizing into the fabric of her tales. For example, the staple of evangelical fiction is the naughty child punished for some infraction like concealment, lying, or cheating. In Mrs. Sherwood, the classic of this mode, the punishments, as we have noted, were positively Draconian, and the reader is often left to feel that if denied a providential early death, an unpunished child will grow up a monster of moral corruption. Under the softening influences of domestic realism, however, Charlotte Yonge can make the same moral lesson a touching little case history in child psychology. Young brother Tom of *The Daisy Chain* first shows disturbing symptoms of dishonesty at home when he looks up answers to lessons he is preparing. Failing to warn their father to reprimand him at this early stage, his brothers and sisters allow him to go off to school ("a scene of temptation"), where, with his bad habits unchecked, Tom lies and gets into trouble. The consequences are painful for everyone. An older brother who assumes the blame to protect him loses a scholarship. But he generously comforts the contrite Tom, "If this sets you on always telling truth, I shan't think any great harm done." The lesson is duly learned, and Tom's repentance and reform are assured:

"'And you'll try and speak the truth, and be straightforward?'

"'I will, I will,' said Tom, worn out in spirits by his long bondage, and glad to catch at the hope of relief and protection.

"'Then let us come home,' and Tom put his hand into his brother's, as a few weeks back would have seemed most unworthy of school-boy dignity" (Pt. I, Ch. 22).

This gift for story-telling, combined with her high moral purpose, made Charlotte Yonge at once both a popular and an "approved" novelist. Although Owen Chadwick surely over-rates her as "one of the true creative novelists of the nineteenth century, with two or three of her books ranking among the best Christian novels of any age," he weighs her reputation accurately in pointing out that she was "in one respect a channel for the most powerful influence which shy and reserved John Keble exercised upon the Victorian churches."[50] The novel in which that influence was most powerfully displayed was *The Heir of Redclyffe*.

The phenomenon of a best-selling novel that could simultaneously appeal to the most naive and sentimental of readers as well as to the highly educated and most mature minds of its age was less rare in the nineteenth century than it would be today. In 1853 *The Heir of Redclyffe* caught the

[50] *The Victorian Church*, II, 215.

attention and affection of the widest conceivable public and held it tenaciously for nearly fifty years. It was a family novel, written in a careful and correct style, with many literary allusions and a general spirit of religious sanctity that marked it as eminently suitable for impressionable young readers, all the more so because it firmly demonstrated the importance of filial obedience and the wrongs of secret marriage engagements. Without excessive moralizing it unequivocally endorsed all the values esteemed by Church, State, and Family—honor, bravery, truth, faith, obedience, and duty. At the same time, it was an easy-reading, spirited novel, full of lively dialogue, enough mild suspense to hold flagging interest, a tender love story, and an appealing romanticism, cooled and tempered from Byronic and Shelleyan flamboyance into a refined aestheticism. Charlotte Yonge's romanticism developed in the age of Prince Albert, not Napoleon. The vestiges of that older romanticism remained in her hero's name, Sir Guy Morville, in his crumbling gothic family manor house, and the family curse that dates back to one of the murderers of Thomas à Becket. But at most this is a pale pre-Raphaelite gothicism, and we learn without surprise that young William Morris and Edward Burne-Jones read it enthusiastically at Oxford and that Dante Gabriel Rossetti "loved and reverenced it."[51]

The new romanticism that *The Heir of Redclyffe* heralds is an introspective, gentle-genteel, somewhat melancholy backward glance at a colorful but long-dead past. The novel captures that moment of transition between Byron's *Giaour* ("bad food for excitable minds," though *Childe Harold* might still be read with profit for "his descriptions of scenery") and Tennyson's *Idylls of the King*. This romanticism found its outlet not in social rebellion, as it had earlier in the century, but in religious reform. The characters in *The Heir of Redclyffe* are lay people; they are not even remotely concerned with theology or problems of religious

[51] Cruse, *The Victorians and their Reading*, p. 52. See Tillotson, *Mid-Victorian Studies*, pp. 49-50.

conflict such as we find in many novels of this period. But they were conceived by an author so thoroughly imbued with religious spirit that her hero was immediately identified as a hero of the Oxford Movement. He is an Anglo-Catholic Galahad (an artist painting his portrait sees him as Sir Galahad kneeling before the Holy Grail), defending the memory of the Stuart Charles I, reading *I Promessi Sposi*, rapt in admiration of a Raphael madonna. Under the influence of her mentor John Keble, Charlotte Yonge had read and, just before beginning this novel, re-read the collection of papers and sermons of one of his students—the *Remains of the Late Reverend Richard Hurrell Froude* that Keble and Newman had edited in 1838. Here was a clerical Guy Morville, whose combination of aesthetic, sentimental, sensitive, and intellectual graces, with "vivid appreciation of the idea of sanctity" and profound faith had inspired Newman "to look with admiration" toward Rome.[52] When Charlotte first conceived the character of Guy and described him to her mother, Mrs. Yonge promptly responded, "Like Mr. Hurrell Froude," to which Charlotte reacted with homely delight at this "sign that I have got the right sow by the ear."[53]

As a romantic hero Guy is admittedly tame and domestic. He is an awkward, lonely adolescent thrust into the lives of a large, hearty family. He makes harmless blunders; he is not especially brilliant or talented, nor is he even strikingly handsome. He falls in love with exactly the right girl, as sweet and loving as he is, and marries her when he has barely come of age. Only a premature death prevents him from settling down to a domestic life as wholesome, though on a somewhat higher social scale, as the one Charlotte Yonge portrayed in *The Daisy Chain*. But Guy also serves higher heroic purposes of self-sacrifice, forgiveness of his enemies, and redemption of the souls of others. He is one

[52] Robert A. Colby, "The Poetical Structure of Newman's *Apologia pro Vita Sua*," *Journal of Religion*, 33 (January, 1953), p. 54.

[53] Coleridge, *Charlotte Mary Yonge*, p. 170.

of those potential saints whose mission, though earth-bound, is spiritual and sacred. *The Heir of Redclyffe* began with an idea suggested to Charlotte by her spinster school-teacher friend Marianne Dyson, who had herself started but then abandoned a story of two characters, "the essentially contrite and the self-satisfied . . . the conceited hero was to persecute the other and finally to cause his death, which was to be to his worldly advantage." The theme was to be the contrition and suffering of this hero—"the penitence of the saints." Miss Dyson's idea fascinated Charlotte, who continued to consult her friend as she shaped her novel. In their letters we can trace the developing domestic and romantic features of what began as a sternly moralistic tale. The emphasis shifts from Miss Dyson's self-satisfied hero, who is Charlotte Yonge's Philip Morville, to the persecuted victim Guy. The family of his guardian becomes prominent: "I *think* there should be some instances of wild escapades of fun together with a tremendous temper, the very vice of the house of Morville. I think a fiery temper would be the thing that would chiefly leave on Guy's mind the impression that he was and must be good for nothing . . . how he finds himself enjoying the lively family too much, and curbs himself sometimes in an odd sudden way which is now and then misunderstood and gives offence."[54]

Charlotte conceived her task as "the playwright work of devising action and narrative." She refers to her characters as "my dramatis personae" and lets them ramble on and grow freely. Peopling her story with the Edmonstone family, she varies, enriches, and vitalizes it—the wise and understanding mother, the hot-tempered but forgiving father, three daughters ranging from young lady down to little girl, an outspoken invalid brother, visiting friends and relatives. Small wonder the novel appealed to all levels of readership and retained its popularity as long as large closely knit family households survived.

[54] *Ibid.*, pp. 162, 171.

196

It is easy to dismiss *The Heir of Redclyffe* as innocent adolescent romance, a sentimental love story full of pathos and Christian moralizing. Charlotte Yonge herself had no more lofty ambitions than to write this kind of novel. But the shaping influences of Evangelicalism produced more than she had anticipated. The intense spirituality of the work, its emphasis on revealed Truth, on scrupulous examination of the conscience and the heart, on the motivations of human actions, and their moral consequences, produced in this most proper and orthodox of Victorian novels some disquieting insights and raised some questions that propriety and orthodoxy could not so easily answer. A hero manifestly intelligent, noble in character, and firm in his religious faith is nevertheless misunderstood, misjudged, and —what is more disturbing—misunderstands and misjudges himself. He is forever struggling in the snares of guilt and doubt. We are told, and he believes, that he has a violent temper. He broods over "the frenzy of his rage and his own murderous impulse," but these passions are never portrayed. Gentle Guy's only weakness of character, at least so far as the reader can observe, is "what some would call a vivid imagination, others a lively faith." He has, to be sure, a tendency to bite his lip when he is provoked and now and then to clench his teeth, but considering how sorely he is tried by his cousin Philip's unjust accusations, it is his self-control rather than his temper that is remarkable. Guy is a Christian hero, far less molded by the family curse of temper than by the Protestant-evangelical habit of self-analysis: "Many a question did he ask himself, to certify whether he wilfully entertained malice, or hatred, or any uncharitableness. It was a long difficult examination, but at its close, he felt convinced that, if such passions knocked at the door of his heart, it was not at his own summons, and that he drove them away without listening to them" (Ch. 18).

His antagonist Philip Morville is an infinitely more complex and troubled figure. To all appearances a model of virtuous and prudential behavior, he is inwardly a sinister and destructive agent, all the more frightening because of his total inability to doubt or question his actions. He is goodness perverted and blinded by self-righteousness. He acts malevolently out of what he believes are benign motives— "I speak for your good," he warns Guy, genuinely convinced that he does. "Philip had been used to feel men's wills and characters bend and give way beneath his superior force of mind. . . . With Guy alone it was not so; he had been sensible of it once or twice before; he had no mastery, and could no more bend that spirit than a bar of steel. This he could not bear, for it obliged him to be continually making efforts to preserve his own sense of superiority" (Ch. 19).

Driven by an almost Puritanical zeal, though he presumably shares the High Church beliefs of his cousins, "firm in his preconceived idea . . . and his own knowledge of mankind," Philip perverts good. When his cousin refuses to account for a large sum of money he has spent, Philip leaps to the conclusion that he is gambling. On receiving news that seemingly confirms his suspicions, "a sudden gleam, as of exultation in a verified prophecy, lighted his eye, shading off quickly, however, and giving place to an iron expression of rigidity and sternness, the compressed mouth, coldly fixed eye, and sedate brow, composed into a grave severity that might have served for an impersonation of stern justice" (Ch. 14). Unshakable in his convictions, he rejects Guy's open-hearted denial of the charge as "his usual course of mystery, reserve, and defiance." Instead of questioning his own conduct, Philip rationalizes and justifies it, thus anticipating by some fifteen years the casuistical evangelical Nicholas Bulstrode of *Middlemarch*, "a man whose desires had been stronger than his theoretic beliefs, and who had gradually explained the gratification of his desires into satisfactory agreement with those beliefs."[55]

[55] *Middlemarch*, Bk. vi, ch. 61. George Eliot had just read the theologian Frederic Denison Maurice's *The Conscience: Lectures on*

In attempting to portray this devious, complex, ambivalent young man, Charlotte Yonge accepted a greater challenge than perhaps at first she recognized. Philip's relentless persecution of Guy begins innocently, in the desire of an upright young man to correct and reform a younger man. But unconsciously Philip harbors two rankling, corrosive prejudices against Guy—one, the family curse of temper, of which he believes Guy guilty even when proved innocent; the other an unconscious jealousy of Guy's riches and his estate at Redclyffe to which Philip has only a remote claim: "He paused at the gate, and looked back at the wide domain and fine old house. He pitied them, and the simple-hearted, honest tenantry, for being the heritage of such a family, and the possession of one so likely to misuse them, instead of training them into the means of conferring benefits on them, on his country. What would not Philip himself do if those lands were his—just what was needed to give his talents free scope? And what would it be to see his beautiful Laura their mistress?" (Ch. 19).

Like the envious Satan, Philip cannot endure happiness in others because it is denied to him. In perfect character, however, with this simple, unmelodramatic family story, he destroys Guy's Eden not by a deliberate act of malice, but out of the same qualities of self-righteousness and moral superiority that have already warped him. Meeting Guy and his young bride Amabel on their honeymoon in Italy, he tries to persuade them to travel with him to a region where fever is raging. When they refuse, he stubbornly sets out alone, catches the fever, and nearly dies. Guy, who comes to nurse him, also falls ill, and as Philip recovers he dies. Thus Philip becomes the heir to the property he has coveted and outlives the man he has envied. But in Guy's noble Christian death, Philip is reborn, contrite and penitent. He has learned his lesson at a terrible price, and al-

---

Casuistry (1868). See Robert A. Colby, *Fiction with a Purpose* (Bloomington, Ind., 1967), pp. 277-87.

though the novel ends with his possession of Redclyffe and his marriage to Laura, we see him as a broken, grieving man, finding consolation only in the little daughter Guy has left behind him.

Charlotte Yonge did not dramatize this struggle in Manichean terms, but, in what they represent, Philip and Guy are men in mortal spiritual conflict. Guy's victory is as inevitable as the reversal of a classical tragedy or the victory of Christ in the Battle of the Angels. In *The Heir of Redclyffe* the battlefield of the Victorian conscience is the family. For all its apparently idyllic blessings, this family is plagued with pain and sorrow: young brother Charlie is a helpless cripple with an agonizing bone disease; sister Laura is frustrated in her lengthy secret engagement; Guy's father had been killed in an accident following a violent quarrel with his grandfather; his mother dies in childbed; his uncle is a shabby musician unable to support his wife and children; Philip's sister is a cold-blooded mercenary shrew; Guy dies on his honeymoon, leaving his wife pregnant; Philip never recovers physically or mentally from the ravages of his fever.

Charlotte Yonge's vision of life, however, was not as morbid as this summary suggests, nor was she, we may confidently assert, slyly preaching cynicism or rebellion. Rather, under an impulse evangelical in its fervor to present Truth as she saw it, she depicted human suffering as conscientiously as she depicted happiness. Accepting unquestioningly the tenets of her Christian faith, she accepted evil, sin, guilt, suffering, and redemption. In such a vision happiness is at best tenuous. Like all evangelicals, the Anglo-Catholic Charlotte Yonge contemplated it with mixed feelings. "Do you recollect," Amabel asks her young husband Guy, "your melancholy definition of happiness years ago?" It was, she reminds him, "Gleams from another world, too soon eclipsed or forfeited" (Ch. 32). It is significant that so relatively large a part of this novel is devoted to the reconciliations that follow Guy's untimely death. The conclusion is a long, tearful epilogue, dwelling in almost microscopic detail on Amy's saintly bravery in her widowhood, on her noble forgiveness of Philip, on his lengthy spiritual and physical convalescence, on the legal details of settling the Morville estate (Charlotte does not ignore the paradox of her title). Faulty as all this is both emotionally and artistically, it is part of the overall evangelical scheme of the novel, translating dogma into the everyday realities of family life and human suffering.

V

THE vogue of the evangelical domestic novel was relatively short-lived. It flourished mainly in the 1830's and 1840's, although in stories written for children and young girls its influence persisted until the end of the century. Both Elizabeth Missing Sewell and Charlotte Yonge lived into the twentieth century themselves, long enough to witness the waning of their popularity. As early as 1861, in a letter to Miss Sewell (with whom she once collaborated on a book of historical readings), Charlotte ruefully quoted the *Morning Post*, "which kindly says that no young people read my books, though their mammas wish them to do so, because they are so emotional."[56] Actually her novels were still thriving at that period. *The Heir of Redclyffe* went into its 22nd edition in 1876, and thanks perhaps to the persistent "mammas" it continued to be read into the present century.[57] Even among her adult contemporaries Charlotte

[56] A.L.S., February 18, 1861, in the Henry W. and Albert A. Berg Collection, New York Public Library, Astor, Lenox and Tilden Foundations.

[57] Among more recent admirers who have written on her are Georgina Battiscombe, *Charlotte Mary Yonge: The Story of an Uneventful Life* (London, 1943); Margaret Mare and Alice C. Percival, *Victorian Best-Seller: The World of Charlotte Yonge* (London, 1948); and Kathleen Tillotson, whose BBC talk given on the centenary of *The Heir of Redclyffe* in 1953 is published in *Mid-Victorian Studies*, pp. 49-55.

Yonge enjoyed enduring respect. In 1861, the same year that the *Post* had commented on her declining popularity, George Henry Lewes bought a copy of *The Daisy Chain* for George Eliot.[58]

The significance of the evangelical novel, however, cannot be charted by sales records. Obviously its vogue declined along with the exhaustion and decline of the evangelical movement itself. But its influence outlived its vogue. Children's literature is notoriously laggard, always at least one generation and often more behind the trends of the times. Guided no doubt by those zealous mammas, evangelical novels found their way into the hands of juvenile readers, thereby unconsciously influencing generations that would consciously reject them. Furthermore, the climate of ideas in which these novels flourished in the first half of the nineteenth century was the same climate in which the major figures of Victorian society and letters were themselves growing up. The Brontës, George Eliot, Buckle, Pattison, Samuel Butler, Kingsley, De Quincey, Ruskin, Macaulay, Jowett, Gladstone, Pusey, Newman, Manning, Elizabeth Barrett—all were evangelical in their family backgrounds, although none of them remained evangelical in later life.[59]

Preeminent among that list of eminent Victorians is George Eliot. With her unfailing conviction that nothing in the experience of life is wasted, she retrieved from the evangelicalism of her youth a profound respect for its power to stir and raise men's souls: "Nevertheless, Evangelicalism had brought into palpable existence and operation in Milby society that idea of duty, that recognition of something to be lived for beyond the mere satisfaction of self, which is to the moral life what the addition of a great cen-

[58] He bought it on Anthony Trollope's recommendation. Gordon Haight observes, "Unfortunately, no comment about it has been recorded" (*George Eliot* [New York, 1968], p. 344).

[59] Ford K. Brown, *Fathers of the Victorians: The Age of Wilberforce* (Cambridge, 1961), p. 6.

tral ganglion is to animal life. No man can begin to mold himself on a faith or an idea without rising to a higher order of experience: a principle of subordination, of self-mastery, has been introduced into his nature; he is no longer a mere bundle of impressions, desires, and impulses" ("Janet's Repentance," Ch. 10).

She had discarded the faith itself long before she began writing her first fiction—not without a certain diffidence and embarrassment, recognizing in that ardent and solemn young girl who "enjoyed" the letters of Hannah More ("the contemplation of so blessed a character as hers is very salutary")[60] a mildly ridiculous figure. Years later she satirized her in the blue-stocking Miss Pratt of "Janet's Repentance" —"I have ever considered fiction a suitable form for conveying moral and religious instruction." But Marian Evans' religious ardor—those years of her adolescence when evangelical Christianity had such a powerful hold on her—is preserved in her fiction. The childish awe that she recalled in a cancelled passage of "Amos Barton"—"Oh that happy time of childish veneration! It is the fashion to regret the days of easy merriment, but we forget the early bliss of easy reverence when the world seemed to us to be peopled with the great and wise, when the old weather-prognosticating gardener was our Socrates, and our spirits quailed before the clergyman without needing to be convinced of the Apostolic Succession. Words cannot convey the awe I felt for every member of the Shepperton choir"[61]—was gently satirized but never forgotten. She mocked the canting clergy, the complacent, self-satisfied bourgeois worshippers, the sectarian bigots, the silly lady novelists who romanticized the "white-neckcloth" ("a kind of genteel tract on a large scale, intended as a sort of medicinal sweetmeat for

[60] *Letters*, I, 7.

[61] This passage is published in Thomas A. Noble's *George Eliot's Scenes of Clerical Life* (New Haven, 1965), p. 46, a study to which I am much indebted.

Low Church young ladies; an Evangelical substitute for the fashionable novel . . ."),[62] but she never denied the staying power of the past and its shaping influence upon the present. Evangelicalism discarded was still experience enduring, feeding upon memory and association so that it remained vital in her art.

Scenes of Clerical Life is neither autobiographical nor reminiscential as, for example, was *The Mill on the Floss*. Drawing on the past mainly because it seemed the only way to begin a novel, she made her first timid attempts in September 1856 with "an introductory chapter describing a Staffordshire village and the life of the neighbouring farm houses."[63] She scrapped that effort, but when she began her first real work of fiction, "The Sad Fortunes of the Reverend Amos Barton," it was set in the past exactly parallel with her own youth—"Shepperton Church was a very different-looking building five-and-twenty years ago." Evangelicalism suffuses this first book more than any other of her novels. It is treated explicitly in two of the three tales and is indeed the main theme of one of them, "Janet's Repentance." Its influence, however, is pervasive in all her work—negatively in her satire and condemnation of bigotry and complacency, positively in her frustrated secular "saints" like Dinah Morris, Maggie Tulliver, and Dorothea Brooke, thematically in her studies of guilt, conscience, self-examination, and moral character development.

Though not a polemic in the cause of evangelicalism, "Janet's Repentance" so loads the case against the opposition that from the outset our sympathies are enlisted for the evangelical clergyman, Mr. Tryan. The bullying, ignorant Dempster and his cohorts represent extreme positions, but they state the anti-evangelical case clearly: " 'That's not the worst,' said Mr. Dempster, 'he preaches against good

[62] *Westminster Review*, 66 (October, 1856), p. 456; reprinted in *The Essays of George Eliot*, ed. Thomas Pinney (New York, 1963), pp. 301-24.

[63] *Letters*, II, 406.

works; says good works are not necessary to salvation—a sectarian, antinomian, anabaptist doctrine. Tell a man he is not to be saved by his works, and you open the flood-gates of all immorality. You see it in all these canting inno-vators; they're all bad ones by the sly; smooth-faced, drawl-ing, hypocritical fellows, who pretend ginger isn't hot in their mouths, and cry down all innocent pleasures; their hearts are all the blacker for their sanctimonious outsides'" (Ch. 1).

In rejecting the Dempsterites the reader finds himself almost automatically embracing the evangelical cause. But George Eliot enlists her reader's sympathy more rationally by demonstrating in this lean and powerfully realistic vig-nette of provincial life that cant and hypocrisy are not the exclusive property of the evangelicals. The "immorality" that Dempster deplores is really the challenge to his own smug authoritarianism. The only floodgates that Mr. Tryan and his fellow evangelicals open are those of truth and en-lightenment. When the unhappy, secretly alcoholic Janet Dempster is guided into that light by Tryan she has an il-luminating vision of her marriage and her self. It sobers her literally as well as figuratively.

Almost as profound is the illumination that evangelical-ism brings to the whole community of Milby—"a dingy-looking town, with a strong smell of tanning up one street and a great shaking of hand-looms up another" that be-comes "a refined, moral, and enlightened town" (Ch. 2). George Eliot is not so naive as to ascribe this transformation totally to the religious influence of evangelicalism. Rather, she makes religion symbolic, a manifestation of a spiritual, psychological, and social change that takes place under the redemptive powers of love and sympathy. Milby reforms because the railroad puts it into the mainstream of com-merce, because prosperous businessmen can educate their children and look a little above and beyond the narrow con-fines of their daily existence. They can even afford the luxury of toleration. The influence of evangelicalism in all this reform is subtle and indirect: "Religious ideas have the fate of melodies, which, once set afloat in the world, are taken up by all sorts of instruments, some of them woefully coarse, feeble, or out of tune, until people are in danger of crying out that the melody itself is detestable" (Ch. 10).

Evangelicalism is simply a medium for the outpouring of those feelings of sympathy, goodness, and love that are often repressed by the grinding conditions of life, especially in provincial towns: "The first condition of human goodness is something to love; the second, something to reverence. And this latter precious gift was brought to Milby by Mr. Tryan and Evangelicalism." This is a religion of humanity rather than a particular sect. As George Eliot wrote to Blackwood, the "collision in the dream is not at all between 'bigotted churchmanship' and evangelicalism, but between *ir*religion and religion."[64]

Through domestic realism George Eliot transforms the poverty of provincial life into the richness of the human comedy itself. In "Janet's Repentance" are the roots of *Middlemarch*; the feuding medical men, the canting hypocrites and village gossips, the timid spinsters and comfortable matrons who populate Milby will flourish again in St. Ogg's and in Middlemarch. And, as in the later great novels, they serve organic functions, part of the social fabric, their lives interrelating and ultimately impinging on the fates of her leading characters. Whether brutalized with ignorance and drink like Dempster or self-consciously and preciously refined like Miss Linnet (on whose bookshelves Hannah More's *Sacred Dramas* shares space with Dryden's *Virgil*, Burke's *On the Sublime and Beautiful*, and Dr. Johnson's *Rasselas*), the citizens of Milby need the redeeming sources of enlightenment that Mr. Tryan can bring them. The effects are immediate in genteel spinsters: "No one could deny that Evangelicalism had wrought a change for the better in Rebecca Linnet's person." A fat lady given to romantic excesses of dress, she now wears a far more softening

[64] *Ibid.*, p. 347. See Noble, p. 77.

and becoming grey gingham. Even more striking is the influence of evangelicalism on that other blue-stocking, Miss Pratt, who moves from the composition of "mere trifles . . . calculated for popular utility" like *Letters to a Young Man on his Entrance into Life* and *De Courcy, or the Rash Promise, a Tale for Youth* (which a reviewer once described as "the light vehicle of a weighty moral") to poems addressed to Mr. Tryan, beginning, "Forward, young wrestler for the truth!" (Ch. 3).

George Eliot extends her treatment of evangelicalism to those areas of purely human experience that transcend religious sects and doctrines. The subject of "Janet's Repentance" is a bitterly unhappy marriage. Its proud, tragic-scale heroine Janet has been reduced to the humiliating existence of an abused wife who has taken to private drinking for solace. The frictions in the Dempsters' marriage are not etched with the precision and delicacy of the disastrous Rosamond-Lydgate marriage of *Middlemarch*, but they are sharply recorded—their childlessness, Janet's efforts to please her worthless husband by sharing his scorn of Mr. Tryan, to conceal her misery from her mother, to conciliate her querulous mother-in-law. The Dempsters are incompatible; the rift between them is profound and irreconcilable. Janet is warm, loving, charitable, selfish only in that universal sense in which every individual is an egoist: "We are all of us born in moral stupidity, taking the world as an udder to feed our supreme selves" (*Middlemarch*, II, Ch. 21). Robert is hard, "callous in worldliness, fevered by sensuality, enslaved by chance impulses" (Ch. 7). Janet can be redeemed, as he can never be, because she is capable of suffering and sharing sympathetically in the suffering of others. A chance meeting with Mr. Tryan in the cottage of a dying consumptive girl paves the way for her salvation far more rapidly than any sermon could have done: "There is a power in the direct glance of a sincere and loving human soul, which will do more to dissipate prejudice and kindle charity than the most elaborate arguments. The fullest exposition of Mr. Tryan's doctrine might not have sufficed to convince Janet that he had not an odious self-complacency in believing himself a peculiar child of God; but one direct, pathetic look of his had dissociated him with that conception forever" (Ch. 12). Later, when she appeals to him for help, he offers religious consolation, but it is his personal account of his own anguished search for God that moves her. And her salvation comes at the moment when she forgets herself and her sorrow: "Ah, what a difference between our lives! you have been choosing pain, and working, and denying yourself; and I have been thinking only of myself" (Ch. 18).

From that point onward, Janet has self-mastery. She finds the strength to face her husband's death and to resist the renewed temptation to drink. The source of that strength is simple faith. The evangelical influence operates, to be sure, but in its largest, most ecumenical sense: "And then she tried to live through . . . the blessed hours of hope, and joy, and peace that had come to her of late, since her whole soul had been bent towards the attainment of purity and holiness." Her moment of religious ecstasy is achieved not in a church but in a solitary evening walk—"one of those baptismal epochs, when the soul, dipped in the sacred waters of joy and peace, rises from them with new energies, with more unalterable longings" (Ch. 25). Significantly, however, the walk follows a conversation with Mr. Tryan. He has shown her the way, although she walks the path alone. Thereafter, "a changed woman," healthy, friendly, social-spirited, she does the practical work that Mr. Tryan's failing health prevents him from doing. As he weakens, she grows stronger and becomes, as it were, his secular deputy and, after his death, his living memorial.

George Eliot had renounced evangelical Christianity at the age of twenty-two. Thereafter she passed through the stages of bitterness and hostility and mockery of her girlhood faith. But in her maturity, happily united with George Henry Lewes and evidently secure in her own spiritual existence, she could look back at the evangelicals with fond sympathy and retrieve from them the important message not only of *Scenes of Clerical Life* but of all her later fiction —"that there was a divine work to be done in life, a rule of goodness higher than the opinion of their neighbours; and if the notion of a heaven in reserve for themselves was a little too prominent, yet the theory of fitness for that heaven consisted in purity of heart, in Christ-like compassion, in the subduing of selfish desires" (Ch. 10). The evangelical novel reaches its artistic peak with her because she was able to distill from it those qualities of human emotion which transcend sect and dogma and penetrate to the very heart of the human condition. As a literary genre it seems to have cancelled itself out by the middle of the nineteenth century. But that thorny path of righteousness, duty, conscience, confession, and repentance along which Hannah More, Mrs. Sherwood, Charlotte Elizabeth, Elizabeth Missing Sewell, and Charlotte Yonge stumbled and bumbled led to a new field for later novelists to explore—the novel of psychological realism.

5

Domestic Devotion and Hearthside Heroism: Harriet Martineau's *Deerbrook* and The Novel of Community

> *Two friends met there, two fam'd*
> *Gifted women. The one,*
> *Brilliant with recent renown,*
> *Young, unpractis'd, had told*
> *With a Master's accent her feign'd*
> *Story of passionate life:*
> *The other, maturer in fame,*
> *Earning, she too, her praise*
> *First in Fiction, had since*
> *Widen'd her sweep, and survey'd*
> *History, Politics, Mind.*
>
> —Matthew Arnold, "Haworth Churchyard,
> April, 1855"

I

It was a graceful compliment Matthew Arnold paid Harriet Martineau in this passage—coupling her with the younger, brilliant Charlotte Brontë—graceful, if a trifle insincere. Arnold's immediate impressions of the two literary spinsters at their meeting at Edward Quillinan's house in December, 1850, had been less reverential than his poem suggests. Twenty-nine, handsome and fashionable, he was understandably cool toward Charlotte Brontë ("past thirty and plain"), and he positively disliked Harriet Martineau, even older and plainer, briskly wielding her ear-trumpet and dominating the conversation with her strong opinions

strongly argued. Arnold found her totally "antipathetic"—
"what an unpleasant life and unpleasant nature," he wrote
of that meeting.[1] Nevertheless, he could not fail to be impressed with her honesty and conviction. He was, after all,
stating only the truth—that she was a gifted, learned, and
influential woman who had won her first fame as a writer
of fiction and then moved on to the larger areas of "History,
Politics, Mind."

What little survives of Harriet Martineau's work today
is in those larger areas. Most of her fiction, in fact, is sub-
sumed under them simply because it is political and economic theory only thinly disguised as fiction. If the title of
her once phenomenally popular *Illustrations of Political
Economy* gives no hint that this is a work of fiction, a hasty
glance at the contents will do little more to persuade one.
There are one or two other works that can perhaps be nar-
rowly squeezed into the category—a historical romance on
Toussaint L'Ouverture, *The Hour and the Man*—and, by
way of contrast, a refreshingly simple children's story, *The
Crofton Boys*. Finally, there is a domestic novel, a story of
love and marriage in a provincial village, *Deerbrook*—altogether a negligible harvest for a nineteenth-century novelist. Yet from this small output of fiction—and from her
Autobiography, a work that demonstrates some of the best
skills of a novelist in spite of its non-fictional nature—we
can trace in Harriet Martineau the emergence of a new and
powerful shaping influence in nineteenth-century English
fiction.

Deerbrook was published in 1839. In the next quarter-
century, the English novel followed a course that this novel

<hr>

[1] Letter to Miss Wightman, December 21, 1850: "At seven came
Miss Martineau and Miss Brontë (Jane Eyre); talk to Miss Martineau
(who blasphemes frightfully) about the prospects of the Church of
England . . . " (*Letters of Matthew Arnold, 1848-1888*, ed. George
W. E. Russell [London, 1895], i, 13; ii, 137. See also Kathleen
Tillotson, " 'Haworth Churchyard': The Making of Arnold's Elegy,"
Brontë Society Transactions (1967), pp. 105-22.

set. The qualities that define the domestic novel are all here. It is bourgeois and anti-romantic. It glorifies the solid values of home and family. It recognizes that the goal of all humans is happiness and self-fulfillment, but it constantly reminds us of the Christian-evangelical imperatives of duty, submission of the individual will, self-sacrifice, and endurance. It emphasizes the importance of compromise, cooperation, and common sense both in the individual's private life and in his public life, as he functions in the social community in which he lives and works. It is the product of many social and literary influences of the early nineteenth century—radicalism, reform, evangelicalism, and romanticism. But these influences are ideological and philosophical, while *Deerbrook* and its successors in the genre of the bourgeois love story are parochial, domestic, filled with the small details of daily living. These novels, it should be noted, are not exclusively feminine in their authorship and readership. The shifting of attention from aristocratic to middle-class family life, from leaders of men to simply employers of men—businessmen, matrons managing their servants, governesses educating their children, clergymen guiding their flock—all this was the material of Dickens, Thackeray, and Trollope as much as of the Brontës, George Eliot, Mrs. Gaskell, and—to put her in such exalted company—Harriet Martineau.

That *Deerbrook* was in its day a pioneering and innovative novel we know from the difficulties its author had in getting it published. In 1838 Harriet Martineau was not an amateur, an unknown quantity, applying timidly to publishers. She was a famous woman. Her *Illustrations of Political Economy*, published in nine volumes in 1834, had been a tremendous success, transforming an unknown little Norwich spinster almost overnight into a national figure, lionized in London society. The Lord Chancellor of England, Lord Brougham, begged her to write more such tales —on taxation and pauperism—which she promptly did. Lord Durham, the coal-mine owner, sought her out to promote his schemes on labor legislation and union organizing. She had also, by this time, won trans-Atlantic fame, and notoriety, with *Society in America* (1837) and *Retrospect of Western Travel* (1838). Distinguished publishers like Murray, Bentley, Colburn, and Saunders bid competitively for these impressions of her exhaustive and exhausting two-year tour of the United States and Canada, during which she had crusaded vigorously for the Abolitionists and thrown herself into numerous controversial issues. In April 1839 Daniel O'Connell appealed to her to come to Ireland to study and report the cause of the Irish people to English readers. On such reputation alone Harriet Martineau should have been confident about the success of anything she wrote. Nevertheless, when she presented the manuscript of *Deerbrook* to John Murray, who had invited her to write a novel for him, he declined it. "He was more than civil,—he was kind, and, I believe, sincere in his regrets. The execution was not the ground of refusal. It was, as I had afterwards reason to know, the scene being laid in middle life."[2]

There, as Harriet Martineau observed, was the root of the trouble. In 1838 a reading public conditioned to romances, high adventure, and the elegances of the "silver-fork" novel was unprepared for a novel of "middle life," with a village apothecary for a hero (no "medical lover" would do, the wag Sydney Smith proclaimed—"If he took his mistress's hand, he would feel her pulse by force of habit; if she fainted, he would have only Epsom salts")[3] and a heroine who came from Birmingham. Young readers in those days, though they were themselves the children of manufacturers and dissenting clergymen, "looked for lords

---

[2] *Harriet Martineau's Autobiography, with Memorials*, ed. Maria Weston Chapman (3 vols., London, 1877; all citations in this chapter are to the third edition, 2 vols., Boston, 1878), I, 398-415; II, 12-13. See also Robert K. Webb, *Harriet Martineau* (New York, 1960), pp. 120-27.

[3] Quoted in Webb, p. 185.

and ladies in every page of a new novel." They were prepared for high life or low life but not middle life. So at least
the publishers believed. Finally another publisher, Moxon,
took *Deerbrook* and was reasonably well rewarded for the
risk. Though not a stunning success, the novel sold respecta-
bly and went through two large editions within a decade of
its publication. In the groundswell of domestic fiction that
followed in the 1840's and 1850's, with so many novels influenced by it and imitative of it, *Deerbrook* was all but sub-
merged. Its literary merits were too fragile to compete with
major talents like Charlotte Brontë, Dickens, Thackeray,
and Mrs. Gaskell. Harriet Martineau herself was aware of
its limitations: "The work was faithful in principle and sentiment to the then state of my mind: and that satisfied me
for a time. I should now [1855] require more of myself, if
I were to attempt a novel." Nevertheless, it had served its
purpose, she concluded, "in overcoming a prejudice against
the use of middle-class life in fiction."[4]

For one so apparently indifferent to the creative urge, so
satisfied and rewarded with her didactic-polemical writing,
it is odd that Harriet Martineau made the efforts she did at
fiction. Her motivation—more accurately her "calling," for
there was a strong spiritual drive in this free-thinking wom-

---

[4] *Autobiography*, I, 415. Kathleen Tillotson calls *Deerbrook* "the
first serious novel of middle class provincial life since Jane Austen"
("Writers and Readers in 1851," in K. and Geoffrey Tillotson, *Mid-
Victorian Studies* [London, 1965], p. 324). The only study of *Deerbrook* in recent years that has come to my attention is Robert Lee
Wolff's essay "The Novel and the Neurosis," in his *Strange Stories
and other Explorations in Victorian Fiction* (Boston, 1971), pp. 69-
141. Wolff's approach, as his title makes clear, is psychoanalytic. He
reads the *Autobiography* as "a clinical treasure house," tracing her
neuroses back to her unhappy childhood, her stormy relationship
with her mother, her jealousy of her sister, and her devotion to her
brother James. He interprets *Deerbrook* as "a clinical study of jealous
possessiveness," the reflection of her frustration in her early years, and
concludes with the confident diagnosis that "Harriet Martineau was
neurotically ill."

an—was powerful, a real sense of mission to teach and to enlighten. As early as 1829, when only twenty-seven, she wrote: "I believe myself possessed of no uncommon talents, and of not an atom of genius; but as various circumstances have led me to think more accurately and read more extensively than some women, I believe that I may so write on subjects of universal concern as to inform some minds and stir up others. . . . Of posthumous fame I have not the slightest expectation or desire. To be useful in my day and generation is enough for me" (*Autobiography*, II, 166).

This is not, of course, the credo of an imaginative artist. Harriet Martineau never deluded herself about the particular drift of her talents. She could admire and even emulate Jane Austen without losing perspective on herself: "She *was* a glorious novelist. I *think* I could write a novel, though I see a thousand things in Scott and her which I could never do. My way of interesting must be a different one" (*Autobiography*, II, 317). Nevertheless she had immortal longings for what she called "the liberty of fiction," and she occasionally chafed at the confining discipline of facts, "the constraint of the effort to be always correct" (*Autobiography*, I, 409). Her earliest writing was devotional, but it took the form of fiction. At nineteen she embarked on a "theologico-metaphysical novel," inspired by the then highly regarded *Tremaine* by Robert Plumer Ward. Good judgment persuaded her that her novel was "excessively dull," and she abandoned it for the more straightforward religious tracts with which she launched her professional career.

But the lure of fiction was always present, and the fine line between fiction and parable, between fact and "tale founded on fact," is one that Harriet Martineau crossed very easily. Indeed, it is to her somewhat questionable credit that she erased that line altogether. Her best work of fiction, *Deerbrook*, had its initial inspiration in an incident from real life, told her by the American novelist Catherine Maria Sedgwick (the basis of Miss Sedgwick's story "Old Maids").[5] Her most ambitious novel, *The Hour and the Man*, was founded on history and conscientiously researched. Her most popular work of fiction bears the forbidding title *Illustrations of Political Economy*, a collection of tales intended to do precisely what, in fact, they did— namely, educate the public in economic theory by demonstrating abstract principles in realistic stories of ordinary life. Tacked to the end of each of the tales is a straight factual summary of the economic principles embodied in the tale. The characters are carefully selected to personify the issues; the plots and dialogues are constructed to advance the lessons as expeditiously as possible. Harriet prepared herself carefully for her work, read widely, travelled to many of the scenes she described, and drew on her childhood memories of her father's manufacturing business in Norwich. Everywhere the tales reflect the ideas of the necessitarian Joseph Priestley and the utilitarians James Mill and Jeremy Bentham. Yet in spite of their solid foundation of research, the *Illustrations* are lively and even, occasionally, entertaining. She was a good story-teller. Recognizing and capitalizing on that talent, she worked so diligently to integrate story and doctrine that she succeeded better than she or her publishers had dared to hope. *Illustrations* was a remarkable success. In their time these tales answered a need—not only the general demand for self-education and self-improvement that characterized the entire nineteenth-century reading public, but also a more specific and urgent

[5] *Autobiography*, I, 411. "Old Maids" was published in *Tales and Sketches of Miss Sedgwick* (Philadelphia, 1835), inscribed to Harriet Martineau, who had become friendly with the author and her family during her American visit. The story, which Miss Sedgwick insisted was "no fiction," concerns a self-sacrificing older sister who gives up the man she loves to her younger sister, who has fallen in love with him. She remains a spinster school-mistress, happily resigned to her lot, and illustrates Miss Sedgwick's theme that the lot of spinsters is noble rather than tragic. For literary authority she cites Scott's heroines who never marry—Flora MacIvor, Rebecca, and Minna Troil (*The Pirate*).

demand for popular education in political and economic subjects. The shock waves of the French Revolution reached out, touching high- and middle- as well as lower-class English society. Adam Smith, James Mill, Ricardo, and Bentham were too heavy reading for the larger public. William Godwin had to translate the abstruse notions of his *Enquiry Concerning Political Justice* into the near-gothic terror of *Caleb Williams* to reach that public. But the demand was there, at every level.

Political Economy, treating as it does the "Production, Distribution, and Consumption of Wealth," was a conception that reached deep into the heart of English society. "Can anything more nearly concern all the members of any society than the way in which the necessaries and comforts of life may be best procured and enjoyed by all?" Harriet Martineau asks this question in her preface, confident of the answer. The economy of the nation and the economy of the individual household are not unrelated; indeed, the analogy is pointed: "Domestic economy is an interesting subject to those who view it as a whole; who observe how, by good management in every department, all the members of a family have their proper business appointed them, their portion of leisure secured to them, their wants supplied, their pleasures cared for; how harmony is preserved within doors by the absence of all causes of jealousy; how good will prevails toward all abroad through the absence of all causes of quarrel."

If "civilised states are [to be] managed like civilised households," instruction in domestic economy must begin early, at home. Harriet Martineau joined a long line of instructors, from Hannah More, Mrs. Barbauld, and Maria Edgeworth to Mrs. Ellis and Mrs. Marcet, turning out teaching materials, tracts, manuals, dialogues, fictionalized exempla. Her immediate inspiration was Mrs. Jane Marcet (1769-1858), author of an educational series—*Conversations on Natural Philosophy, Conversations on Vegetable Physiology, Conversations on Chemistry*, and *Conversations on Political Economy*—textbooks read, Harriet writes in a sketch of her, by "tens of thousands of young republicans," and distinguished by their "simplicity, the apt language, the absence of all condescension, and the avoidance of lecturing."[6] Macaulay may have had tongue in cheek when he declared in his "Essay on Milton" that "every girl who has read Mrs. Marcet's little *Conversations on Political Economy* could teach Walpole or Montague many lessons in finance," but the effectiveness of her instruction had many witnesses. One of these was Mrs. Barbauld's niece, herself a woman of letters, Lucy Aikin, who, coming upon Mrs. Marcet when she was already grown up but still admittedly ignorant of the subject, "found myself shamed into opening the leaves, studying it from end to end with great attention, and confessing that I found it well worth the pains."[7]

Harriet Martineau also came late to Mrs. Marcet, discovering her in 1827 after she had already written several stories on economic themes: "It struck me at once that the principles of the whole science might be advantageously conveyed in the same way,—not by being smothered up in a story, but by being exhibited in their natural workings in selected passages of social life" (*Autobiography*, I, 105). To render the principles more graphic, so that the uneducated man might grasp them and share the complex interests of political economy—this became her purpose. She scorned the mere exemplum used "as a trap to catch the idle readers," remembering how, in her own childhood, "we grew sick of works that pretend to be stories, and turn out to be catechisms of some kind of knowledge which we had much rather become acquainted with in its undisguised form" (Preface to *Illustrations of Political Economy*).

What she envisioned was something rather different from anything that had come before—"sketches of society, in narratives of those who labour and earn and spend, who are

---

[6] *Biographical Sketches* (London, 1869), I, ch. 8.

[7] *Miscellanies by the Late Lucy Aikin*, ed. P. H. LeBreton (London, 1864), p. 107.

happy or otherwise, according as the institutions under which they live are good or bad"—in other words, vignettes, slices of life cut out of reality but shaped to fit the economic theories she was teaching. The destinies of her characters are determined by forces larger than they, forces beyond their control—at least without the knowledge for controlling them which Harriet Martineau offered. With their immediacy, their relevance to the lives of their readers, their lively action and brisk style, it is little wonder that the tales delighted the public who could thus imbibe education and morality in an especially palatable form.

In 1833, while the *Illustrations* were still being issued in monthly parts, Edward Bulwer-Lytton hailed her work, observing that few have attempted the necessary business of educating the public in politics: "It is to perform to political morals the same task as Addison fulfilled with domestic. Miss Martineau, in the excellent fictions she has given the world, has performed this noble undertaking. . . ." Bulwer found their author inferior to Maria Edgeworth in wit and characterization—as well as lacking in her racy local color. But the mere coupling of her name with so eminent a figure as Miss Edgeworth was impressive, as was his appreciation of her style—"fresh, nervous, graphic, and full of homeliness or of poetry as the subject may require"—and of her "nameless and indefinable power of sustaining interest in the progress of her tale."[8] Some critics even feared that her power of "sustaining interest," the charm of the stories themselves, might obscure their serious didactic purpose. The *Edinburgh Review* (April, 1833), for example, warned that "the usefulness of the several stories may be injured by their beauty." In evidence one might note the comment a decade later in the *Christian Remembrancer* (November, 1843), on the ineffectuality of polemical religious novels:

[8] "Our Moral Fictions: Miss Martineau's Illustrations of Political Economy," *New Monthly Magazine*, 37 (Jan.-Feb., 1833), pp. 146-51. The article is unsigned; Professor Walter Houghton of the *Wellesley Index* has assigned it to Bulwer.

"We find, from experience, that the young of both sexes read them as mere tales, as we used to do Miss Martineau's series in political economy, with a fixed resolve to shirk the principles and all that purported to have a didactic aim." In 1862 Charles Knight, discussing Miss Martineau in a chapter on novelists in his *Popular History of England* (where he ranks her with Bulwer, Ainsworth, Dickens, and Thackeray), concluded that her story-telling gifts—"her great power of assimilation, by which local images and scenes were reproduced as if they had been the result of actual observation,—her skilful admixture of narrative and dialogue—her ability to conceive a character and to carry it through with real dramatic power"—may actually have defeated her educational purposes. Thousands of her admiring readers, he claimed, "rose from the perusal of her monthly volumes without the 'Principles' having taken the slightest hold upon their minds. Her triumph as a novelist was the more remarkable as her purpose was a mistake in art."

Knight overestimated Harriet Martineau's "triumph as a novelist." But he correctly singled out her distinct novelistic skills, all of which are displayed, modestly but unmistakably, in the *Illustrations*. Like the professional she was, she wrote methodically, with outlines, plans, research. She claimed that she deliberately restrained herself "from glancing even in thought towards the scene and nature of my story till it should be suggested by my collective didactic materials" (*Autobiography*, I, 147). Not until she had laboriously composed her Summary of Principles did she allow herself to set the scene of the story and select the characters. But once the imaginative element entered, the work began to fly—"the story went off, like a letter." A mysterious power that the necessitarian-utilitarian Harriet Martineau could never quite account for seemed to take over. All human actions, she maintained, had discoverable antecedents. Yet she could not explain fiction making, creating a plot, "a task above human faculties . . . the same power as that of prophecy" (*Autobiography*, I, 179). At best in her fiction Harriet Martineau achieved only the verisimilitude of good journalism, but that she should have achieved even this much in a work as forbidding as *Illustrations of Political Economy* is a sign of her considerable ability.

Fiction springs out of these tales almost spontaneously. In a letter to W. J. Fox in 1832 she described the rapid pace at which she worked: "Now (in VI) the British Fisheries being established close by (a fact) they rise & multiply, (a fact) till a bad season or two pinches them, (a fact) & then comes an epidemic, (a fact) thins them & helps up the survivors. Here is room for bustle, in contrast to the last, for uncommon scenery & varied incident, & for showing the miseries of the positive check."[9] Facts feed her imagination —"bustle," "uncommon scenery & varied incident"—the story takes form. Unhappily, for the modern reader at least, the professional in Harriet Martineau kept her didactic purpose uppermost. One must dig for the more purely entertaining qualities, but they are there.

They are there precisely—and almost ironically—because she was not striving for literary and aesthetic effects, because both her sympathies and her previous writing experience directed her toward actuality, the strictest observation and recording of fact. After systematic preparation and planning, she wrote swiftly, without revising and polishing. Her mentor was William Cobbett, who had advised: "Know first what you want to say, and then say it in the first words that occur to you" (*Autobiography*, I, 93-94). She found expression by words "as easy as breathing air," with generally happy results—a crisp, natural prose making no claims to high literature. She writes engaging passages of description, dialogue, and characterization even in the chilly depths of exposition on political economy.

The social-documentary story was yet unknown, but the vivid sketches of the degradation and demoralization of the poor that emerged in Disraeli (*Sybil*), Dickens, Kingsley,

[9] Quoted in Webb, p. 115.

Mrs. Trollope (*Michael Armstrong*), Charlotte Elizabeth, and Mrs. Gaskell are anticipated by Harriet Martineau. Except Dickens, none of these novelists was more skillful at integrating the materials of fact and fiction. Mrs. Gaskell wrote *Mary Barton* out of passion and conviction but made no pretense at economic analysis: "I know nothing of Political Economy, or the theories of trade. I have tried to write truthfully. . . ." If her novel was read as a social document, it was because it "has received some confirmation from the events which have so recently [1848] occurred among a similar class on the Continent" (Preface). When she attempted a more explicit presentation of economic issues in *North and South*, she resorted to the stiff lecture-discussion clumsily introduced into her fine and sensitive study of purely human relationships (the proud Margaret Hale grudgingly learning to respect and love the factory owner Mr. Thornton):

" 'You seem to have a strong objection to acts of parliament and all legislation affecting your mode of management down here at Milton,' said Mr. Hale.

" 'Yes, I have; and many others have as well. And with justice, I think. The whole machinery—I don't mean the wood and iron machinery now—of the cotton trade is so new that it is no wonder if it does not work well in every part all at once. Seventy years ago what was it? And now what is it not? Raw, crude materials came together; men of the same level, as regarded education and station, took suddenly the different positions of masters and men, owing to the mother-wit, as regarded opportunities and probabilities, which distinguished some, and made them far-seeing as to what great future lay concealed in that rude model of Sir Richard Arkwright's. The rapid development of what might be called a new trade, gave those early masters enormous powers of wealth and command. . . .'

"Margaret's lip curled, but somehow she was compelled to listen; she could no longer abstract herself in her own thoughts" (Ch. 10).

There are similar lectures and debates in *Illustrations of Political Economy*, but, thanks to the form of the work, with its Summary of Principles, Harriet Martineau was often able to separate the more strictly factual material from the narrative. As a result she is readable and lively. Her characters evolve from personified economic abstractions into human beings: "Mr. Farrer was bustling about, apparently in a state of great happiness. His brown wig seemed to sit lightly on his crown; his shoes creaked very actively; his half-whistle betokened a light heart, and he poked the fire as if he had forgotten how much coals were a bushel" ("The Farrers of Budge Row"). In "Homes Abroad" an impoverished cottager who, with his family, will ultimately illustrate that the solution to farm poverty is emigration to Australia, assumes genuine fictive qualities: "Among the grumblers was Castle; a man who, without fault of his own, was, in the full vigour of life, reduced from a state of comfortable independence to the very verge of pauperism. . . . He had married a second time, a woman much younger than himself, who had never known hardship, and was little prepared to meet it, however gay her temper seemed before there was anything to try it. She did nothing for her husband but bring him children and nurse them till they died, which they almost all did, as times grew worse and comforts became scarce. . . . Castle was now almost invariably low and peevish; and at five-and-forty had the querulous tone, wrinkled face, and lagging gait of an old man. The effect of hardship had been even worse upon his wife than upon himself. Instead of being peevish, she seemed to have lost all feeling; and while her husband yet worked as long as he could get anything to do, she was as lazy as if she had been brought up to live on parish bread" (Ch. 1).

Dialogue, when it is not devoted to expository speeches on economic theory, is natural and dramatic. Here Castle's daughter, who is going to Australia ahead of the others, comes to say goodbye. She finds her father "leaning against the wall" in despair:

" 'Where's your money?' he asked. 'You had need take care of money, when you have got it. All the rest is moonshine, to my thinking.'

" 'There is very bright sunshine where we are going, if they all say true,' said Ellen; 'and that you will find, father, before a year is over. You may trust Frank and Mr. Jackson, I am sure; and so—'

" 'I trust nobody. I have had enough of trusting people,' cried Castle. 'All this is your doing, remember, both of you; So never cast it up to me. Go, go. 'Tis getting very late. Where's your money, I ask you, child?'

" 'Safe, father, sewed into my stays. But, father, what *can* happen to us so bad as living here, as—as—we have done lately?'

" 'Go, children, go, and leave off talking about our meeting again at the other side of the world. If I go to the bottom half-way, Ellen, it will be none the worse for you, but the better, except that Frank must go too, and you would not like that so well.'

" 'O father—!'

" 'Well, one kiss more; and God bless *you*, whatever becomes of me" (Ch. 3).

This is the fiction of domestic realism. Its heroes are laborers, farmers, merchants, and bankers; its heroines include a "princess of fishwomen" (Ella of Garveloch) and shopkeepers' daughters. On economic disasters hang not only the welfare of the state but the happiness of young lovers. Harriet Martineau shuttles between one and the other without the slightest self-consciousness: "This evening was the brightest of the whole spring in the eyes of Fanny and Melea. The bank had only sustained a loss, instead of being about to break" ("Berkeley the Banker"). Teas are prepared by matrons in their best black silk; currant wine is sipped and seed cake is nibbled, while they talk of rising prices, the dangers of banks' issuing more paper money, the effects of the tariff on local trade, and the need for crop diversification.

Since the lives of real people are affected by economic developments and since people do talk a good deal about prices and business, her fundamental approach to realistic domestic fiction can hardly be faulted. When, unfortunately, her characters talk too much (as their author herself often did, to the dismay of many who knew her), when they slip into lecture and polemics, her stories suffer. Admittedly they carry a burden of didactic purpose too heavy for any first-rate work of fiction to bear. For all her earnest dedication to exposition, Harriet Martineau was sensitive to the pitfalls of her task. In one of the most interesting of the *Illustrations*, "For Each and For All," a wife remarks to her husband, who has been declaiming on taxation's effect on wages: "What we want then is, a regulation of the supply of the labour market, a lightening of taxation, and a liberal commercial system. But, Henry, where is the eloquence of all this?—that which is commonly called eloquence? It seems to me more like a lecture than a speech." As the reader applauds this eminently fair observation, the husband, a member of Parliament, agrees: "And so it was; but these are days when, to the people, naked truth is the best eloquence." He proceeds to describe to her the excitement of political meetings, and she replies enthusiastically: "I can imagine it. The true romance of human life lies among the poorer classes; the most rapid vicissitudes, the strongest passions, the most undiluted emotions, the most eloquent deportment, the truest experience are there" (Ch. 9).

These words, modified perhaps to include the middle classes, might be the credo of the emerging domestic novel. "For Each and For All" indeed has peculiar literary interest both for its characters and for its theme. The only one of the *Illustrations* to deal with the aristocracy, it begins in a style and manner of the fashionable or "silver-fork" novel with passages worthy of Mrs. Gore: "The season was more than half over, and was about to be pronounced remarkably dull, when a promise of novelty was given out in the shape of a rumour that Lord F-- and his lady, who had been travelling

225

abroad from the day of their marriage, had arrived in town, and that the bride's first appearance would take place at the Duke of A--'s ball on the 20th." Adding piquancy to this opening is the fact that Lady F-- had been an actress before her brilliant marriage: "The curiosity was not confined to mothers and daughters, to whose observation an extraordinary marriage is the most exciting circumstance that life affords; in this case, the interest was shared by their husbands and fathers."

We are quickly assured, however, that Lady F-- is eminently genteel, having gone on the stage only after her father's death had left her impoverished. She is, moreover —and ideally for Harriet Martineau's didactic purposes— intelligent and prudent: "The bride fancied little, and feared nothing. She had been conversant with many ranks of society, and had found them all composed of men and women; and she never doubted that in that with which she was about to become acquainted, she should also have to deal with men and women." Being sensible too, she enjoys the luxuries of her new life without abusing or over-rating them.

Her equally sensible mate listens attentively to her advice, especially on the evils of idleness, and becomes actively engaged in business and in politics: "The time is coming when no class of society may be called idle," she prophetically warns. But reformation not revolution is their goal. They remain aristocrats—Harriet Martineau and her fictional mouthpieces affirming that there will always be distinctions of rank and merit. At the end, rich and socially prominent, happily awaiting the birth of an heir, they nevertheless extol the virtues of simple domestic life: "If the aristocracy cannot, by their own experience, get to know all that life is,—though they are born, love, marry, suffer, enjoy, and die, let some idea be given them of it by true images held up in the mirror of their studies. . . . Let us have in books, in pictures, and on the stage, working men and women, in the various periods of their struggle through life."

Lord F-- finally asks his sibyl-wife: "What, for instance, could a weaver of fiction make of our present life?" She prophesies a time when "writer and readers must be contented with little narrative; contented to know that what passes within us, since so little happens to us. Would there be nothing to instruct and gratify in pictures of our position, in revelations of our hearts, and records of our conversations?" And he replies, "Let us comfort ourselves, Letitia, with deciding that it must be the fault of the recorder if there were not" (Ch. 9).

"The true romance of human life" is thus defined and illustrated. If Harriet Martineau has not quite formulated a "poetics" of the genre, she has at least established its ground-rules. She made her most distinguished contribution to the form, however, not in a work of fiction but in a literally "true romance of human life"—her *Autobiography*, published posthumously in 1877 but written twenty-two years earlier in one of the several periods of her life when she believed, on good medical authority, that she was dying. Romance of course must be understood in the nineteenth-century sense as a work concerned with spontaneous feelings and natural emotions, rather than in the sense of distant time and place, exotic adventure and passionate love. Yet in telling the story of an almost incredible career, a rise from obscurity to fame, complicated infinitely by her sex, her ill health and deafness, her plain appearance and socially abrasive personality, and most of all by her outspoken reforming zeal—in all this Harriet Martineau's *Autobiography* is a Victorian domestic romance. Its candor, sensitivity, and frank self-exposure rank it with many other Victorian works that all but break down the lines between imaginative literature and autobiography—*Jane Eyre, The Mill on the Floss, David Copperfield, Great Expectations, The Prelude, Father and Son, The Way of all Flesh*. Charlotte Brontë told Harriet Martineau that she had read her autobiographical reminiscences in her earlier book *Household Education* "with astonishment. . . . It was like meeting her own fetch,—so precisely the fears and miseries there described the same as her own, told or not told in 'Jane Eyre'" (*Autobiography*, II, 22).

Granted the limitations of the book—its lack of charm and imagination, its harshness of judgment on others, its complacency and dogmatism—the *Autobiography* is nevertheless a fascinating and sometimes very moving record, from its Wordsworthian opening—"My first recollections are of some infantine impressions"—to the unaffected simplicity of its closing pages, as Harriet Martineau contemplated death: "And now that I am awaiting it at any hour, the whole thing seems so easy, simple and natural that I cannot but wonder how I could keep my thoughts fixed upon it when it was far off. I cannot do it now. Night after night since I have known that I am mortally ill, I have tried to conceive, with the help of the sensations of my sinking-fits, the act of dying, and its attendant feelings; and, thus far, I have always gone to sleep in the middle of it" (*Autobiography*, II, 105).

The outlines of Harriet Martineau's career trace a fictional success story, and the details that fill it in conform remarkably to the patterns of numerous Victorian novels. Like the evangelical autobiographers—Mrs. Sherwood, Charlotte Elizabeth, Elizabeth Missing Sewell—she had an extraordinary power of recall and could evoke out of a vivid memory the joys and agonies of childhood: "the coarse feel of the sheets" in the bed of a poor farm cottage where she had been sent as a child for her health, the "rough bark" of a tree that she grasped as a toddler, the unconscious cruelty and misunderstanding of parents, the child's terrors of the unknown.

In common with little Jane Eyre and Maggie Tulliver, with Pip and David Copperfield, she found in recalling childhood experience a wealth of psychological insight and aesthetic delight: her irrational fears (a magic lantern show that set her shrieking and "brought on bowel-complaint"), her hypersensitivity and feelings of anguish and guilt at minor thoughtless rebukes from her elders, her first religious speculations ("My idea of Heaven was a place gay with yellow and lilac crocuses. . . . While I was afraid of everybody I saw, I was not in the least afraid of God"), her brooding morbidity ("Being usually very unhappy, I was constantly longing for heaven, and seriously, and very frequently, planning suicide in order to get there"), her sense of the injustice of life ("Justice was precisely what was least understood in our house in regard to servants and children"), her desire to run away from home ("I used to lean out of the window, and look up and down the street, and wonder how far I could go without being caught. I had no doubt at all that if I once got into a farm-house, and wore a woollen petticoat, and milked the cows, I should be safe, and that nobody would inquire about me anymore" (*Autobiography*, I, 12-14).

Out of the developing consciousness of a child, Harriet Martineau traces the emergence of a free spirit—the Victorian heroine of Charlotte Brontë and George Eliot. That spirit is the product of painstaking and often painful self-analysis and self-discovery. She remained outwardly obedient and submissive, but she smoldered in quiet resentment. Ultimately, as with the fictional heroines, there was overt rebellion, a declaration of independence from family ties and even, in Harriet's case, from religion. Like her fictional counterparts, too, she had to learn self-mastery. For her the problem was complicated by the deafness that manifested itself in her childhood and further alienated her from her family and from society. That she finally was reconciled to her handicap gave her, understandably, pride and self-satisfaction: "Yet here am I now, on the borders of the grave, at the end of a busy life, confident that this same deafness is about the best thing that ever happened to me; —the best, in a selfish view, as the grandest impulse to self-mastery; and the best, in a higher view, as my most peculiar opportunity of helping others, who suffer the same misfortune without equal stimulus to surmount the false shame, and other unspeakable miseries which attend it" (*Autobiography*, I, 59).

The *Autobiography* was potentially a first-rate Victorian novel. But even on what she believed was her deathbed, Harriet Martineau was too vigorous, too absorbed in the problems of "History, Politics, Mind," to distill a novel from autobiography. She had had, moreover, by 1855 too much success with her non-fiction and too little with fiction to encourage her in that direction. In 1851, at Charlotte Brontë's urging, she sent the manuscript of the first volume of a new novel to Smith, Elder. But she submitted it anonymously, as "a foolish prank," and to her embarrassment, George Smith rejected it. Never one to brood over lost opportunities, she destroyed the manuscript and went on to other work.[10] Thus *Deerbrook* remains her only important novel. Measured against the achievement of her successors, it is a very minor one. Yet like so much of Harriet Martineau's work that we tend nowadays to dismiss or to approach patronizingly, it bears study and offers surprises and even occasional rewards of pleasure. Furthermore it represents a pioneer effort in the sociological novel—the novel that studies individual character as it is shaped by the society in which it lives—the novel of community.

---

[10] *Autobiography*, II, 65-66. See also Kathleen Tillotson, *Mid-Victorian Studies*, p. 324, for an account of this episode. Smith's grounds for rejection were, interestingly, its favorable presentation of Catholicism in a period of intense anti-Catholicism. Harriet Martineau's tolerant views on the controversial issue of papal aggression provoked her negative comment on *Villette*, a novel that generally she admired: "She goes out of her way to express a passionate hatred of Romanism. It is not the calm disapproval of a ritual religion. . . . We do not exactly see the moral necessity for this (there is no artistical necessity) and we are rather sorry for it, occurring as it does at a time when catholics and protestants hate each other quite sufficiently . . . " (review of *Villette*, *Daily News*, February 3, 1853).

II

SURVEYING the novels of early Victorian England, the sociologist-critic Raymond Williams observes that "the exploration of community, the substance and meaning of community," was a central issue in many of them. This was a period, he points out, in which the solid social structures of the past were coming under challenge. What fascinated the novelists was the human reaction to these challenges and to the sweeping social changes that the new industrial civilization was bringing to the old rural communities: "What community is, what it has been, what it might be; how community relates to individuals and relationships; how men and women, directly engaged, see within them or beyond them, for but more often against them, the shape of a society; these related themes are the dominant bearings. For this is a period in which what it means to live in a community is more uncertain, more critical, more disturbing as a question put both to societies and to persons than ever before in history. The underlying experiences of this powerful and transforming urban and industrial civilisation are of rapid and inescapable social change. . . . People became more aware of great social and historical changes which altered not only outward forms—institutions and landscapes—but also inward feelings, experiences, self-definitions. These facts of change can be seen lying deep in almost every imagination."[11]

Understandably there was a tendency to evade the issues, to retreat into the safety of the fixed past, and to portray village life in idylls like Miss Mitford's *Our Village*. A political and social realist, Harriet Martineau wrote *Deerbrook* in direct reaction to such trends. She admired *Our Village* but ranked it as merely "the representative of household cheerfulness in the humbler range of the litera-

[11] *The English Novel from Dickens to Lawrence* (New York, 1970), p. 12.

ture of fiction."[12] Nevertheless she perceived that Miss Mitford was on the right track—first, because however idyllic her scenes, her descriptions were "graphic," drawn from life, fresh. Secondly, Miss Mitford's sketches "appealed to a new sense," a popular demand for vividness, simplicity, and verisimilitude (*Autobiography*, I, 316). Though schooled in the formal conventions of the eighteenth-century prose essay, Miss Mitford emphasized in *Our Village* the new romantic sensibility of one of her favorite poets, Wordsworth—dwelling on the natural, spontaneous joys of life, "the kindly and unconscious influence of habit." Her vision is enclosed, parochial, intimate: "Even in books I like a confined locality, and so do the critics when they talk of the unities. Nothing is so tiresome as to be whirled half over Europe at the chariot-wheels of a hero, to go to sleep at Vienna, and awaken at Madrid; it produces a real fatigue, a weariness of spirit. On the other hand, nothing is so delightful as to sit down in a country village, in one of Miss Austen's delicious novels, quite sure before we leave it to become intimate with every spot and every person it contains. . . ." Her favorite adjectives are "tiny" and "tidy" and their synonyms. "Of all situations for a constant residence that which appears to me most delightful is a little village far in the country; a small neighbourhood . . . with inhabitants whose faces are as familiar to us as the flowers in our garden; a little world of our own, close-packed and insulated like ants in an ant-hill, or bees in a hive, or sheep in a fold, or nuns in a convent, or sailors in a ship" (*Our Village*, Ch. 1).

This unnamed village is a fairyland. Three Mile Cross, the real-life Berkshire cottage in which Miss Mitford wrote

[12] *Biographical Sketches*, I, ch. 4. For the judgment of a more recent student of Miss Mitford, see J. C. Owen: "There is a very special charm about a thoroughly good-humored, thoroughly competent, not quite first-rate writer" ("Utopia in Little: Mary Russell Mitford and *Our Village*," *Studies in Short Fiction*, 5 [Spring, 1968], p. 245).

her book, working under desperate financial pressure to support an idle, improvident father and an ailing mother, was a "gaunt and cheerless" house, constantly in need of repair, next to a public-house from which the owner's pigs came wandering to wreck her little garden.[13] But in the bucolic landscape of *Our Village* nature is sweet, charming, and endlessly benevolent. The book is, to be sure, "true"— to the extent that the reader may easily visualize its scenes and even occasionally recognize them—but this is a selected and edited truth. When her artist friend Sir William Elford asked if her characters and descriptions were true, she responded heartily: "Yes! yes! yes! As true as is well possible. You, as a great landscape painter, know that in painting a favourite scene you do a little embellish, and can't help it; you avail yourself of happy accidents of atmosphere, and if anything be ugly you strike it out, or if anything be wanting, you put it in. But still the picture is a likeness. . . ."[14]

The sketches of *Our Village* were so popular that they were extended ultimately to five volumes, published between 1824 and 1832. Ironically, Miss Mitford, who had long struggled for literary success by writing tragedies for Charles Kemble and Macready, won her fame with simple, homely potboilers. She had no skill as a novelist, no idea of plot or characterization. Once, she confessed in a letter to Elford in 1830, she tried to write a novel, drafting about one hundred pages, until "I came to a dead stop for want of invention. A lack of incident killed the poor thing. It went out like a candle."[15]

Village life for Miss Mitford is merely a decorative setting in which her decorous people (they hardly merit the designation "characters") move. Some of her sketches, in

[13] W. J. Roberts, *Mary Russell Mitford: The Tragedy of a Blue-stocking* (London, 1913), ch. 14.

[14] *Ibid.*, p. 239.

[15] *The Letters of Mary Russell Mitford*, ed. R. Brimley Johnson (New York, 1925), p. 167. *Atherton* (1854), her only full-length novel, a story of a young girl who inherits a fortune, was a totally undistinguished book.

fact, were written to match pictures in the annuals—"which many bought to look at and few cared to read."[16] The realities of the Industrial Revolution, the Napoleonic Wars, plague, crop failure, personal boredom and despair, drunkenness, ignorance and superstition—concerns of such eighteenth-century village poets as Goldsmith, Crabbe, and Burns—never touch Miss Mitford's country folk. Yet successful as her sketches were with the public, she dimly sensed their limitations. She called them "my airy nothings," and attempted in later years to add some little social substance by extending her focus in *Belford Regis* (1835) from rural village to country town, "a class of the community which, whilst it forms so large a portion of our population, occupies so small a space in our literature, and amongst whom, more perhaps than amongst any other of English society, may be traced the peculiarities, the prejudices, and the excellences of the national character."[17] The results were no more substantial and perhaps less charming than *Our Village* largely because of Miss Mitford's overall limitations as a writer of fiction. The characters are mere stock types, more variegated as to interests and occupations than her villagers but rendered lifeless by her moralizing and sentimentalizing. Nevertheless, Miss Mitford's perception that in country town life one might trace, better than in any other segment of English society, the qualities of "the national character" was absolutely correct.[18] She had discov-

---

[16] Preface to *Atherton and Other Tales*, 3 vols. (London, 1854).

[17] Preface to *Belford Regis, or Sketches of a Country Town*, 3 vols. (London, 1835).

[18] She recognized the possibilities in French as well as in English literature, observing in a letter to Charles Boner in 1845 that Balzac's sketches of peasant life are failures because "he has no love for the people . . . a great mistake in these days, when they are rising in importance every hour. Georges [sic] Sand and Eugène Sue are wiser, as well as the great old Bard; and they will have their reward. . . . Even Mrs. Gore, who may be looked on as a sort of weather-cock to show which way the wind of popularity blows, has just put forth a Christmas Story in which the scene is laid in a farm house, and the squire's son marries a clerk's daughter" (*Letters*, p. 199).

ered the social microcosm though she lacked the skill to develop the idea in her own writings.

The essence of community—whether in personal, human relationships like marriage and the family or in social relationships like work, law enforcement, and civil government —is a mutuality of interests, responsibilities, and rewards. In the village, where private lives tend to be more intimately connected than in cities, the Victorian novelist found an ideal setting for his social microcosm. Within the manageable limits of a small group of characters with a small range of possible actions, he could explore human nature and interpret character in greater depth than he could on a larger scale. But he had also to keep his novel moving forward and to retain his reader's interest in what was, superficially at least, routine and ordinary. Here again *Deerbrook*, in contrast to the all but static *Our Village*, offers an early example of how domestic fiction met these problems. In a delightful chapter, "Sophia in the Village," Harriet Martineau describes how the news of Hester's engagement is spread through the town. Beginning, "Deerbrook was not a place where practical affairs could long be kept secret," she proceeds with an account of the Greys' young daughter Sophia broadcasting the news. With short, breathless sentences, Harriet captures the spirit of provincial life—Sophia hastening into town on a series of totally unnecessary errands to blurt out the news wherever she can:

"On the way she met Dr. Levitt, about to enter the house of a sick parishioner. Dr. Levitt hoped all at home were well. All very well, indeed, Sophia was obliged to him. Her only fear was that the excitement of present circumstances might be too much for mama. Mama was so very much attached to cousin Hester, and it would be such a delightful thing to have her settled beside them! Perhaps Dr. Levitt had not heard that Hester and Mr. Hope were going to be married. No, indeed, he had not. He wondered his friend Hope had not told him of his good fortune, of which he heartily wished him joy. How long had this happy affair been settled? Not long, he fancied? Not very long; and perhaps Mr. Hope did not consider that it was quite made public yet: but Sophia thought that Dr. Levitt ought to know" (I, ch. 13).

At the sight of a new face in the butcher shop, Sophia's young heart "leaped up" and she busily seeks out other hearers for her news. Finally, exhausted, she gives up—"nobody remained to be informed. She could only go home, put off her bonnet, and sit with her mother, watching who would call, and planning the external arrangements which constitute the whole interest of a wedding to narrow minds and apathetic hearts."

As the village novel evolved from Miss Mitford's little sketches and other prose idylls and pastorals into the realistic novel of social community like *Deerbrook, Cranford,* and *Middlemarch,* it became increasingly a register of the interdependency of human lives in society. Sophia, flitting about Deerbrook with her news of a marriage, is broadcasting gossip, but she is also communicating news, spreading among a group of mutually concerned people information that is interesting to them all. Even the "narrow minds and apathetic hearts" will in some way respond to the marriage of their neighbors, Hester and Mr. Hope. In her *Illustrations of Political Economy* Harriet Martineau had made explicit the prevailing economic theory of the nineteenth century—that men live and work together in community for mutual advantage. Profit-making was as natural to mankind as love-making or any other instinct, and its legitimate exercise was essential to the healthy harmonious existence of the state and its populace. Drawing an analogy between society and the family, she had observed that if the social community might be run as simply as the family, there would be none of the glaring abuses of poverty and inequality from which the state presently suffers. "Such extremes as these are seldom or never to be met with under the same roof in the present day, when domestic economy is so much better understood than in the times when such sights were actually seen in rich men's castles; but in that larger family,—the nation,—every one of these abuses still exists, and many more."

"That larger family,—the nation," the concern of political theorists and social philosophers, was too large an area for the domestic novelist. But the village was an ideal medium for projecting English society, the microcosm that could enclose and encapsulate those vaster problems of society in which the domestic novelist and his reader were as deeply interested as the political economist. The village, as Julia Patton wrote in her study of English village literature, was "close to humanity and close to nature . . . and small enough to be grasped imaginatively, as a city with its vast complex of interests and institutions and activities cannot be."[19] The rural community of the early nineteenth century, like the family unit that it so closely resembles—small, enclosed, self-contained yet mutually dependent—was compact, fixed in time, firmly established by tradition and social order, yet sufficiently varied in customs and personalities to provide rich material for the newly emerging novel of domestic realism. Miss Mitford exploited its picturesque charm, its quaintness and tranquility—qualities especially valued by readers already stifled in the gloom and smog of industrial towns. For the working classes, regional dialect, rustic characters, the often authentic details of daily village life, were a new form of romantic escapism, vastly different, to be sure, from the Byronic and gothic coloration of conventional romances but refreshing and delightful in their own way.

In his survey of the popular fiction of the lower classes, Louis James singles out a novel by Thomas Miller, *Gideon Giles the Roper* (1841) as especially appealing: "Good is shown in all the characters, even the villains, in a way that mars the plausibility of the story . . . [but] Miller was clearly writing from an overflowing good humour and delight

[19] *The English Village: A Literary Study, 1750-1850* (New York, 1919), p. 1.

in the world, which he communicates to the reader."[20] That good humor is a reflection both of his humanitarianism and of his delight in nature. The author of a number of books on the beauties and pleasures of the country (*Rural Sketches, Beauties of the Country, Pictures of Country Life and Summer Rambles in Green Places*), Miller worked closely with his illustrators (Samuel Williams, Edward Lambert), "to make the scenery and characters thoroughly English." Even when, as in *Gideon Giles*, his subject is the inequity of an English law that punished a man for peddling his own goods without a license, Miller is determined to prove the fundamental soundness of English justice. His realistic detail is striking, breathing life into a polemical tale with a heartiness that Miss Mitford sadly lacked. His country inn is peopled with earthy, "comfortable" villagers like fat Ben Brust: "Ben was married; his wife was a thin, spare, coarse-grained little woman, with a sharp vinegar aspect, so thin that she was nicknamed 'Famine,' while Ben was called 'Plenty'; he would have bumped down three wives the size of his own, in any fair scale in England. Famine went out to work, while Plenty lay sleeping in the sunshine; she was 'scratching and saving,' washed and cleaned for people in the village; Plenty sat on gates and stiles, whistling, or sometimes standing on the bridge would spit in the water and watch it float away" (Ch. 1).

Ben is not a generalized eighteenth-century character type, yet he is a representative of his class and his community. For Miller, Ben and his fellow rustics are indeed the masses of humanity. When a young Cambridge-educated gentleman dines with Ben on friendly terms, Miller comments approvingly: "The world would be all the better if the fetters which were worn by 'high society' were broken; if rich and poor were to meet together on a more equal footing. . . . Rank requires a necessary distance, but assuredly it would lose nothing if the chain was not always kept at full stretch" (Ch. 2).

[20] *Fiction for the Working Man, 1830-1850* (London, 1963), p. 104.

The village thus truly becomes the social microcosm. The homely domestic detail that individualizes also universalizes. It brings men together as they share in specific interests and activities. Miss Mitford's villagers are idealized and generalized. She firmly disclaimed the use of real-life models: "General truth of delineation, I hope there is," she wrote in her Preface to *Belford Regis*, "but of individual portrait painting, I must seriously assert that none has been intended." Her villagers live in a curious isolation from each other and from the reader. Hers is less a community than a picture gallery with separate canvasses. This effect is not so much the result of the sketchbook form of *Our Village* (Mrs. Gaskell's *Cranford*, also in the form of a series of sketches, is an integrated novel with a strong central theme), as it is a failure on her part to develop the idea of community and the inter-relationship of human beings in the course of their daily domestic lives.

III

> ... With good
> Still overcoming evil, and by small
> Accomplishing great things, by things deem'd weak
> Subverting worldly strong and worldly wise. ...
> —*Paradise Lost,* xii (Epigraph to *Deerbrook*)

By its very nature the domestic novel negates the romance. Concerned with the reality of what happens or what might conceivably happen in everyday life, it cannot co-exist in the literary world with romance. So, at least, the nineteenth-century novelists believed. They tell us repeatedly that their tales are "founded on fact." They insist that their characters lead ordinary lives; Mrs. Trollope prepares the readers of *One Fault* (1840): "The persons of the story I am about to tell were neither of high rank, nor of distinguished fashion; and, worse still, the narrative cannot by possibility be forced to become one of romantic interest.

Ordinary everyday human beings and ordinary everyday events are my theme. . . . That they shall be such men and women as I have seen and known is the only fact concerning them that can be urged as an apology for introducing them at all." As one novelist complained: "Novel-writing has completely changed its character. From its high-flown, elaborate style, it is now fallen into its opposite extreme; from improbabilities, always impalpable, sometimes gross, now, in their place, we find nothing but the hum-drummeries of reality" (Mrs. E. C. Grey, *The Little Wife* [1841]). The challenge to novelists was to make the "hum-drummeries" themselves interesting and significant. If readers were to survive their rude wrenching away from romance, they must be prepared by learning to accept in their fiction a new, clear-eyed vision of reality.

In spite of all such firm resolve, however, to strip away the "unrealities," the romance in prose survived. But it survived in new forms, in the imaginative fiction of the Brontës, George Eliot, and Dickens. This new romanticism in fiction was realistic and domestic in its setting and circumstances. What made it romantic essentially was its emphasis upon the imagination—from the nightmare fantasies of Yorkshire farmers like Heathcliff and the hallucinatory visions of schoolteacher Lucy Snowe to the adolescent fairytale-making of Pip and David Copperfield, and the childhood daydreaming of Maggie Tulliver. Gothic terror and ghostly visitations were replaced by the ragings of guilty conscience—Carker and the locomotive, the river rats of the Thames, Lady Deadlock in flight, Bulstrode contemplating the unconscious form of Raffles. No serious Victorian novelist, however deep his devotion to facts and his contempt for mere escapism, could have denied the function of the imagination in fiction. What is indeed striking about so much Victorian domestic fiction, major and minor, is its preoccupation with the conflicts that our all too human tendency to imagine, to dream, to fantasize produces in our daily lives.

Harriet Martineau certainly shared this concern—to the point of making it the principal theme of *Deerbrook*. She approached the writing of her novel with a well-articulated theory of realistic fiction ("every perfect plot in fiction is taken bodily from real life") and expectations no more lofty than telling her simple tale with pathos and honesty: "I know the book to have been true to the state of thought and feeling I was then in, which I now regard as imperfect and very far from lofty:—I believe it to have been useful, not only in overcoming a prejudice against the use of middle-class life in fiction but in a more special application to the discipline of temper; and therefore I am glad I wrote it" (*Autobiography*, I, 415).

Modest as its conception was, *Deerbrook* did not fail to tackle the serious problems of life. Typical of domestic fiction, its plot lacks all elements of sensationalism. The closest it comes to violence is a village riot in which some windows are broken; the closest to suspense, an episode in which the heroine falls through the ice while skating on the village pond. The life-death cycle is fully treated: babies are born, a child dies of fever, old people die, younger ones struggle for work, for financial security and prestige in the community, and for the purely personal satisfactions of love and marriage. The interest of the novel lies not in the extraordinary events of life but in the complicating of the very ordinary ones. And Harriet Martineau achieves these complications—as did most Victorians in their domestic fiction —by showing the effects of the undisciplined or improperly disciplined imagination on average human life. The problems of the characters in *Deerbrook* are those of the romantic imagination—the confusion of appearance and reality, the chain reactions of human misunderstandings—acted out in a scene of domestic life. The solutions are those of a practical Christian ethic—submission to the will of God and acceptance of the duties and obligations of living in a community with other human beings.

The plot of *Deerbrook* is based on a misunderstanding,

a confusion of appearance and reality arising from a man's marriage to a woman whom he does not love. She *thinks* that he loves her; he *thinks* that he loves her sister. Ultimately he discovers that he loves his wife, but a series of potentially tragic misunderstandings has been unleashed. Nothing is quite as it appears because it is human nature to mistake and misinterpret reality. Even the idyllic village of Deerbrook, which so enchants the two city-bred heroines, is not what it seems. The greenery and shrubbery conceal "the timber and coal yards and granaries." Later this same lovely spot is the scene of nasty gossip, mob violence, crop failure, and—surely not without symbolic significance —plague. The inhabitants constantly confuse appearance for reality—from the sensitive hero whose marriage bodes so much evil, the two sweet Ibbotson sisters whose lives become entangled with his, to the malicious village gossip who is so deeply entrapped in her own lies that she comes actually to believe them. Village life itself, as Harriet Martineau observes in her opening chapter, is conducive to daydreaming and myth-making. As the Grey family awaits the visit of the Ibbotson sisters from Birmingham, "the ladies were evidently in a state of expectation—a state exceedingly trying to people who, living at ease in the country, have rarely anything to expect beyond the days of the week, the newspaper, and their dinners."

When the sisters appear and one of them, Hester, proves to be a beauty, the well-meaning Mrs. Grey leaps to the conclusion that the local doctor Mr. Hope will fall in love with her. The fact is that he has fallen in love with her less striking sister Margaret. But the human failing of hasty judgment and miscalculation, fed by the human ego, which convinces one of the correctness of his errors, is the essence of the appearance-reality conflict: "It is a fact which few but the despisers of their race like to acknowledge, and which those despisers of their race are therefore apt to interpret wrongly, and are enabled to make too much of— that it is perfectly natural,—so natural as to appear necessary,—that when young people first meet, the possibility of their falling in love should occur to all the minds present" (I, ch. 1).

Mrs. Grey goes busily to work as a matchmaker, and when Hope protests that he has no "intentions" regarding Hester, she accuses him of trifling with the girl's affections. Her confusion compounds his. A man of delicate conscience, he reacts with deep concern: "There was nothing to him so abhorrent as giving pain; nothing so intolerable in idea as injuring any human being: and he was now compelled to believe that through some conduct of his own, some imprudence, in a case where imprudence is guilt, he had broken up the peace of a woman whom, though he did not love, he respected and warmly regarded!" (I, ch. 11.) He proposes; Hester, who genuinely loves him, accepts; and Margaret innocently rejoices in their supposed bliss. She meanwhile has fallen in love with Philip Enderby, and that romance flourishes until again delusion causes near-disaster. Enderby accidentally discovers that Hope had once loved Margaret. Blinded by this revelation, he misjudges innocent actions, heeds malicious gossip from his sister Mrs. Rowland, and weaves a web of misunderstanding that is almost fatal to the happiness of all.

In every instance the misunderstandings are the result of over-active minds and imaginations. Hope meets the Ibbotson sisters and his fancy immediately begins to churn: "His thoughts already darted forward to the time when the Miss Ibbotsons would be leaving Deerbrook. It was already a heavy thought how dull Deerbrook would be without them. He was already unconsciously looking at every object in and around the familiar place with the eyes of the strangers, speculating on how the whole would appeal to them. In short his mind was full of them" (I, ch. 5). With such impetuosity, it is less incredible that Hope, a man of intelligence and good will, should make his disastrous decision to marry.

243

Self-delusion follows a natural course for Hope. Self-betrayed, he blames no one but himself. Fortunately, because he is a rational creature, he not only survives, but he spares his wife the pain of ever discovering his secret. After due suffering, he even comes to love her. Philip Enderby, another man of intelligence and good will, sees his errors too and in the end happily marries Margaret. But self-delusion takes a more unnatural and sinister course in his sister Mrs. Rowland, whose malice blinds her to reality. In the hands of a more gifted novelist than Harriet Martineau, Mrs. Rowland might have become a fascinating study in neurotic behavior. Her jealousy of her neighbors the Greys and their friends (hence the Ibbotson sisters and Mr. Hope become her enemies) is unmotivated. Harriet can portray her only as a monster—possessive, domineering, shrill, fanatical. Presumably sane, she is so blinded by jealousy that she creates her own reality. When Philip announces his engagement to Margaret, she simply refuses to accept the fact, announcing: "I shall deny the engagement everywhere." The study of abnormal psychology was outside Harriet's scheme, but she must have been at least dimly aware of the potential depths of Mrs. Rowland's character. Philip, for example, conjectures that his sister's obduracy "comes from internal torture." She persists, however, until her child lies dying of plague, and Hope and his family, the victims of her malice, rally to her aid. They cannot save the child, but in grief and remorse she at last confesses her lies, clearing the way for a happy ending.

Although Harriet Martineau was writing a warning against the snares and delusions of appearance, she was a firm believer in the ideals of love and romance. The domestic love story, of which *Deerbrook* is not only an example but very possibly the archetype, presupposes every bit as noble an idealism as the romances of chivalry, but it is an idealism transferred to the realities of hearth and home. Chivalry had its charms, but its absurdity, its "irrelevance" in the modern world, had been displayed more than two centuries earlier in *Don Quixote*. To cling to its vestiges in sentimentalized courtship and love-making was only to be caught in the metaphysical trap of confusing appearance and reality. Is there a place for romance in nineteenth-century utilitarian society? Philip Enderby raises this question in a playful conversation with Hester and Margaret.

Margaret Ibbotson, although a girl of deep feeling and sensibility, is a realist. She distrusts allegory: "There is a pleasure in making one's way about in a grotto in a garden; but I think there is a much higher one in exploring a cave on the sea-shore, dim and winding, where you never know that you have come to the end—a much higher pleasure in exploring a life than following out an allegory." She warns of the dangers of making fancies and "mysteries" of human emotions. Philip protests laughingly that she would thereby outlaw courtship: "You surely would not overthrow the whole art of wooing? You would not doom lovers' plots and devices?" Margaret replies that such artifices are demanded only by silly, vain women—"suitable enough five centuries ago" but false to the realities of married life: "But I certainly think those much the wisest and happiest, who look upon the whole affair as the solemn matter that it really is, and who desire to be treated, from the beginning, with the sincerity and seriousness which they will require after they are married." To this her sister Hester echoes: "If the same simplicity and seriousness were common in this as are required in other grave transactions, there would be less of the treachery, delusion, and heart-breaking, which lie heavy upon the souls of many a man and many a woman" (1, ch. 6).

Harriet Martineau's readers might quietly add—"But there would also be fewer love stories." Yet in reviewing the great Victorian love stories that came after *Deerbrook* we note how prophetic she was. The passionate heroine who lives only for her love—Catherine Earnshaw, for example— is doomed. The frivolous girls who demand "wooing" and live by false standards of flirtation and vanity are invariably viewed with a cold eye. Charlotte Brontë has no sympathy for Ginevra Fanshawe or Blanche Ingram; George Eliot sees only disaster for Hetty Sorrel and for the man who loves Rosamond Vincy; Dickens gently ridicules Dora Spenlowe; Thackeray is far less gentle with Blanche Amory and Beatrix Esmond. Marriage, the domestic novelist insists, imposes serious demands, and to pretend otherwise is stupid or dishonest. None of these novelists is blind to the charms of love; they simply wish to transpose these from the delusions of myth to the substantial reality of home and daily life. Thus Harriet Martineau—author of a non-fiction work called *Household Education*, the subject of which, she wrote, "is important in its bearings on every one's happiness"—celebrates in fiction the simple joys of furnishing a house. If her readers failed to see the romance of domesticity in this, it was not through lack of conviction on her part. She describes the almost sacred nature of the future wife's tasks: "Both the sisters were surprised to find how much pleasure they took in the preparations for this marriage. They could not have believed it, and, but that they were too happy to feel any kind of contempt, they would have despised themselves for it. But such contempt would have been misplaced. All things are according to the ideas and feelings with which they are connected; and if, as old George Herbert says, dusting a room is an act of religious grace when it is done from a feeling of religious duty, furnishing a house is a process of high enjoyment when it is the preparation of a home for happy love" (i, ch. 14).

Hester is furnishing a modest village house, not a rose-covered bower or a fashionable town-house in Mayfair. The reader knows how much rent will be paid, the terms of the lease, how the furniture will be arranged. But the scene is not without its romantic aura—the cool shade and fragrance of the summer garden, the cozy warmth of fireplace and drawn curtains on winter evenings—in short, the domestic intimacies of marriage are given added seriousness and dignity: "Here will they first feel what it is to have a home of their own—where they will first enjoy the privacy of it, the security, the freedom, the consequence in the eyes of others, the sacredness in their own."

This domesticating of the love story, probably the most interesting feature of *Deerbrook*, is also the source of its artistic failure. Perhaps from Victorian reticence or her own sexual innocence (in one of her political economy tales she urges birth control by conjugal abstinence), Harriet Martineau shrinks from acknowledging the real problem of this ill-conceived marriage and focusses instead on the externals of life. Not that she was unaware of the sexual implications of her subject. She dwells at some length on Hope's anguish as he confronts his (on his side) loveless marriage, his terrors that his bride will suspect the truth, or that he will be unable to conceal his feelings for Margaret, who, true to real-life Victorian practice, lives with the couple after their marriage. Returning home from his wedding journey, he spends a sleepless night: "There was no escape. The peace of his wife, of Margaret—his own peace in theirs—depended wholly on the deep secrecy in which he should preserve the mistake he had made. It was a mistake. He could scarcely endure the thought but it was so" (I, ch. 16).

It is a dilemma that Harriet Martineau cannot translate into the easy domestic terms of most of her novel. Impetuous flight, impassioned confrontations, suicides—these are ruled out by the nature of her work. Yet these domestic tensions demand powerful description and penetrating psychological analysis that she is simply incapable of producing. All that she can do is to raise her authorial voice, to use strikingly inappropriate language ("throbbing pulses," "quivering nerves," "wrung hearts"). Hope soliloquizes in the clichés of theatrical melodrama: " 'So this is home!' thought he, as he surveyed the room, filled as it was with tokens of occupation, and appliances of domestic life. 'It is home to be more lonely than ever before—and yet never to be alone with my secret! At my own table, by my own hearth, I cannot look into the faces around me, nor say what

I am thinking. In every act and every word I am in danger of disturbing the innocent—even of sullying the pure, and of breaking the bruised reed. . . . I am in bondage every hour that I spend at home. . . . I am guilty; or rather, I have been guilty; and this is my retribution' " (II, ch. 3).

Happily, both for the author and for her characters, Harriet Martineau does not preserve the fustian mood but quickly slips back into the steadier rhythms and idioms of natural speech. Hope practices his profession, faces crises caused by gossip and the ignorance of the villagers, and eventually overcomes his foes. Meanwhile he achieves self-mastery, encourages Margaret's marriage to Philip, and develops a genuine love for his wife.

The domestic love story portrays lovers, especially after they marry, as solid citizens. Hope's therapy and salvation lie in constructive work, duty, activity in the community, which he serves as a doctor. No man survives in isolation and no couple, however deep their love, can live exclusively in that love. At best they live happily ever after—in a society, with children, relatives, friends, neighbors, and fellow workers. Victorian families were large, but houses (except among the very rich) were small. Lives constantly impinged on one another. School, church, an occupation or profession, were as interesting to readers of novels as the more intimate personal problems of love and marriage. Even the melancholy romantic giants of Victorian fiction operated in some kind of community. Heathcliff was a landlord and a farmer, with tenants, servants, and a few neighbors. He might despise them, but his life was touched by them. Lucy Snowe lives in a school community. Jane Eyre and Mr. Rochester enjoy temporary isolation, but they are to have children and a religious life. The characters in Dickens, Thackeray, and Trollope move in many communities simultaneously. Provincial life, constricted as it was, was nevertheless a microcosm of all human society. The sheltered ladies living in the cozy security of Mrs. Gaskell's village of *Cranford* cling to the vestiges of the past in a rapidly changing society only twenty miles from "the great neighbouring commercial town of Drumble." They survive only with compromise and cooperation, as the railroad rushes by, the bank fails, and the old class structure all but topples. Lady Glenmire is happy to exchange her title for marriage to the plain-named village doctor Mr. Hoggins; a one-time milliner, Betty Barker, entertains the ladies at tea; genteel Miss Matty is temporarily reduced to shop-keeping. Cranford loses its isolation and becomes a community as its citizens draw together in crisis.

Although Anthony Trollope's Barset is more a church community than a total society, it too is a center and a mirror for domestic life, for mutual dependency, for confrontations with the actualities as opposed to the possibilities of human existence. The cross-sectioning within the church hierarchy is far more secular than clerical, and the characters are certainly more memorable in their roles as human and social beings than as clergy. (Trollope's object, he writes in the Conclusion to *The Last Chronicle of Barset*, "has been to paint the social and not the professional lives of clergymen.") Bishop Proudie is first and foremost a henpecked husband, Archdeacon Grantly a proud and headstrong patrician, Dean Arabin a troubled intellectual, Dr. Harding a sweet and sensitive old gentleman, Reverend Josiah Crawley an unhappy, moody man on whom "the troubles of the world seemed to come with a double weight," Mr. Slope a social climber. Their idealism, their self-deception, their impulsiveness, their fallibilities produce the problems and the solutions of the novels. But it is their existence within a community that unites them in action and makes those actions significant. In *The Last Chronicle of Barset* as in *Deerbrook* a community is united first in delusion and error—when the citizens of Barset reluctantly but confidently accept the evidence of Josiah Crawley's guilt—and then in reparation, when they acknowledge his innocence. The issues cross social lines and force into mutual interaction everyone from Bishop Proudie and Archdeacon Grantly down to the humble laborer who advises Crawley to endure—"It's dogged as does it." In between, all manner of personal and domestic dramas take place, but the community remains the stage on which the main drama is acted out. The scene shifts, in Trollope, to London in a clumsy subplot. Characters from "outside" are introduced, including the attorney Mr. Toogood, who is so instrumental in saving Crawley. But the community theme —the microcosm of Barset—holds firm.

In still another Victorian provincial community, Mrs. Margaret Oliphant's Carlingford, an idealistic clergyman sees both his romantic and his vocational aspirations crushed and learns to accept the middle road of resignation and compromise (*Salem Chapel*), while the shopkeeping bourgeoisie rise in social position (*Miss Marjoribanks* and *Phoebe, Junior*), and a whole town, briefly torn by rumor and scandal, unites in a spirit of forgiveness and cooperation (*The Perpetual Curate*). Even in the remote West Riding of Yorkshire, in Charlotte Brontë's *Shirley*, a community slowly and painfully begins to shape itself through mutual understanding and love. "The throes of a sort of moral earthquake were felt heaving under the hills of the northern counties" (Ch. 2), and the social, economic, and emotional crises that ensue separate then unite the inhabitants. Laborers and mill-owners learn to live as well as work together for their mutual benefit. Idealists like Caroline Helstone and Shirley Keeldar mature with suffering and adjust to reality. At the happy ending all come together in a common union, appropriately symbolized in the marriage ceremony: "On this day the Fieldhead tenantry dine together; the Hollow's Mill workpeople will be assembled in a like festal purpose; the schools have a grand treat. This morning there were two marriages solemnised in Briarfield Church."

Finally, as George Eliot so impressively demonstrated in *Middlemarch*, social institutions like marriage and the family themselves are communities that demand a sharing of interests and duties and that thrive only when, like society as a whole, they achieve a proper balance between responsibilities and rewards. *Deerbrook* was published some thirty years before *Middlemarch*. Although George Eliot declared her respect and admiration for other books by Harriet Martineau, we do not know whether or to what extent she was influenced by the earlier novel.[21] The Hope-Lydgate plots have interesting parallels. Both are medical men who alienate their communities by their enlightened practices (Hope is suspected by the ignorant villagers of body-snatching) and by their involvement in unpopular political causes. Both experience marital crises. Beyond that there is no comparison—except, perhaps, the most significant parallel of all, the sense of how individual lives become intertwined in social community. Many novelists before Harriet Martineau had recognized the effects of the social environment on the nature and behavior of their characters, from Moll Flanders' Newgate to Emma Woodhouse's Highbury. But she was one of the first English novelists to create an imaginative community as a setting out of which, almost

[21] George Eliot's highest praise was in a letter of June 2, 1852, where she referred to Harriet Martineau's contributions to the *Westminster Review*: "After all, she is a *trump*—the only English woman that possesses thoroughly the art of writing" (*Letters*, II, 32). Although in later years their relationship was distant, George Eliot had been impressed by Harriet on their first meeting in 1845 and saw her frequently thereafter: "Her conversation is delightful, and her manners so perfectly easy and lady-like. . . . She is a charming person—quite one of those great people whom one does not venerate the less for having seen" (*Letters*, I, 188-89). She was deeply moved by Harriet's story of schoolboy life, *The Crofton Boys*: "I have had some delightful crying over it. There are two or three lines in it that would feed one's soul for a month" (*Letters*, I, 192). There is no mention of *Deerbrook* in her published letters, but it seems unlikely that she had not read the novel. George Henry Lewes evidently shared her admiration for Harriet Martineau. He published her story "The Old Governess" in *The Leader* (November 9, 1850), a story that, he told Charlotte Brontë, "touched him and made him cry" (Shakespeare Head Brontë, III, 183-84).

organically, the characters and their conflicts emerge. Her center is Deerbrook—the community to which people come to meet their destinies. The novel is *about* Deerbrook; the plot concerns people who happen to live in Deerbrook and who have no fictional existence outside of it. The novel begins with a description of Deerbrook and the arrival of the two heroines. It ends with some characters leaving it, but with others who remain behind, recalling the legend (of a stream where deer came to drink) that gave the village its name. In between, like a protagonist, Deerbrook undergoes crises of crop failure, popular discontent and brief rebellion, pestilence, then rebirth—the last chapter is entitled "Deerbrook in Sunshine."

Not being the artist George Eliot was, Harriet Martineau fails to give life to her villagers, although she attempts to use some of their commentary as a chorus. They remain essentially disembodied—a mob, "a multitude of feet and voices." The social cross-sectioning is also lifeless. The baronet and his wife, who encourage the mob violence against Hope because of his political activity, are merely types—snobbish, arrogant people with no real malice but also no personality. Farmers and workmen are colorless and give no sense of the quality of their speech or work. Only those who move within the orbits of the leading characters —the Greys, the Rowlands, old Mrs. Enderby, the servant Morris—have identity, and of these only the children are characterized convincingly. Yet, thanks to her community scheme, Harriet Martineau gives breadth to her novel and makes this pioneering work a model for many later novels. She breaks out of the confines of the purely domestic scene and personal love story, moving freely from the hearth to the marketplace and the village green. Deerbrook is not the complex social web that Middlemarch is, but it has life as a community and its characters achieve through their existence within it a stature that they would not otherwise have had.

But above and beyond their social existence as members

of the community of Deerbrook, these characters must also achieve some stature as individuals. Harriet Martineau, like all writers of moral and artistic sensibility, knew that the novel demanded more substance than a mere chronicle of daily routine within a social framework. The noble heroic exploits of the older romantic fiction had inspired noble heroic sentiments. But when heroes and heroines do nothing more noble than accept and adjust to the demands of simple existence in reality, they must still be capable of feeling lofty emotions and of living noble lives. The humble village of Deerbrook must serve as an arena for the display of the Christian virtues, testing morality and courage less dramatically perhaps but just as rigorously as a metropolis like London or Paris, or a battlefield, or the dangerous high seas. Dedicated from her youth to becoming "a forcible and elegant writer on religious and moral subjects," Harriet Martineau carefully developed *Deerbrook*'s theme of romantic delusion versus reality along the lines of homely but profound moral values. The reality that eludes her characters—thereby producing the confusions and misunderstandings that constitute her plot—is ultimately achieved. It is a reality seized happily by the fortunate lovers in the book, who go forth to build new lives. But it is also a reality that demands, for others, sacrifice, resignation, and fortitude.

In the real world of the domestic novel problems do not end with marriage, and marriage itself is not always attainable. As another novelist and schoolteacher Elizabeth Missing Sewell soberly taught her pupils: "Romance says, 'And so they were married and lived happily ever after.' Reality says, 'And so they were married, and entered upon new duties and new cares.' "[22] The only certainty in life is suffering; the only Christian solution is recognition of this condition as part of God's scheme.

[22] *Principles of Education drawn from Nature and Revelation and applied to Female Education in the Upper Classes*, 2 vols. in 1 (New York, 1866), ch. 23.

No character in *Deerbrook*, in fact few characters in Victorian fiction, more typically represents this spirit of resignation to suffering than Maria Young, friend and confidante of Margaret Ibbotson. Crippled, confined to a dreary existence as a governess, she can remember a happier past when she was pretty and rich and secretly attracted to Philip Enderby. But a carriage accident and the death of her father force her into the sidelines of life, where she must witness the joys of others denied forever to her. Maria is one of the earliest in that long line of suffering governesses, but unlike the rebellious Jane Eyre and Lucy Snowe, who were certainly influenced by her,[23] she has resigned herself to her lot: "Let a governess learn what to expect," she tells Hester; "set her free from a hankering after happiness in her work, and you have a happy governess" (i, ch. 3).

Maria has learned that happiness is a delusion and that its pursuit is futile and dangerous. Yet she does not despair. Not a Christian-martyr type like the characters in Miss Sewell's evangelical novels, Maria is fatalistic and stoical, consoling herself with memory and imagination ("The delight of a happy mood of mind is beyond everything at the time; it sets one above all that can happen; it steeps one in heaven itself"—i, ch. 5) and in service to others. Thus she encourages the courtship of Margaret and Philip: "Her duty then was clearly to give them up to each other with such spirit of self-sacrifice as she might be capable of" (i, ch. 6). Like Charlotte Brontë's Lucy Snowe, she has observed that there are some who are destined for happiness ("They marry their loves and stand amazed at their own bliss, and are truly the happiest people upon earth, and in the broad road to be the wisest") and others who will know

[23] See Charlotte Brontë's letter to Harriet Martineau, accompanying a presentation copy of *Shirley*: "When Currer Bell first read 'Deerbrook' he tasted a new and keen pleasure, and experienced a genuine benefit. In his mind 'Deerbrook' ranks with the writings that have really done him good, added to his stock of ideas, and rectified his views of life" (Shakespeare Head Brontë, iii, 56).

only suffering, yet will transcend their pain ("They rise to the highest above them. Some of these must be content with having learned more or less what life is, and of what it is for, and with reconciling themselves to its objects and condition"—I, ch. 15). Ultimately Maria voices the primary purpose of the domestic novel: to teach the acceptance of life by displaying life as it truly is, neither terrible nor glorious, but part of the greater destiny, the Divine plan. She asks why we should demand "that one lot should, in this exceedingly small section of our immortality, be as happy as another; why we cannot each husband our own life and means without wanting to be all equal. Let us bless Heaven for your lot, by all means; but why, in the name of Providence, should mine be like it?" (III, ch. 14.)

Deerbrook is a modest novel in its scope and in its achievement. Its vision of life is confined to the reality of ordinary people, the world of the petty bourgeois. Yet there is something vastly ambitious in what Harriet Martineau was attempting to do in this book. Fully to appreciate that attempt, one must look ahead to the major works of nineteenth-century English fiction—to *David Copperfield* and *Little Dorrit, The Newcomes*, and *Middlemarch*. All these novels deal mainly with bourgeois society and the struggles of ordinary people in ordinary life; but their authors recognized that in the very nature of human life there is something divine and sublime—and that is love. The special contribution of the Victorian novelist is that he saw love in a new way—not exalted and heightened by romance, but simply and lucidly displayed in the domestic lives of men and women. There are many celebrations of domestic love in nineteenth-century poetry, ranging in quality from grossly sentimental to touching and beautiful—from Patmore's *The Angel in the House* and Clough's *Mari Magno* to Meredith's *Modern Love*. It is in fiction, however, that the values and institutions of bourgeois domesticity—courtship, marriage, children, parents, neighbors—found their most natural expression. The extent of Harriet Martineau's contribution to this discovery is considerable. In *Deerbrook*, a novel that foreshadowed the best work of the great novelists who followed her—Charlotte Brontë, Mrs. Gaskell, Trollope, George Eliot, Dickens, and Thackeray—Harriet Martineau established the domestic love story as a valid literary genre. Equally important, she framed the social microcosm in the English village, bringing together within its modest borders and applying to the lives of its ordinary citizens those concerns of "History, Politics, Mind" that Matthew Arnold summed up as the principal achievement of her career.

Conclusion

THE ephemeral minor fiction of an age often reflects, on a reduced but accurate scale, its major novels. Its influence, as many critics have observed, is not always direct. Rather, it serves to reconstruct the age and atmosphere in which the major novels were shaped—formed, as they were, in the always mysterious processes in which the creative imagination works. In this study we have examined a number of neglected novels of the first half of the nineteenth century, not for the purpose of tracing the history of the novel, but for emphasizing and analyzing certain significant trends in the development of an emerging art form. From the bulk of popular fiction we have concentrated upon novels of domestic realism, the work mainly of women simply because its subjects were closest to their recognized interests and abilities. These are novels that, we believe—by their seriousness, their emphasis upon truth-to-life and upon basic questions of human and social values—did much to erase the stigma of idle romance and to enhance the dignity and respectability of the novel as literature.

The best of them—and even among the second-rate there is much that is solidly good—were the seedbeds for the flowering of the major Victorian novels. In the career of a single novelist like Mrs. Gore, for example, we noted the rejection of the frivolity and glitter of fashionable life in favor of the bland but solid domestic virtues—a mirror of that changing spirit of the times from the Regency to the reign of Victoria which so fascinated Thackeray among the major novelists. In the strictly utilitarian tales of Maria Edgeworth, written to illustrate and disseminate her fa-

257

ther's theories of education, we noted the emergence of new interest in the personality of the child, his early education at home as preparation for his entire adult life. Her close observation of real children and her sympathetic imaginative recreation of their emotional and psychological responses to the experiences of daily life produced a fiction that anticipates the *Bildungsroman* and the preoccupation of the major Victorian novelists—the Brontës, Dickens, and George Eliot in particular—with the childhood of their characters as it shaped the course of their adult lives.

Still another concern—the child's moral and spiritual growth—inspired religiously oriented novelists from the writers of evangelical tracts and simplistic moral tales like Hannah More and Mrs. Sherwood to writers of lively, realistic novels of family life like Charlotte Yonge. All shared a common concern for the soul and conceived salvation as a matter of individual conscience and self-examination. Hence their anticipation of the so-called psychological novel, with its probings of guilt, anxiety, self-understanding, and identity. The great Victorian novels with their crises of conscience—Jane Eyre's renunciation of the married Mr. Rochester; Maggie Tulliver's renunciation of her cousin's fiancé Stephen Guest; Dickens' harried conscience sufferers from innocent Pip and Arthur Clennam to dark villains like Carker, Bradley Headstone, and John Jasper; Trollope's agonized Reverend Josiah Crawley; George Eliot's self-analytical characters like Dorothea Brooke and the casuistical Mr. Bulstrode; Thackeray's contrite Colonel Newcome—all share something of this evangelical passion.

Finally, in the recognition that men must live together in social as well as personal harmony, working for mutual good that at times demands the sacrifice of personal good, the novel of domestic realism achieved perhaps its richest fulfillment. Rejecting the conventionally romantic love story for studies of human relationships in their subtler, more complex, but also more homely and real aspects—courtship, marriage, the problems of supporting and raising a family

—the novel became at last universal and microcosmic. Its focus remained the individual within the domestic scene, but the isolation and insularity of the English hearth and home were proved to be illusory. In the social community of Harriet Martineau's provincial Deerbrook, Mrs. Gaskell's snug Cranford, Trollope's Barset, and, supremely, George Eliot's Middlemarch, the domestic microcosm is complete. From here it could develop no further. The family unit and the social unit alike, as well as the harmony of the individual living in a secure relationship with a personal and benevolent God, could not survive the disruptive influences of modern technology, urbanization, and scientific materialism. The microcosmic unity was fragmented, and the literary genre of domestic realism survived only in the much altered forms of social realism and literary naturalism. Its life span was therefore relatively brief, but it left a lasting heritage in English fiction.

Index

Eliot, George (*cont.*)
255, 258, 259; *Mill on the
Floss, The,* 25, 141, 181-82,
190, 204, 227, 228, 240,
258; *Scenes of Clerical Life,*
202-209: "Amos Barton,"
203, 204, "Janet's Repentance," 159, 203, 204-208;
and Harriet Martineau, 251n
Ellis, Mrs. Sarah Stickney, 35,
37-38, 217; *Daughters of
England, The,* 38, 52; *Pictures
of Private Life,* 37-38
Ensor, R. C. K., 145
Esterhazy, Princess, 71
evangelical literature, 5, 147,
149-63, 166-67, 170, 174,
175, 186, 192, 197-99, 201;
evangelical novel, 145-200.
See also tracts
evangelicalism, 50, 145-53, 159,
161, 166-74, 176-84, 200-209,
212, 258. *See also* religion

family novel, 83-84, 129, 130,
132, 134, 138, 186-91, 194,
196, 200, 259
Farrar, F. W., *Eric; or Little
by Little,* 140-41
fashionable novel, 41-85. *See
also* "silver-fork" novel
female domination, 4-5, 35, 48-
50, 62, 67, 70-80. *See also*
women
Ferrier, Susan, 5, 98-106;
Destiny, 17, 100-101;
Inheritance, The, 100-101;
Marriage, 99, 100-101
Fielding, Henry, *Tom Jones,*
92, 134-35
Fitch, Sir Joshua, 138n
Fitzherbert, Mrs., 49
Fordyce, Dr. James, *Sermons
to Young Women,* 113
Fox, W. J., 221

Foxe, John, *Acts and Monu-
ments,* 147, 159
Frith, William, 9
Froebel, Friedrich, 142
Froude, Hurrell, 168, 195
Froude, James A., 168-69
Frye, Northrop, 28
Fullerton, Georgiana, 147

Gaskell, Mrs. E. C., 3, 186,
212, 214, 256; *Cranford,*
236, 239, 248-49; *Mary
Barton,* 175, 222; *North and
South,* 222; *Wives and
Daughters,* 23-24, 87n
Genlis, Madame de, 123
George III, 47
George IV, 50, 69; as Prince
of Wales, 47, 62
Gettmann, R. A., 60n
Gibbon, Edward, 130n
Gladstone, W. E., 202
Godwin, William, 217
Goethe, J. W., *Werther,* 29, 123
Goldsmith, Oliver, 234; *Vicar
of Wakefield, The,* 7-9, 12,
18-19, 40
Gore, Mrs. Catherine, 5, 17,
22, 41-48, 112, 127, 225,
234n, 257; *Cabinet Minister,
The,* 47, 76; *Cecil, or The
Adventures of a Coxcomb,*
47, 54, 55-57, 59-70, 73, 74,
81, 85; *Cecil, a Peer,* 65, 66;
Dowager, The, 60; *Fair of
May Fair, The,* 77; *Hamiltons,
The,* 82-84; *Memoirs of a
Peeress,* 62n, 70; *Modern
Chivalry,* 64; *Money Lender,
The,* 48; *Mothers and
Daughters,* 76, 77-78; *Mrs.
Armytage, or Female Dom-
ination,* 77, 79-81; *Pin Money,*
73, 75; *Preferment,* 64-65;
Progress and Prejudice, 64;

LIBRARY OF CONGRESS CATALOGING IN PUBLICATION DATA

Colby, Vineta.
 Yesterday's woman: domestic realism in the English
novel.

 Includes bibliographical references.
 1. English fiction—19th century—History and criticism.
I. Title.
PR871.C6   823'.03   73-2469
ISBN 0-691-06263-3